AF207800

God and the Pandemic,

A Judaic Reflection on the Coronavirus

Rabbi Michael Leo Samuel

First Edition Design Publishing
Sarasota, Florida USA

God and the Pandemic, A Judaic Reflection on the Coronavirus
Copyright ©2020 Michael Leo Samuel

ISBN 978-1506-909-28-8 PRINT
ISBN 978-1506-909-29-5 EBOOK

LCCN 2020911423

July 2020

Published and Distributed by
First Edition Design Publishing, Inc.
P.O. Box 20217, Sarasota, FL 34276-3217
www.firsteditiondesignpublishing.com

Dedicated to the memory of all those who have died from
COVID-19

Additional titles by Rabbi Michael Leo Samuel

Maimonides' Hidden Torah Commentary
Genesis 1-21

Maimonides' Hidden Torah Commentary
Volume II – Genesis 22-50

Maimonides' Hidden Torah Commentary
Exodus 1-20

A Shepherd's Song: Psalm 23
Shepherd Metaphor in Jewish Thought

Gentle Judaic Wisdom For A Troubled World

Rediscovering Philo of Alexandria,
A First Century Torah Commentator (Vol. 1-5)

Torah from Alexandria:
Philo as a Biblical Commentator (Volume 1-3)

The Lord is My Shepherd: The Theology of the Caring God

Birth and Rebirth through Genesis:
A Timeless Theological Conversation Vol. 1: Genesis 1-3

Table of Contents

Part One
The Mythic Journey & A Brief History of Ancient Pandemics

Part Two
Struggling with Faith

Part Three
Understanding "Acts of God" & "Acts of Man"

Part Four
Pastoral Issues: God & Suffering

Part Five
The Poetics of Space Social Distancing & Pastoral Issues

Part Six
Wisdom from the Bible, Mishnah & Talmud

Part Seven
Practical Questions Concerning Jewish Law & Other Assorted Queries
Concerning the Coronavirus

Part Eight
Jewish Issues & Concerns

Foreword

Pandemics have existed from time immemorial. Seemingly few, however, have had the maturity and wisdom to navigate these destructive forces intelligently and successfully. Rabbi Samuel wisely opens his lens widely to give us a valuable historical panorama of the history of plagues and pandemics. Samuel skillfully examines and critiques various responses to pandemics. He exposes the inadequacies and fallacies of simplistic explanations. His work is deep and wide showing what ancients, medievalists and moderns have written on this troubling topic. Penned as a Judaic guide to understanding and coping with this current Covid-19 crisis, Samuel's words are also highly relevant to Christians and those of other religious traditions seeking knowledge for these difficult times.

Rabbi Samuel's work is keenly attuned to Scripture, tradition, history, psychology, social science and pastoral concerns. Seeking to make sense of a worldwide disaster is no mean task. But this sage scholar presents a richness and variety of perspectives that will inform the thinker and inspire the one in need of encouragement by putting the pandemic in temporal and eternal perspective. By exposing various myths, the rabbi's well-chosen and balanced words will provide comfort in the storm and sensible help to all people seeking to cope and to remain people of hope.

In characteristic rabbinic style, Samuel's work is filled with striking stories, vivid illustrations and practical guidance in helping to shepherd others through the complexities and challenges of this pandemic crisis. I am a fan of Rabbi Michael Leo Samuel because in this book, as in his many previous publications, he displays the unusual ability to bring theology, science, psychology, health and medical dimensions of real life struggles right down to earth. In short, he knows how to "put the cookies on a shelf" that all readers can grasp and digest. *God and the Pandemic* is a balanced, mature work by a veteran scholar that embraces a world and life view that will remain relevant, sensible and sane reading long after this present pandemic subsides. I highly recommend this book.

Marvin R. Wilson, Ph.D.
Professor Emeritus
Department of Biblical and Theological Studies
Gordon College

Author Notes to the Reader

A Brief History of the Problem

The coronavirus has been known to the scientific and medical communities since the 1960s, but only rarely has this little-known virus become widely recognized in the last fifty years. In 2003, the Severe Acute Respiratory Syndrome Coronavirus (a.k.a. the acronym SARS-CoV) also occurred in mainland China and in Hong Kong. Another type of coronavirus broke out in the Middle East in 2012 where it became known as the Middle East Respiratory Syndrome Coronavirus (MERS-CoV), and this occurred in Saudi Arabia, the United Arab Emirates and the Republic of Korea, and in other countries.

Fortunately, in both instances, these outbreaks were contained thanks to a combination of human intervention and still unknown natural circumstances. What we do know is that viruses mutate and adapt, much as we do as human beings. And the problem remains, coronaviruses will continue to change. We can blame that on evolution. And although scientists know a great deal about human coronaviruses, there is still much to be known.

In 2005, research scientists think that one of the viruses that they discovered—one that is responsible for a common cold—jumped from cattle to humans, leading to what they described as a pandemic of respiratory disease recorded around 1890 in human history. If this identification is accurate, the coronavirus has probably been making mischief throughout much of recorded history, but physicians of the past did not know how to identify it.

As one physician observed:

The researchers argue that in the second half of the 19th century a highly infectious respiratory disease with a high mortality rate, now known as contagious bovine pleuropneumonia, affected cattle herds around the world. Even though most industrialized countries mounted massive culling operations in the period between 1870 and 1890 and were able to eradicate the disease by the beginning of the 20th century, it is plausible that the culling personnel, animal handlers and farmers could have been exposed to coronavirus-infected bovine respiratory secretions.

There is still so much to learn. . .[1]

We might still wonder: How do we differentiate the symptoms of the cold or flu, seasonal allergies from the coronavirus? While many strains of the coronavirus produce mild symptoms similar to the common cold, COVID-19 causes severe illness in certain groups, e.g., older people, people of all ages who have underlying health conditions such as heart or lung disease, diabetes. To date, there is no vaccine yet for COVID-19, but within the year, we may well have several choices to choose from.

Why Did I Write this Book?

Once the public became aware of the coronavirus, governors across the country began implementing social distancing guidelines. One day, the thought occurred to me to write a series of articles to the San Diego Jewish World newspaper based on questions many of my congregants and friends have asked. Being a regular weekly columnist, I figured the articles would afford me an opportunity to share some of my daily thoughts on the nature of the pandemic and its religious and theological implications about our earthly journey in this world that often includes suffering and despair.

The topic led me to familiarize myself with many of the great pandemics in recorded history. I wanted to know and understand how the earlier generations dealt with this problem. I have observed and read many articles expressed by other religious leaders and their respective faith traditions. Regardless of our point of origin, the questions I encountered are all the same: What is the nature of suffering in a just universe? How does suffering alter our perceptions of God, our experiences of faith? What might we learn from one another?

How has the coronavirus altered our way of experiencing a particular faith? What are the healthy images and dysfunctional images of God that we have encountered during this time? How might we learn wisdom from the social-distancing and the retreat into our inner space—our home? How do we communicate a spiritual message when it is impossible to gather and pray at the church/synagogue/ or mosque and ashram?

From all the responses I discovered, each minister, rabbi, imam, roshi, and philosopher expressed his approach to the pandemic through a cultural and religious prism. The God images that we carry within our psyche inevitably colors the type of God we see and experience in the world. Some people hold on to a stern image of God who exacts retribution at the slightest offense. Others portray a God who is aloof, perhaps even distant. The list of God-images and its impact upon a suffering community is discussed in Chapter 11 of this book, entitled, "Rereading the Book of Job." One of the lessons emerging from Job is how he ultimately gives meaning to suffering by ministering toward those around him who were stricken with disease and suffering. You could say Job's experience of woundedness became his strength. Through Job's pain, he came to better understand his purpose in Creation. But knowledge always comes with a fee, as it says, "Much wisdom, much grief; the more knowledge, the more sorrow. (Eccl. 1:18).

Most of that particular chapter comes from an earlier book I wrote on Psalm 23, but I rewrote much of the material concerning how the faith community ought to consider acting in this time of national crisis and danger. The COVID-19 virus has united all of us; we are fighting a new world war, but this time it is the human race that must stand together against a determined foe that is indifferent to our existence. As I wrote these articles in my personal blog, I wondered: If the great spiritual teachers of the past were alive today, what kind of wisdom would they impart to us? As clergy, what are the new ways we might convey inspiration at this dangerous time? The coronavirus has made us much more aware of our vulnerabilities and of our mortality.

Facing human pain and healing must prove redemptive. The Talmud tells us a remarkable story about Rabbi Joshua, who one day met up with the Prophet Elijah. He asked him, "When will the Messiah come?" Elijah replied, "God ask him yourself. "Rabbi Joshua asked further, "But where can he be found?" Elijah said, "He will be sitting at the gates of Rome."[1]

When Rabbi Joshua arrived, he discovers the Messiah is sitting among the lepers, ministering to each of them, carefully tending to each of their individual wounds. In Levitical law, the leper conveys the most severe form of ritual impurity. Normally a healthy person must keep his distance from the leper. But the Messiah could care less about the ritual status of the leper; his only concern is to facilitate healing among them, one wound at a time. This Talmudic story provides the roadmap of how we as a nation will pass through the wilderness of the coronavirus. All of us have become a little bit like lepers. But even lepers need healing. By standing together as a community, tending to the wounded's lesions, we will emerge as wounded healers for the future.

A Coronavirus Prayer

Oh God Who dwells among us as in Heaven,
grant us wisdom, understanding and knowledge;
help us eradicate the coronavirus that threatens all people.
Assist the angels of healing,
the doctors, nurses, first-responders, and caregivers!
Grant them the insight, the intuition,
humility and steadfast spirit they need at this time
Endow and fortify the spirit of those who are sick with the virus
with inner strength and faith; may they receive the proper
medical care that they require for a speedy recovery.
As we walk through the valley of darkness,
we will not fear evil; because You are with us.
Help us conquer our anxieties and fears of what we do not know.
Let us come together in the spirit of a common humanity;
Let us work on creating the ties that bind our families
and communities together.
We pray for Divine Compassion in fighting this pandemic.
Give us the faith and vision to persevere
And the wisdom to learn the valuable lessons
that we all belong to one human family;
we need each other's support.
And for those who have lost loved ones,
Let us as a community to offer our love and support.
May God's Shekhinah look after the survivors,
And give them the strength they need at this time.
The Lord is our Shepherd
We shall not want.
Healer of all flesh!
Hearer of all prayer!
And let us say, "Amen!"

Part 1
The Mythic Journey & A Brief History of Ancient Pandemics

CHAPTER 1

"And once the storm is over, you won't remember how you made it through, how you managed to survive. You won't even be sure whether the storm is really over. But one thing is certain. When you come out of the storm, you won't be the same person who walked in."

Haruki Murakami

Beginning Our Heroic Journey

There once lived a famous Roman slave who became one of the most celebrated Stoic philosophers of his age—his name was Epictetus (ca. 50-C.E.-130 C.E.). His biography is all the more remarkable—especially when we consider his humble origins. Born to a slave-woman in the Phrygian city of Hierapolis in Asia Minor, Epictetus won his freedom from a master who also once lived the life of a slave. People from all over the Empire gathered regularly to hear Epictetus speak. This wise Sage captivated the hearts of those who heard his genuine wisdom, a wisdom that was born from a life of personal suffering. He wrote:

> What would have become of Hercules, do you think, if there had been no lion, hydra, stag or boar – and no savage criminals to rid the world of? What would he have done in the absence of such challenges? He would have just rolled over in bed and gone back to sleep! So by snoring his life away in luxury and comfort he never would have developed into the mighty Hercules. And even if he had, what good would it have done him? What would have been the use of those arms, that physique, and that noble soul, without crises or conditions to stir him into action? [2]

Every heroic story begins with an adventure that will test the limits and inner strength of an individual's capacity. Anyone aspiring to become a hero cannot afford to remain stationary—especially in the face of a challenge. A hero must resist the temptation to "playing it safe" by living according to other people's expectations.

The 19th century chess champion Wilhelm Steinitz used to say, "Chess is not for timid people."

And neither is life.

The personal message of Epictetus' homily is clear: God did not put us in this world to be mediocre, but to become exceptional people. There is nothing ordinary about the life God has granted us. But to realize this potential, Epictetus encourages us to embrace and accept our uniqueness, and ability to rise above adversity. The ordeals and hardships we face define our place in history now and for the future. Our life experiences become a historical record for posterity.

That's what it means to live heroically.

Hercules was the mythic hero most admired by Cynic and Stoic philosophers. His labors embodied their belief that it's more rewarding to face hardship voluntarily and cultivate strength of character than to take the easy option by embracing comfortable living and idleness. But no hero can ever be born without obstacles challenging one's resolve. The hero's journey on a psychological level requires that he overcome the darker impulses and passions—his "inner savage," as it were. This journey commits the protagonist to live a life of self-discovery, where one comes to discover one's destiny and life-purpose. The hero's insight is never an end in and of itself; his path leads him to better the human community around him; he seeks to redeem society itself.

Moreover, it is impossible to become a hero without first facing something dangerous and threatening. Hercules might have considered going to sleep after succeeding in his first ordeal, but Providence demanded that he regularly face ominous challenges, each one more difficult than the other. The hero's journey, when seen from this perspective, anticipates a triumphant return from the realm of darkness and death to light and life—from unconsciousness to a state of pure consciousness.

Epictetus' illustration of Hercules reminds us that on a psychological level, each of us has an inner hero that we must self-actualize. The heroic journey we experience will inevitably lead to a greater understanding of ourselves. In most hero myths, the hero sets out to bring a treasure to one's country or the world. But the journey inevitably involves facing one's inner demons and other obstacles that serve as rites of initiation. In virtually all hero stories across the globe, the hero must prove his worth, the caliber of his ideas and his character in a variety of dangerous ways that will test the limits of mortality.

In the end, God has endowed each of us with the time, talent, and treasure to make our life extraordinary. The hero is such a person that will always push the limits of his mortality in order to affirm life in the face of danger.

The story of the hero is told in every culture and period of human history. Each of these stories share several common themes. Heroes are never passively born; heroes are made and shaped by the circumstances surrounding them and by the moral decisions they make. This pattern is not unique to Greek myth, but also occurs throughout every biblical story—from Adam to Job. What was true regarding Abraham, Isaac, and especially Jacob, is no less true with their descendants. God grants each of us certain talents, abilities, strengths, and skills to help actualize our human potential in this world. The adversities we face serve to spur us to use these skills. In Jungian terms, human individuation is something only we can do for ourselves—nobody else can.

Hillel and Epictetus

Hillel the Elder (110 B.C.E-10 C.E.) expressed the following thought: "If I am not for myself, who will be for me? And if I am only for myself, then what am I, and if not now, when?" (*Avoth* 1:14). Hillel's remark bears a likeness to the thought Epictetus comment about Hercules. For Hillel and Epictetus, living heroically requires that we wake up from our lethargy and believe we can and must make a difference. "If I am not for myself, who will be for me?" In a word: Nobody. An actualized human being is always challenging and pushing oneself to be creative in overcoming obstacles. Epictetus would have concurred with Hillel's last question: If not now, when? Life is short as it is; we cannot utilize God's gift without focused attention and a steely determination to triumph over our challenges.

Epictetus' Advice for Facing COVID-19

Everything Epictetus described about Hercules could just as easily apply to our country, the United States of America. As the world's number one economic and military superpower, the United States possesses the stature of a Hercules on the world stage for over 170 years. As Americans, we sometimes take our country's history and greatness for granted. No other nation in the history of the world has liberated more countries from tyrannies than the United States. Although our great country has sometimes made tragic mistakes in our past, we have learned from these errors and remain committed to evolving as a country.

In one of Epictetus' most valuable lessons, he borrows a theme from Socrates, and argues that every human being is like a sculptor; the quality and self-actualization of human's life is not a given. Rather, each of us must make something out of our life experiences when it comes to the art of living. As one modern Stoic scholar observed:

> Epictetus compared philosophy to artisans: As wood is to the carpenter, and bronze to the sculptor, so are our own lives the proper material in the art of living. Philosophy is not reserved for wise old men, it's an essential craft for everybody who wants to learn how to live (and die) well. Every life situation presents a blank canvas or a block of marble that we can sculpt and train on, so that over a lifetime we can master our craft. That's basically what Stoicism does, it teaches us how to excel in life, it prepares us to face adversity calmly, and simply helps us sculpt and enjoy a good life.[3]

The situation our country is presently undergoing offers the opportunity of a life-time to recast the way we experience our world. The current pandemic in this country tests our ability to unite as a nation and form a singular identity with purpose and resolve. Defeating an invisible foe capable of claiming millions of lives requires that our nation—from the President to the common citizen—work together for the common good. We have opportunity to embrace the hero archetype and make the decision to live beyond ourselves.

CHAPTER 2

*"Those who cannot remember the past are
condemned to repeat it."*

George Santayana
The Life of Reason

The Pandemics of Late Antiquity

We are not only products of the present. Contemporary events are invariably influenced by a hidden historical process that has left its imprint on every current decision made. And those who fail to learn from history's errors risk letting their present reality be enslaved by it. As the philosopher George Santayana observed, problem-solving in the present is impossible if we refuse to discern the lessons learned from the past. Historical insight allows people to chart a different course and choose a different destiny. By meditating upon history, we can gain insights into the issues concerning people whose lives once resembled our own in many remarkable ways.

Rather than reinventing the wheel, let us draw inspiration from the past.

The Jewish philosopher Moses Maimonides (1138-1204) explains that when a person has succumbed to an illicit temptation, God will retest the individual's moral resolve by confronting him with a similar situation. Has this person learned from his previous mistakes? Or will he repeat them once again when confronted by a comparable temptation? We can apply his insight to the challenges that a nation face. Countries today must decide how to react in times of national crisis. Political leaders must choose wisely and not repeat the errors of the past.

We must learn from the embers of the past—not its ashes.

Scientific progress becomes possible only if we can understand how the earlier generations went astray in their scientific assumptions. Einstein had to have a complete grasp of the physics of his day before exposing its weak points. Wisdom is ascertained only through trial and error; the acquisition of knowledge comes with tuition gained from experience—and sometimes the price of education can be steep. Wisdom is not something inherited but is an acquired quality. In metaphorical terms, think of learning as the threads, and wisdom is like the weaver who creatively weaves the threads through his loom. Wisdom, by definition, must continuously be challenged, questioned, refined, and subject to revision; it must be woven and rewoven again and again. The art of weaving is a profound metaphor for understanding the workings of the universe and our place in it.

Santayana's aphorism might be expressed positively, "People capable of remembering wisdom from the past are free to reapply it." By looking at the positive models that have improved the lives of society, we can implement many of these same techniques in how we respond to a serious crisis. A people's memory based on significant events that have formed its past can serve as a model and paradigm for improving our world provided, we can tether that message to our present-day reality.[4]

This point especially applies to how we study the history of pandemics, which challenge the viability of an empire and nation. There is considerable wisdom we can learn from the past, provided we are open-minded and curious. In this book, we cannot examine all the great pandemics of human history, but we will touch upon some of the most critical pandemics that changed history. How the ancients responded to these pandemics might surprise moderns—and as you will see, there are many valuable lessons to be learned from the periods dating back to Late Antiquity. This depiction also applies today to our country and other countries who have suffered great economic chaos since the beginning of the coronavirus.

Before proceeding, let us begin by defining some basic terms. The term epidemic derives from Greek ἐπί (*epi*) "upon or above" and δῆμος (*demos*) signifies "people." It characterizes the rapid spread of disease to a large number of people in a given population within a short period of time; it can describe any problem that has grown out of control. It can affect a wide geographic area and affects a broad cross-section of a region's population." A pandemic (from Greek πᾶν, [*pan* = "all"] and δῆμος [*demos* = "people"]) is an epidemic that has spread across multiple continents affecting a substantial number of people of a whole country, or even the entire world.

The Background to the Antonine Plague

Lucius Verus and his adoptive brother Marcus Aurelius served as co-emperors of the Roman Empire during its Golden Age. In the first four years of their reign, Rome experienced good times and prosperity. But all that changed in the year 165 C.E., which proved to be a watershed moment of Roman history. A formidable Parthian army decided to invade the Kingdom of Armenia, a province of Rome. The Roman legions did not take this incursion lightly, and they attacked and eventually repelled the Parthian invasion. At the same time, the Germanic armies believed Rome had overextended itself and attacked Rome along her northern borders. But as challenging as both these adversaries were, they could not compare to the most perilous foe of all—a pandemic that would ultimately bring the mighty Roman Empire to its knees.

Historically, three pandemics weakened the foundation of the Roman Empire, which ultimately contributed towards its eventual demise: The Antonine Plague (165-180 C.E.), the Plague of Cyprian (249-262 C.E.) and the Justinian Plague (541-542 C.E.). The culprit is believed to have been caused either by smallpox, measles, possibly the bubonic plague, or some other disease that produced hemorrhagic fever. Determining the specific disease is difficult given the paucity of information that is available from that time. According to the immunologist Michael B. A. Oldstone, the ancients had considerable difficulty distinguishing between the measles virus infection from smallpox virus infection. The spread of the disease had much to do with the formation of urbanized cultures. He observes:

> Undoubtedly the great river valley cultures, dominant over 6,000 years ago in Mesopotamia and along the Tigris-Euphrates Valley, were the first to suffer measles virus epidemics. Indeed, some have conjectured that the plague of Athens in 4 B.C., in Antonine of the Roman world in the second century A.D., in China in 162 and 310, and in Tours in Southern France in the sixth century were associated with or consequences of measles virus infections. The formation of these urbanized centers as large, complex, organized, and densely populated cities brought together diverse people, some with resistance and others with susceptibility to the measles virus.[5]

Let us parenthetically add that in the Peloponnesian War (431–404 B.C.E.) fought between Athens and Sparta, an epidemic ravaged the people of Athens. The plague killed between 75,000-100,00 people and the urban environment most likely contributed to these high numbers who lived in the city during the war. The cause of the plague is unknown, although thirty pathogens have been considered.[6]

The Antonine Plague: A Chinese Connection?

It is significant the Antonine Plague began at a time when Rome and China established the first Silk Road, an ancient trade route that connects China to Eurasia.[7] Some historians think the plagues afflicting the Eastern Han Empire during the reigns of Emperor Huan of Han (r. 146–168 C.E.) and Emperor Ling of Han (r. 168–189 C.E.) might have been connected to the Antonine Plague on the western end of Eurasia.[8] Both the Han Dynasty of China and the Roman Empire did not know about the pathogens that created this pandemic. The Antonine Plague lasted from 165-180 C.E. Although the Roman roads and highways helped transformed Rome into a mighty empire, yet it would one day make it vulnerable to foreign diseases. Still, the interaction of these two civilizations might have given birth to the pandemic.

The historian William H. McNeil observed, "Religious history also offers another striking parallel between Rome and China. The Buddhist faith began to penetrate the Han empire in the first century C.E., and soon won converts in high places. Its period of official dominance in court circles extended from the third to the ninth centuries C.E. This obviously parallels the successes that came to Christianity in the Roman empire during the same period. Like Christianity, Buddhism explained suffering. In the forms that established themselves in China, Buddhism offered the same sort of comfort to bereaved survivors and victims of violence or of disease as Christian faith did in the Roman world."[9]

Another Theory Concerning the Antonine Plague

Alternatively, during the reign of Roman emperor Marcus Aurelius Antoninus (r. 161–180 C.E.), Roman legions came into contact with the disease during the siege of Seleucid, a city located off of the Tigris River. As the soldiers returned from the wars in the East, the disease spread northward to Gaul and among troops stationed along the Rhine River. The ancients believed that pestilence occurred because of the sin of impiety. Although he was a philosopher, Marcus Aurelius believed the gods must be respected at all times.

In the *Historica Augusta* (*Augustan History*) contains a series of biographies about the Roman Emperors and other significant figures of Roman history. It spans across the period 117 to 284. The information regarding Marcus Aurelius is illuminating. The writer of this valuable Roman historical work claims Lucius Verus' death was not coincidental; the gods punished him and the Empire for disrespecting the gods.

> It was his fate to seem to bring a pestilence with him to whatever provinces he traversed on his return, and finally even to Rome. It is believed that this pestilence originated in Babylonia, where a pestilential vapor arose in a temple of Apollo from a golden casket which a soldier had accidentally cut open, and that it spread thence over Parthia and the whole world. Lucius Verus, however, is not to blame for this so much as Cassius, who stormed Seleucia in violation of an agreement, after it had received our soldiers as friends. . . [10]

When Marcus Aurelius heard about the desecration of Apollo's Temple, he became irate. The Emperor had good reason to feel fearful. Although Apollo is identified as a god of healing, he was also a bringer of plagues. The Emperor believed the deity chose to ravage Roman because of Verus' men's lack of respect. So devastating was this plague, the religious institutions quickly organized their cults to placate the gods. In the city of Hierapolis, several Roman cities across sent delegations to Apollo, asking for the god's advice about how they might survive. The priests and priestesses believed the god could be appeased by making sacrifices, and having the people donate their wealth to the local shrines. But all the homage and sacrifices proved ineffectual.

Verus' soldiers sinned by treating the deity's statue as if it were a work of art and not religious devotion. Consequently, the gods punished Verus and his kingdom. The Greeks and Romans identified Apollo as not only the god of healing but also as the bearer of plagues and epidemics. The wise monarch believed that if mortals could properly pacify him, perhaps the calamities could be averted.

As a philosopher, Marcus Aurelius was a man for all seasons. Yet, like many people living today, he believed that the gods often strike back at people for failing to show proper respect and loyalty. Despite millennia of human progress, this attitude remains embedded in our psyche. Instead of

Apollo taking issue with mortals, today, pious people identify God of the Bible as the bringer of plagues and pandemics. Today, as the coronavirus spreads across the world, religious leaders have sounded the clarion, "We have sinned against God's Law, and He is punishing us for our sins."

This is not a new story.

We have walked this path before.

The Plague of Galen

Many ancient Roman thinkers such as Cicero, Lucretius, and Seneca had a secular view about God and nature. They believed reality could be understood without the need not to posit the existence of God, gods, angels, or the like. Galen was such a thinker. As the Romans offered their sacrifices and made the appropriate prayers to their deities, the physician Galen scoffed at this widespread attitude. He believed there was a scientific reason why the pandemic spread—and it had nothing to do with gods who became offended. Galen attributed the disease to what he called μίασμα ("miasma"), believed to be a physical contagion that is airborne. The stench touched everything, and it became embedded in every part of Roman life. The condition of the air infected many people who shared the same living space, as Galen insists, "caused by the interaction between the surrounding air and individual constitutions." Note that the miasmic theory of disease was attributed to an invisible vapor arising from filth, contaminated water, foul air, and poor hygienic conditions, and decaying flesh; it was believed to be easily transmissible. To Galen's credit, only in the late 19th century did medical science finally reject the theory of miasma.

But as medicine progressed, medical science eventually developed the germ theory of disease, which is the currently accepted scientific theory for many diseases. It states that microorganisms known as pathogens or "germs" can lead to disease. Germs are microscopic that the human eye cannot see without a microscope. They invade lifeforms—humans and non-human. When they take root in a host organism, they cause disease. "Germs" are not limited to only bacterium, but can include any type of microorganism or even non-living pathogens, as we see with viruses, prions, or viroids.

The Antonine Plague soon became known as the "Plague of Galen" because he is the first physician to leave documented notes regarding its symptoms. Galen described it as a rash, which he called exanthem, from the Greek ἐξάνθημα ("exanthema") "a breaking out." This symptom is commonly seen in those afflicted with smallpox. He also commented on how the illness affects the alimentary tract, particularly diarrhea and black stools. Galen observed that if the stool was very black, the patient did not survive. Besides, Galen served as Emperor Marcus Aurelius' physician. Many historians believe Marcus Aurelius' also died from the plague.[11]

The Antonine Plague proved to be a defining moment in Roman history. Some historians think the total deaths have been estimated at 5 million. In some areas, the disease killed as much as one third of the population and it also destroyed much of the Roman army. The might of the Roman Empire dissipated over time—largely because of the Antonine Plague.

Marcus Aurelius: Mastering the Chaos—A Lesson for Today

Marcus Aurelius found himself in an awkward situation. How was he going to protect his people from the social chaos ensuing from the Antonine Plague that was destroying the Empire? His background in Stoic thought gave him the inspiration to lead. Stoic philosophy, he exclaimed, "Be like the rock that the waves keep crashing over. It stands unmoved and the raging of the sea falls still around it. It's unfortunate that this has happened. No. It's fortunate that this has happened and I've remained unharmed by it—not shattered by the present or frightened of the future. It could have happened to anyone. But not everyone could have remained unharmed by it."[12]

Marcus Aurelius understood that life is full of accidents that are often unpreventable. But rather than succumbing to despair, the individual must summon his inner strength and deal with the hand he has been dealt with. Aside from being a brilliant philosopher, Marcus Aurelius proved to be a capable administrator. He realized that death is the great equalizer. It did not matter what strata of society one belonged to; rich and poor suffered alike.

With resurgent German tribes threatening Rome from the North, something novel had to be done. The wise Emperor knew the mighty Roman Empire's aura of invulnerability had been punctured by a mysterious disease that could not be understood. The depletion of the Roman legions to the pandemic led the Emperor to make sweeping social changes previous leaders would never have considered. With the scarcity of soldiers that remained, the Emperor recruited liberated slaves and gladiators, Roman society pulled itself under Marcus Aurelius, and the

Empire endured. In his writings, the philosopher-king cautioned his people to banish fear whenever confronted by a dangerous situation. Although we cannot control what happens to us in the world, we can control how we react.

When we look at the impact the coronavirus is having on our nation's psyche, Marcus Aurelius' words of wisdom emerge as a shining light. Although he could see how Rome was rapidly deteriorating into a state of chaos, immorality, and violence, the Emperor offered these pithy words in his *Meditations* that moderns ought to familiarize themselves with:

> Real good luck would be to abandon life without ever encountering dishonesty, or hypocrisy, or self-indulgence, or pride. But the next best voyage is to die when you've had enough. Or are you determined to lie down with evil? Hasn't experience even taught you that—to avoid it like the plague? Because it is a plague—a mental cancer—worse than anything caused by tainted air or an unhealthy climate. Disease like that can only threaten your life; this one attacks your humanity."[13]

Marcus Aurelius was right. Hysteria indeed can be more damaging than any plague. Whether it be the Antonine Plague or the coronavirus, we must respond to the challenge with clarity and determination. Throughout it all, the Stoic Emperor always maintained his focus and purpose. Was Marcus Aurelius indirectly referring to the Antonine Plague in mind when he wrote, "Time is like a river made up of the events which happen, and a violent stream; for as soon as a thing has been seen, it is carried away, and another comes in its place, and this will be carried away too"?[14] Probably. Marcus Aurelius believed that having unrealistic expectations about life is a disappointment waiting to happen.

We must be prepared for anything!

We might also think the Marcus Aurelius never experienced hardship. But this was not the case. The Stoic historian Donald Roberson points out that Marcus Aurelius did not live a relaxed life:

> Marcus was a naturally loving and affectionate man, deeply affected by loss. Over the course of his life, he increasingly turned to the ancient precepts of Stoicism as a way of coping when those closest to him were taken.

Now, as he lies dying, he reflects once again on those he has lost. A few years earlier, the Empress Faustina, his wife of thirty-five years, passed away. He'd lived long enough to see eight of their thirteen children die. Four of his eight daughters survived, but only one of his five sons, Commodus.

Death was everywhere, though. During Marcus's reign, millions of Romans throughout the empire had been killed by war or disease. The two went hand in hand, as the legionary camps were particularly vulnerable to outbreaks of plague, especially during the long winter months. The air around him is still thick with the sweet smell of frankincense, which the Romans vainly hoped might help prevent the spread of the disease. For over a decade now, the scent of smoke and incense had been a reminder to Marcus that he was living under the shadow of death and that survival from one day to the next should never be taken for granted.[15]

When we look at how the Roman Emperor conducted himself, he emerges as a wonderful model for how future political leaders of nations ought to act. He possessed a moral clarity that united the Empire. Marcus Aurelius behaved as a wise shepherd in looking after the welfare of his people. Let us pray that Democrats and Republicans learn from this great man—whose legacy will never be forgotten. Unfortunately, the chaotic leadership that came after Marcus Aurelius did not follow the guidelines the gentle Emperor recommended, and Rome swiftly perished.

The Plague of Cyprian

Before Emperor Constantine, Roman emperors took a dim view toward the early Christian Church. Although Marcus Aurelius possessed many exceptional attributes and was blessed with wisdom, his hatred and persecution of the Christians remained a terrible legacy. When the plague seized Rome, Christians often became the scapegoat, much like the Jews became after Rome had converted to Christianity. It is ironic; the Roman emperors considered the early Christians to be much like the Jews, whom they regarded as atheists since they rejected the Graeco-Roman pantheon of deities. In addition, they were perceived as "haters of humanity"[16] since they did not honor and appease the gods.

It is not known whether this pandemic was a continuation of the Antonine Plague, but it soon became known as the Plague of Cyprian. As with the Antonine Plague, it is unclear what it was that caused it. Among the diseases considered, it too may have included smallpox, pandemic influenza, and viral hemorrhagic fever (filoviruses) like the Ebola Virus. But as we mentioned before, deciphering the disease was limited by their limited knowledge of medicine.

The Roman historian Dio Cassius (155-235 CE) estimated 2,000 deaths per day in Rome at the height of the initial outbreak. At the height of the second epidemic between 250 and 266 C.E., as many as 5000 people a day died in Rome[17]—causing widespread manpower shortages for food production and a further weakening of the Roman army.

The name "Cyprian" commemorates the St. Cyprian, bishop of Carthage, an early Christian writer who witnessed and described the plague. Cyprian's biographer, Pontius of Carthage, wrote of the plague at Carthage:

> Afterwards there broke out a dreadful plague, and excessive destruction of a hateful disease invaded every house in succession of the trembling populace, carrying off day by day with abrupt attack numberless people, everyone from his own house. All were shuddering, fleeing, shunning the contagion, impiously exposing their own friends, as if with the exclusion of the person who was sure to die of the plague, one could exclude death itself also. There lay about the meanwhile, over the whole city, no longer bodies, but the carcasses of many, and, by the contemplation of a lot which in their turn would be theirs, demanded the pity of the passers-by for themselves. No one regarded anything besides his cruel gains. No one trembled at the remembrance of a similar event. No one did to another what he himself wished to experience.[18]

Despite appealing to the gods for relief, Roman leaders did not know how to prevent the spread the contagion. The situation had become so serious, nobody treated the sick, much less buried the dead. The historian of Early Church history, Gary Ferngren made several significant observations that I will briefly summarize. And as the plague swept through

Carthage in North Africa, the corpses piled up throughout the streets, as the flesh rotted. The families of the dead could not be found. But the forms of religious piety continued unabated. Emperor Decius ordered all the Christians of the Empire to Carthage's bishop to offer sacrifices to the Roman deities. However, Cyprian came up with a brilliant stroke of religious genius; he urged the city's Christians to give aid to their persecutors and to care for the sick. He urged the rich to donate funds and the poor to volunteer their service for relief efforts.

Cyprian instructed his followers to minister to believers and pagans alike. And under Cyprian's administration, the Christians buried the dead left in the streets and continued caring for the sick and dying. Cyprian demonstrated remarkable courage and organized this relief effort for five years. One could argue that Cyprian's legions became the template that later inspired the Red Cross. It is significant the men that Cyprian mobilized risked their lives to minister and heal those who stood at death's door. These men and women became the world's first responders.

Ferngren's comments here are especially poignant:

> And Cyprian was not the only hero from that era. Much later, in Alexandria, Egypt, in about 416, the Christian patriarch of that city organized a corps of men recruited from the poor classes to transport and nurse the sick. They were called the *parabalani,* the "reckless ones," because they risked their lives by exposing themselves to contagion while assisting the sick. Already in 312, during a widespread plague, Christians in many Eastern cities were performing similar tasks.
>
> In the face of epidemics, they seem often to have formed ambulance corps, making up for municipal authorities' failure to help the sick and dying. Such large-scale organized emergency efforts did not emerge from nowhere. For centuries Christians had been developing infrastructure in their own churches to help the sick. The diaconal (deacon-led) care that the churches offered the sick was usually palliative, since it was administered for the most part by people with little or no medical training or experience. But we know today that in the absence of professional expertise and even medications, a basic

regimen of nursing care including food, water, and rest can cut mortality during epidemics by two-thirds or even more.[19]

Aaron as the Archetype of Healing Ministry

St. Cyprian's behavior can serve as a wonderful illustration to a lesser-known biblical story. We read:

> On the following day, the whole community of Israelites were muttering against Moses and Aaron and saying, 'You are responsible for killing the LORD'S people!' Now, as the community was banding together against Moses and Aaron, they turned towards the Tent of Meeting, and there was the cloud covering it, and the glory of the LORD appeared. Moses and Aaron then went to the front of the Tent of Meeting.
>
> The LORD spoke to Moses and said, "Get away from this community. I am going to destroy them here and now." They threw themselves on their faces. Moses then said to Aaron, 'Take a censer, put fire in it from the altar, place incense on it and hurry to the community to perform the rite of expiation for them: for retribution has come from the LORD, plague has broken out.' Aaron took it as Moses said and ran into the middle of the community, but plague had already broken out among the people. He put in the incense and performed the rite of expiation for the people. Then he stood between the living and the dead, and the plague stopped. There were fourteen thousand seven hundred victims of the plague, apart from those who died because of Korah. Aaron then went back to Moses at the entrance to the Tent of Meeting; the plague had been halted.
>
> Numbers 16:46-50

Rashi dramatically pointed out, "Aaron seized the angel of death and held him against his will."[20]The famous Jewish medical historian Julius Preuss (1861–1913), thinks that the phrase, "stood between the living and the dead" indicates he managed to separate the healthy from the unhealthy, which at that time might have been considered as a practical, hygienic measure.[21] This passage might suggest the possibility that Aaron resorted to the practice commonly known as triage, which is the process of determining the priority of patients' treatments by the severity of their condition or likelihood of recovery with and without treatment.

Aaron's use of the incense in combatting a mysterious epidemic may illustrate how its fragrance might have served as a disinfectant; the incense contained essential oils that could kill a virus and bacteria on contact. Some Native American Indians used a technique called "Smudging," which involves the burning of sacred herbs or resins whose smoke is aimed at parts of the body that are diseased, such as the face, head, feet, along the spine. Inhaling the vapors of these essential oils are directly absorbed through the skin. It is believed to have healing properties. When we think about the doctors and nurses taking care of the coronavirus patients, they too are standing between two worlds, we cannot help but think that the spirit of St. Cyprian is evident in the care given by all the physicians, caregivers, and first responders.

The Fate of Rabbi Akiba's Disciples

It is surprising neither the Babylonian or Jerusalem Talmud make any direct reference to the great pandemics that crippled the Roman Empire. Had Josephus (37-100 C.E.) lived in the late to early 2nd-3rd century, he would have written about the plagues that destroyed Rome. It would have been natural—even understandable for the Sages living in the Land of Israel to argue God was punishing the Roman Empire for its many sins committed against the Jewish people and their religion. But this was not the case. When it does speak of pestilence, the Sages pointed out that a city that had "Even in the case of such a great city as Antioch, if three corpses were produced on three successive days, i.e., that is a sign of pestilence."[22]

Mar Samuel (165-257 C.E.) lived during the Antonine Plague and the Plague of Cyprian; it is conceivable he was well-aware of the pandemic that gripped the Roman Empire. "When Mar Samuel heard that pestilence was raging in the far-away place called *Be Hozae* [is a province in southwestern Iran], he ordained a fast of supplication because he feared its spread to his town since an active caravan traffic (*sheyara*) existed between the two places that the pestilence accompanied."[23]

One reason for the Talmud's omission might suggest that by the time the Talmud was redacted, the redactors had long forgotten about what happened to Rome. But the statement from Mar Samuel does fit with how the Roman pandemics spread across the Empire. Some have argued that the Talmud in BT Yebamoth 62b records that R. Akiba had 24,000 students from Gevat to Antipatris (a city built during the first century by Herod the Great, who named it in honor of his father, Antipater). They all died in one period of time because they did not treat one another with respect."

But R. Adin Steinsaltz observed in his commentary,

> It appears from the Gemara that most of Rabbi Akiba's disciples died in a plague. However, Rav Sherira Gaon explains in his letter that this was a *shemada*, meaning their death was due either to governmental persecution or to war. If so, this would appear to be related to the Bar Kokhba revolt, of which Rabbi Akiba was an ardent supporter. It is reasonable to surmise that Rabbi Akiba's students served as soldiers under Bar Kokhba and when the Romans suppressed the revolt with great brutality, these students were killed. the image depicts an engraving that was prepared by the Roman senate in honor of Hadrian after he succeeded in suppressing the Bar Kokhba revolt. It is currently at the Israel Museum in Jerusalem.

There is no evidence they died from a plague, but it is more likely, as R. Sherira Gaon (906-1006) observed, they died as soldiers who joined the Bar Kokhba revolt. His son, Rabbi Hai Gaon of Pumbedita, Iraq (939-1038), also argued that Rabbi Akiba's students supported Bar Kokhba revolt against Rome and were all killed. [24] The association between Rabbi Akiba and the Bar Kokhba revolt is significant for he endorsed Bar Kokhba's ambition to free Judea from the hegemony of Rome.

By encouraging his students to fight against Rome, the Roman legions killed them. The historical tragedies of the failed revolt were many. Emperor Hadrian believed that Judaism was the root cause of the Jews' rebellions against Rome. Hadrian ceremonially burned the Torah on the Temple Mount. Perhaps most famously, he renamed Judea with name Palaestina (Palestine) in honor of Israel's ancient enemies—the Philistines.

Part 2
Struggling with Faith

CHAPTER 3

"Dear God, we paid for all this stuff ourselves,
so thanks for nothing."

Bart Simpson's Thanksgiving Prayer

"If we are honest, we will admit that most modern Jews
in the period before Hitler cared little about God and
expected almost nothing of God in history... relying on
God was old-fashioned and medieval. We relied on
ourselves, on humanity, to a messianic extent."[25]

Eugene Borowitz,
Reform Judaism Today

The Myth of Self-Sufficiency

The coronavirus pandemic of 2020 has shaken our society to its core. Its negative impact has led to millions of people losing their jobs and businesses. People have become fearful and suspicious of one another. People can be seen fighting in the local Costco stores because someone did not observe the rules of social-distancing.

It is amazing how quickly our lives can turn upside down.

Before the advent of this new danger confronting us, most of us did not feel any imminent threat; we shook hands and hugged each other with no fear. Guests came to our homes, as well as our places of worship. We never imagined that the social fabric of our societies could unravel and change in what seems like the twinkle of an eye. We could go to the supermarket and always buy what we needed for the week. We never imagined modern people would be fighting over toilet paper. Some enterprising individuals hoarded thousands of toilet paper rolls, offering to sell it on Amazon.com and eBay for $4.00.

Toilet paper?

Sometimes our world seems like a dystopian novel. What has happened to us and our sanity? Suddenly the supermarket shelves looked like the supermarkets we have seen in places like Venezuela, or the old Soviet Union. I will never forget the scarcity these shelves conveyed. The cities look like deserted ghost towns and in some places in the world, lions and tigers can be seen lying down peacefully on the streets.

Yes, we live in fear.

We Need to Rediscover Our Faith in God

Although we pride ourselves on being vastly more sophisticated than the ancients, there's much we can learn from our primal forbearers. For example: Ancient farmers have always recognized that the success of a crop depended upon weather conditions that were completely out of one's control. The farmer knew that in a matter of minutes that a severe rainstorm could cause damage to both his crops and freshly cultivated soil. Mildew, infestations of beetles, locusts, and other insects likewise can destroy a harvest. Droughts in agricultural and pastoral areas are often more damaging and widespread than brush fires. Early man's keen sense of vulnerability led the farmer to rely on a Supreme Being who would look after him and his needs.

Modern farmers have more tools available in combatting traditional problems such as locusts and other pests. Still a sudden change in weather can adversely affect the success of a crop, e.g., an unexpected drop in temperatures, or a heavy rain can cause physical damage to crops, but the real threat is mold. After heavy rainfall, the cool night temperatures can create the perfect conditions for spore germination and propagation, and once that occurs, curing the infection becomes almost impossible. Consumers become aware of the problem when they see a sudden price-increase at the local market. Despite our technological prowess, we are more vulnerable to these meteorological than we might consciously realize.

The Philosophy of Scientism

Although the phenomena of plagues are well-attested throughout the annals of recorded history, we would like to think that in a highly-technological society that we have everything under control. But no sooner will after we conquer the present coronavirus, we now hear warnings about the next variant of coronavirus. Not only has the pandemic turned the world economies upside-down, it has a pervasive anxiety that is impacting our psychological and spiritual well-being of people everywhere. Our feelings of powerlessness, angst, and unease do not seem to be abating, as we face an uncertain future.

In a scientific age, it is not uncommon to hear the philosophy of scientism asserted in the university and public-school classrooms. The mere mention of God is forbidden to discuss when speaking about how the universe came into being. We no longer need God to explain the order of the universe. Nature operates according to certain impersonal laws. Science alone is the only rational guide to truth. All else is mere belief and opinion. Today, we regard scientists and medical community's leadership much like the ancients regarded the high priests of their societies, modern-day secular shamans who act as the purveyors of truth. Man has become comfortable assuming the role of God, but only superficially.

The Chinese have a wise saying, "Be careful what you wish for, you might just get it." Just as every coin has two sides, every outcome also has a positive and negative potential. People often dream of being wealthy, but they fail to realize that wealth creates envy; people who suddenly find themselves wealthy beyond their dreams after winning the lottery often end up poorer than they were before winning the lottery ticket. The ancient Minoan story of King Midas and his golden touch illustrates this same problem. Wanting to be God may seem tantalizing at first sight, but there are aspects of this desire that could make human beings miserable.

Elie Wiesel's Parable: When Man Became God

Elie Wiesel tells us a parable about God and man exchanging places; this parable is as suggestive as its beginning. Wiesel narrates:

> Legend tells us that one day man spoke to God in this wise. "Let us change about. You be man, and I will be God. For only one second." God smiled and asked him, "Aren't you afraid?" "No." "And you?" "Yes I am," God said. Nevertheless, he granted man's desire. He became a man, and the man took his place and immediately availed himself of his omnipotence; he refused to revert to his previous state. So neither God nor man was ever again what he seemed to be.

. . . Years passed, centuries, perhaps eternities. And
suddenly the drama quickened. The past for one and the
present for the other, were too heavy to be borne. As the
liberation of the other, they renewed the ancient dialogue
whose echoes come to us in the night, charged with hatred,
remorse, and most of all, with infinite yearning. [26]

Wiesel's haunting parable describes the Promethean age where human
beings have usurped the role of God, while the Divine has taken on the face
of the victim who suffers in the face of unspeakable evil. As a result of this
exchange, neither God or man ever remained the same. With infinite power
comes infinite responsibility—more responsibility than human beings are
willing to take on. The last part of his parable illustrates that once man
assumed the position of God proved more than he wanted to handle; he
became weary of the gift of omnipotence; simply put, he lacked the wisdom
and patience to use it properly. Although secular culture strives to become
God, our culture has discovered that being God is not exactly what we
thought it would be. Karl Marx claimed, "religion is the opiate of the
people," but nowadays, it is opiates that serve as the religion of the people.

Secular culture has failed to deal with problem of meaninglessness in our
lives. The absence of the Divine has often driven people to madness, cults,
and sometimes to religious fundamentalism. The appeal for the latter is
strong because modern man has become dissatisfied with the superficiality
of modern life. By the same token, for "God to become man," according to
Wiesel, proved to be no less daunting even for God.

Wiesel's story has an interesting parallel in the theological comedy,
"Bruce Almighty" that was released in 2003. While man may wish he were
God; God grants the protagonist Bruce Nolan (played by Jim Carrey) his
desire; in actuality the job is infinitely more challenging than the
protagonist imagined. In the end, he freely relinquishes his God-like powers
and in the process finds contentment as a human being.

Viruses have a way of dethroning our arrogance as a species.

The Atheistic Challenge

One is reminded from the famous scene from Macbeth:

> She should have died hereafter;
> There would have been a time for such a word.
> — Tomorrow, and tomorrow, and tomorrow,
> Creeps in this petty pace from day to day,
> To the last syllable of recorded time;
> And all our yesterdays have lighted fools
> The way to dusty death. Out, out, brief candle!
> Life is but a walking shadow, a poor player
> That struts and frets his hour upon the stage
> And then is heard no more. It is a tale
> Told by an idiot, full of sound and fury
> Signifying nothing.
> *Macbeth* (Act 5, Scene 5, lines 17-28)

A more recent paraphrasing of this famous passage reads:

> The days creep slowly along until the end of time. And every day that's already happened has taken fools that much closer to their deaths. Out, out, brief candle. Life is nothing more than an illusion. It's like a poor actor who struts and worries for his hour on the stage and then is never heard from again. Life is a story told by an idiot, full of noise and emotional disturbance but devoid of meaning.

It is intriguing to compare Macbeth's words to the ideas expressed in later existential philosophical thought. The "brief candle" signifies the limited days of our life in this temporal world. But Macbeth asserts life has no meaning or ultimate purpose. His statement conveys a sense of pure cynicism, as well as a sense of existential despair. But Macbeth's remark is nothing more than a recipe for nihilism. And considering how he lived his amoral life, it is understandable.

Some have argued that "Gods are saviors for many, the ones they pray to throughout the year for protection. But when humanity is in peril, it is usually the gods who flee first . . ."[27] Judaism teaches that God made us stewards of our world, and it is our moral imperative to improve upon God's Creation—a world that was never perfect even from its inception. This is a point we shall discuss later in this book.

That being said, it is important to note atheists may share more in common with their theistic cousins than they realize. Non-theistic people also have beliefs, as well as questions pertaining to, "How do we make sense of what has happened?"

Jewish tradition differs from Christianity in one basic respect. Christians by and large wish prefer having certainty that they are "saved" and are going to Heaven after they die. Answers are more important than questions. But in Judaism, the question is more important than the answer. Answers come and go and may be reformulated in time. But a great question will never change; it will challenge the thinking of today's generation much as it has with generations who lived thousands of years ago. Great questions will continue to challenge the future as well.

Atheists and agnostics claim that their values derive from science and secular humanism. They often tend to believe in humankind's nobler impulses, namely, the evolutionary imperative will eventually enable human beings to live in a more civilized world.

As you can see, this statement requires a leap of faith that one might expect from a theist. As a theistic person, I am not a great believer in man's innate goodness—especially given what my father experienced in Auschwitz. Yet, I believe that the objections posed by people of the atheistic bent—especially now during this great pandemic—raises legitimate and existential questions every thinking person cannot honestly ignore.

The Holiness of Atheism

Rabbi Abraham Isaac Kook (1865-1935) was an Orthodox rabbi, the first Ashkenazi Chief Rabbi of British Mandatory Palestine. In addition, he was a mystic and scholar; his receptivity to the sciences helped him articulate a philosophy of Judaism was compelling. When his followers asked him about atheism, he refused to consider it as a depraved cultural force. Even atheism possesses a spark of holiness because it challenges the religious status quo to purse itself of its dross. Atheism can serve to help people abandon ideas about God that are unhealthy, "Atheism has a temporary legitimacy, for it is needed to purge away the aberrations that attached themselves to religious faith because of a deficiency in perception and in the divine service." He adds further:

> Atheism arises as a pained outcry to liberate man from this
> narrow and alien pit, to raise him from the darkness . . .

Atheism has a temporary legitimacy, for it is needed to purge away the aberrations that attached themselves to religious faith because of a deficiency in perception and in the divine service. This is its sole function in existence— to remove the *particular* images from the speculations concerning Him who is the *essence* of all life and the source of all thought . . . [Its purpose is to] uproot the dross that separates man from the truly divine light, and in the ruins wrought by atheism will the higher knowledge of God erect her Temple. To cleanse the air of the arrogant and evil aberration of focusing thought on the divine *essence*— a preoccupation that leads to idolatry—a thoroughgoing atheism arises, in itself no better than the former but opposed to it in absolute terms . . .

The violence of atheism will cleanse away the dross that accumulated in the lower levels of religious faith, and thereby will the heavens be cleared and the shining light of the higher faith will become visible, which is the song of the world and the truth of the world. Whoever recognizes the essence of atheism from this perspective embraces the positive element in it and traces it back to its origin in holiness. He glimpses the awesome splendor in the ice-like formations upon the celestial horizon (Cf. Ezekiel 1:22).[28]

According to Hasidic tradition, R. Jacob Isaac of Pzhysha, known as the "Holy Jew" once taught his disciples that there is nothing on earth without its good aspect; there are "holy sparks" of divinity in everything waiting to be revealed. A clever student asks, "What good is there in atheism?" He answered, "When it comes to man's social duties and obligations, he should behave as if he were an atheist, assuming God does not exist to help the poor and the needy, so that if he did not help them, they would remain impoverished. "Faith is a virtue when applied to one's own life. It is wrong to have it on behalf of others, there is yet something of value in atheism, for even the believer has to be a small doubter when called upon to alleviate human suffering."[29]

For those who question or struggle with faith, Maimonides has long taught that before we can know what God is, we must first determine what

God *is not*. Modern theologians call this the *via negativa*, the path of negation. By emancipating ourselves of the childish perceptions of God that we have inherited, we can become open to the God of Life and Infinite possibilities. Atheism challenges believers to let go of their immature perceptions. In the words of Hamlet,

> *"There are more things in heaven and earth, Horatio,*
> *Than are dreamt of in your philosophy.*

Hamlet (1.5.167-8)

In the end what matters is that people of all backgrounds and creeds work together—theists, agnostic, and atheists together can work toward the common good.

Young Martin Buber's Epiphany

As professional clergy, we tend to think robotically and uncritically about our faith. In some ways, the atheists speak like biblical prophets; they challenge us to ask and demand we articulate in clear terms what we ought to believe in. I enjoy reading books and articles written by atheists. Whereas many theistic people like myself are willing to take a leap of faith, I have found atheists also take a leap of faith—they assume there is no God, nor is there an objective meaning or purpose to the universe. They assume we are living in the realm of the absurd, and that we must live heroically and accept the fact that life has no intrinsic meaning (Camus, Sartre).

As a young teenager learning about Jewish philosophy, I wanted to answer my agnostic friends' questions and convince them why they ought to believe in God. But what I have learned over the decades is that most folks are not merely interested in having a theological debate; they are searching for an answer that is spiritually deep and relevant.

For those people who have suffered through the coronavirus, questions about God's Reality or Presence are real and existential in nature. Glib theological answers will not satisfy a searching soul. People are looking for something more. The great 20th century Jewish philosopher Martin Buber recalls that shortly before World War I, a young man came to see after he had experienced a morning of mystical ecstasy. Buber was friendly and attentive; he answered his youthful visitor. However, in human communication, sometimes it is not always the question that is expressed that matters, but rather it is the silent question that a person cannot express, or does not know how to articulate.

For this reason, Buber realized that he was not entirely "present" to the young man in spirit, who died in battle shortly after. When he heard about the news, Buber felt dissatisfied with how he interacted with the man, who came to him for spiritual guidance.[30] Buber learned that being emotionally present to someone seeking guidance is what he failed to do. The presence of a concerned and listening heart—not discursive philosophical repartee, is what the young man really needed. Buber's realization soon led to his formulation of his most significant spiritual work, "I and Thou."

For ministers of all faiths, the story about Martin Buber offers a valuable lesson about the power of listening. Not every question people ask about God is necessarily intellectual in nature. When people feel as though they have reached the end of their earthly journey, they need an answer that is pastoral and healing in spirit.

There is a charming Sufi tale that illustrates this point. "Once there was a man whose marriage was in trouble sought his advice, the Sufi Master said, "You must learn to listen to your wife." The man took this advice to heart and returned after a month to say he had learned to listen to every word his wife was saying.

Said the Master with a smile, "Now go home and listen to every word she isn't saying."

In the art of communication, we must learn to listen to the unarticulated need and question.

Pascal's Wager

The seventeenth-century French philosopher, mathematician, and physicist, Blaise Pascal (1623–1662) came up with a clever way how an agnostic or non-believer might consider thinking about faith. Pascal argued that, while it's impossible to prove whether or not God exists through reason alone. The next best thing is to live your life as if God exists, which He certainly does! If we live as though God exists and we discover that God truly does exist, we win eternal bliss in heaven. However, if we make the wager that God does not exist and He does, Pascal points out that we will spend all eternity in damnation.

But what if we are not sure? If we live as though God exists, and He does indeed exist, we will have gained eternal life. If He doesn't exist, we have lost nothing. If, on the other hand, we live as though God does not exist and He really does exist, we have gained hell and punishment and have lost heaven and bliss. Pascal claims that when you consider the odds, clearly the rational choice to live as if God exists is the better of the possible choices. The relative paybacks that come with believing are greater than the payback or risks of not believing in God. Perhaps when we living as if we have faith, someday we might eventually come to have faith. [31]

Critiquing Pascal's Wager

Pascal's argument has little appeal to Jews. Jewish tradition has long taught, "Be not like servants who minister to their master upon the condition of receiving a reward; but be like servants who minister their master without the condition of receiving a reward; and let the fear of Heaven be upon you" (*Avoth* 1:3). When we worship God to receive a reward, we are no longer serving God, but ourselves. There is a name for that, it's called, "idolatry." Rabbinic thought would certainly concur with the early 20th century psychologist William James, who candidly noted, "Those who engaged in such egotistic reasoning might be among the first that God would exclude from heaven." Elihu asks Job, "If you are righteous, what do you give him, or what does he receive from your hand?" (Job 35:7).

Christopher Hitchens argues that the wager makes a mockery of the idea of God. How are you going to venerate God as the greatest possible being to exist, and who can read your thoughts and judge them, and then turn around and say God isn't smart enough to see through false beliefs made "just in case?" It is "religious hucksterism." It's a sly way of saying, "Hey, come on over to my shop, I have a special price just for you, but come in through the side door." It assumes God is a moron. If this wager were a real possibility for eternal salvation, then it's all the more reason not to believe in the God it represents. Richard Dawkins' counter-argument also makes more sense:

> There is something distinctly odd about the argument, however. Believing is not something you can decide to do as a matter of policy. At least, it is not something I can decide to do as an act of will. I can decide to go to church and I can decide to recite the Nicene Creed, and I can decide to swear on a stack of bibles that I believe every word inside them. But none of that can make me actually believe it if I don't. Pascal's Wager could only ever be an

argument for *feigning* belief in God. And the God that you claim to believe in had better not be of the omniscient kind or he'd see through the deception.

But why, in any case, do we so readily accept the idea that the one thing you must do if you want to please God is believe in him? What's so special about believing? Isn't it just as likely that God would reward kindness, or generosity, or humility? Or sincerity? What if God is a scientist who regards honest seeking after truth as the supreme virtue? Indeed, wouldn't the designer of the universe have to be a scientist?

Bertrand Russell was asked what he would say if he died and found himself confronted by God, demanding to know why Russell had not believed in him. 'Not enough evidence, God, not enough evidence,' was Russell's (I almost said immortal) reply. Mightn't God respect Russell for his courageous skepticism (let alone for the courageous pacifism that landed him in prison in the First World War) far more than he would respect Pascal for his cowardly bet-hedging? And, while we cannot know which way God would jump, we don't need to know in order to refute Pascal's Wager. We are talking about a bet, remember, and Pascal wasn't claiming that his wager enjoyed anything but very long odds. Would you bet on God's valuing dishonestly faked belief (or even honest belief) over honest skepticism?[32]

It is utterly preposterous and theologically scandalous to suggest that God may choose to reward honest disbelief and punish blind or feigned faith. Scriptures makes this point clear: "For the LORD, your God, is the God of gods, the LORD of lords, the great God, mighty and awesome, who has no favorites, accepts no bribes" (Deut. 10:16). In other words, we are not doing God any favors by believing in His existence. This is precisely the kind of dross R. Abraham Isaac Kook warned us about in the previous section that needs to be purged from the religious consciousness of the believer.

Victor Frankl's Reinterpretation of Pascal's Wager

Perhaps there is another way of salvaging Pascal's idea. If we think of religion as a meaning-making system, then let us propose s different reconstruction of Pascal's Wager via the prism of Victor Frankl's belief in the importance of discovering meaning in our lives. While Frankl was in the concentration camp at Auschwitz, he taught his fellow inmates that one way they could find meaning in their lives was to make a "bet" that their suffering had some kind of redemptive meaning. There was no way they would know whether this bet would pay off. But the belief that life has meaning—even in the death camps—gave them the ability to make it from day to day. Conversely, those who lost their sense of meaning—even though they may have had more food to eat—perished more quickly than those who believed life has meaning. Frankl helped my father with this philosophy, and he instructed him to divide his food portions into half and save part of it for the evening when everyone went to bed. He came to regard the extra food-portion as a treat, and it gave him something to look forward to.

Although Pascal's wager may not be the most convincing path, when applied to Victor Frankl's psychological approach, it makes perfect sense. Make a wager. Assume that there is purpose and meaning to our existence in the universe. If you are correct, look at what you gain—a life that has purpose and direction. If you assume that there is no purpose and no meaning to your existence in the universe, what difference does it matter whether you live or die?

What if you are not sure whether there is purpose and meaning to your existence in the universe? Then take the risk that there is. For, in the end, you will feel more fulfillment and happiness, a Victor Frankl believed that a spiritual life that is imbued with belief in the meaning of life grants the person a spiritual quality that cannot be attained in any other way. It is preferable to a belief that in nihilism and meaninglessness. When we assume there is a purpose, we know we can find the strength to conquer all obstacles that are in our path. We will perceive the unexpected events in our lives as a challenge and that we know we can cope and eventually triumph. This is an existential way of reformulating Pascal's Wager.

It is the wager I am willing to believe in; it worked for my father who endured the horrors of Nazi torture and abuse in Auschwitz. It also works for me. Perhaps it can work for you too. What we need is a purpose driven life. I realize this approach may not work for everybody. But this approach gives me the hope we can find a purpose for even the bad things that occur in this world—such as the coronavirus. In a godless universe, there is no morality. Anyone with the strongest will-to-power to achieve one's goal can trample over as many lives as it takes to reach the pinnacle of power. Nietzsche (and Adler) believed power to be the main driving force in humans, and for many it is.

Drazin's Bet

My dear college and friend Rabbi Dr. Israel Drazin has offered these additional comments that I would like to share with the reader.

> I have a different approach, one that we can call "Drazin's Bet."
>
> Unlike Pascal's wager, Drazin's Bet focuses on behavior, not belief. It recognizes, as Maimonides taught, that it is usually impossible or at least difficult to force people to believe something contrary to their nature, training, and inclinations. Also, unlike Pascal's wager, the bet addresses religious people rather than atheists.
>
> According to Drazin's Bet, if a person believes in God, two possibilities exist. The first is that God wants people to sit back, relax and depend on divine help. Like a parent or king, God will take care of humanity and bring a messianic age. God will feed the poor, clothe the naked, and ensure that war, pestilence, ignorance, and spoiling the environment do not destroy the world. The second possibility is that God wants people to do these things.
>
> In my opinion, the first view is misguided. I propose Drazin's Bet. I suggest that even if people are convinced that God will take care of everything and that there is no need to act, they should still hedge their bets. For it is possible, contrary to their understanding, but consistent with that of Maimonides, God wants people to act. The bet states that whenever there is a need for something to be done – to help people, society or the world in general – people should behave as if there is no God who is involved in human affairs and nothing will be done to resolve the

problem at hand unless they themselves do what must be done.

The bet takes into account that if God is present as a parent, ready, willing and able to resolve the problem, since God knows that the individual who assumed the divine role is behaving for a good reason, God will be pleased with the person's behavior.

The bet goes one step further. It supposes that God would be displeased with people who contend that they should sit back, pray, read religious texts, and not work to improve themselves, society and the world.

Thus, the bet is a sure thing; there is no way of losing. If I am right that God expects people to perform these acts, the individual is performing God's will. If, on the other hand, God does all that needs to be done, God will still be satisfied with the person who assumes the divine role.

However, the pious person who does not take the bet and who sits back performing devotional deeds, expecting God to remedy human and societal needs, when God expects people to perform these acts, will suffer divine wrath.

Part 3
Understanding "Acts of God" & "Acts of Man"

CHAPTER 4

"In ridiculing a pathetic human fallacy, which seeks explanation where none need be sought and which multiplies unnecessary assumptions, one should not mimic primitive ontology in order to challenge it. Better to dispose of the needless assumption altogether. This holds true for everything from Noah's flood to the Holocaust."

Christopher Hitchens

Defining "Acts of God"

Although there exists a separation between Church and State in our country, nevertheless, God is frequently invoked in our legal tradition whenever the law speaks about "Acts of God" whenever unexpected disasters occur. When Hurricane Katrina flooded New Orleans in 2006, the insurance companies associated this flood as an "act of God."

For insurance purposes, one might wonder: If an Allstate Insurance Company surveyed the damage of Noah's flood, would it also qualify as an "act of God"? You might say, "Wait a minute! The flood in the story of Noah is an act of God! Did not God announce He was going to destroy sinful and violent people? But the insurance industry is not interested in theology; it is only interesting in establishing liability. When a lightning causes a fire to burn a house down, or when a tree fell upon homes after a tornado breezed through town, the implicit assumption is that nobody is at fault here—only God. Insurance companies fully know that whenever an "act of God" occurs—they are responsible to compensate the insured party. God cannot be sued. Parenthetically I would add that in Jewish tradition, pious Jews have often "sued" God for a variety of alleged offenses—from failing to provide a dowry for a poor man's daughter to the allowing the Holocaust to occur. In every story, God was always a "no-show" at the trial. Collecting from an Almighty Deity is not something any collection agency is empowered to do.

Yet, "acts of God" and "apocalyptic" continue to be figures of speech that permeate secular language. The ancients frequently spoke about the "gods being angry" whenever they beheld something disastrous. Given the capriciousness of these natural disasters, it was only natural for primal man to believe that God was "fickle" and could turn against a person on a dime. Biblical stories often depict God as having a quick-temper and is always ready to exterminate evil doers. When Noah left the ark, the first act of devotion to God involved offering God several sacrifices (Gen. 8:20). Most commentators think Noah wished to express his gratitude for being rescued with his family and animals. Let us propose a different deconstruction of the text. Noah felt God might someday lose His temper and destroy the world again. To prevent this from happening to his descendants, Noah offers the sacrifice as a bribe. The anthropologist E. B. Tylor (ca. 1832-1917) proposed the theory that sacrifice was essentially a business transaction between mortals and the gods based on the principle of *do ut des* ("I give so that you will give in return"). In modern terms, we refer to this bartering principle as, *Quid pro quo* ("something for something" in Latin). In other words, "You scratch my back, I'll scratch yours!" The sacrifice functions as a mutual exchange.

Maimonides on "Act of God"

In the ancient realm, everything in nature constituted an "act of God." Maimonides noted that the ancients regarded God as the "ultimate" reason why something occurred in nature. But as the ancient Greek scientists and mathematicians began observing the natural order, the "act of God" was simply another way of saying "natural phenomena." The more the human being progressed over the centuries, the field of geology taught man that one could account for all the seismic activities, hurricanes, tornadoes, and other natural disasters without ever having to evoke God into the picture. Modern scientists often assert that the world makes perfect sense without God. Anthropologists taught the ancients used God as a way of explaining phenomena we otherwise do not understand. Moreover, as science's precise and powerful way explained more of what humankind did not understand in the pre-modern era, the value of God as the explanation for how the universe functions diminished. In the end, insofar as science and religion contend head to head, whether in explaining the origin of the species or why droughts and famine occur, secularists claim that religion consistently comes out the loser every time. Compared to the precision of the laboratory, it appears as muddled superstition. We, however, disagree with this position.

The Lisbon Earthquake of 1755

With the birth of modernity, the association between angry deities as the source of natural disasters was summarily rejected, even though this perception remained embedded deep in the psyche of ministers, rabbis, imams, other religious representatives, and the masses. When a disaster, or in this case, the coronavirus pandemic began, a chorus of religious leaders immediately began citing scripture and blamed the deaths of innocents on the nations' sinfulness.

If we time-traveled to Lisbon on November 1, 1755, shortly after the famous earthquake that destroyed 30,000 people, we would have heard a similar theological discussion to the coronavirus pandemic of our time. Besides the earthquake, a tidal wave followed and caused considerably more damage to the city. Aside from the earthquake's immediate damage, fires also broke out throughout the city and completed the work of destruction. It was a virtual trifecta disaster.

Religious pundits claimed that the offenses of Lisbon were legion; it was a city that was famous for its brothels—and God punished their wanton ways with an earthquake. Yet, this explanation proved wanting. Although the earthquake destroyed the city's churches, the brothels were spared! Among Christian scholars of that era, the English cleric John Wesley (1703-1791) attributed Lisbon's destruction to Portugal's role in supporting the Spanish Inquisition that expelled the entire Jewish population. Yet, Spain and Italy were spared, despite being the primary instigators of the Inquisition![33] If Wesley were correct, the rest of Europe should have also been punished for expelling and persecuting the Jews who lived peacefully in their lands. Wesley's answer is too theologically facile to take seriously. It is no wonder why no European intellectual took a dismissive attitude toward Wesley's theory.

Voltaire Reflects on the Lisbon Earthquake

Voltaire was one of France's most celebrated intellectuals. He was a free-thinker who did not care much about institutional religion. Voltaire believed in God, but denied God had any interest in the affairs of mortals. Voltaire took an interest in a couple of famous earthquakes of world history.

In 1556, Shaanxi China experienced an earthquake that killed 830,000 people. Voltaire also recalled hearing about another earthquake that occurred in China that resulted in 400,000 dead. Historically, China has experienced more than its fair share of earthquake tragedies.

In any event, Voltaire's letters raised serious theological questions about God's rulership of the world; God's management of the world did not seem to be concerned itself with man's best good, as Leibnitz argued in his *Theodicy*. Voltaire thought of Leibnitz as a Catholic medievalist. The French thinker would have approved of Hitchens' earlier remarks that such speculation is utterly useless—especially as the bodies of the Lisbon dead were still yet to be buried. Voltaire's pen proved to be a mighty weapon in challenging the theological status quo of his era.

In his poem, "An Examination of the Axiom: All is well,'" Voltaire wrote:

Oh, miserable mortals!
Oh wretched earth!
Oh, dreadful assembly of all mankind!
Eternal sermon of useless sufferings!
Deluded philosophers who cry, "All is well,"
Hasten, contemplate these frightful ruins,
This wreck, these shreds, these wretched ashes of the dead;
These women and children heaped on one another,
These scattered members under broken marble;
One-hundred thousand unfortunates devoured by the earth,
Who, bleeding, lacerated, and still alive,
Buried under their roofs without aid in their anguish,
End their sad days!
In answer to the half-formed cries of their dying voices,
At the frightful sight of their smoking ashes,
Will you say: "This is the result of eternal laws
Directing the acts of a free and good God!"
Will you say, in seeing this mass of victims:
"God is revenged, their death is the price for their crimes?"
What crime, what error did these children,
Crushed and bloody on their mothers' breasts, commit?
Did Lisbon, which is no more, have more vices
Than London and Paris immersed in their pleasures?
Lisbon is destroyed, and they dance in Paris!

Voltaire wondered, did the volcanic activity that caused the earthquake really have to be part of the Creation? Can the people of Lisbon derive any solace knowing that their city's destruction served a positive purpose in God's grand-scheme of things? One could almost hear the ghost of the ancient pre-Socratic thinker, Epicurus, who famously declared, "Is God willing to prevent evil, but not able? Then he is not omnipotent. Is he able, but not willing? Then he is malevolent. Is he both able and willing? Then whence cometh evil? Is he neither able nor willing? Then why call him God?"

Jean-Jacques Rousseau's Thoughts on the Lisbon Earthquake

Voltaire was not the only lone voice of France whose words captivated the hearts and minds that read his words with enthusiasm. Jean-Jacques Rousseau (1712-1778) was also a French philosopher, writer and composer. His political ideas helped to inspire the French and the American Revolution.

Although Rousseau was also a deist, but unlike Voltaire, Rousseau's concept of God differed considerably from Voltaire, whose view depicts a deity who acts malevolently toward His creation:

> Everything seemed to cooperate in drawing me out of my sweet and foolish reverie. I was not cured of my attack when I received a copy of the *Poem on the Ruin of Lisbon* which I assumed had been sent to me by the author. That gave me the obligation to write to him and to speak to him about his piece. I did so by means of a letter that was printed a long time afterwards without my assent, as will be said below. Struck at seeing this poor man burdened down, so to speak, with prosperity and glory nevertheless declaiming bitterly against the miseries of this life and always finding all to be evil, I formed the senseless project of making him return into himself and of proving to him that all was good. While always appearing to believe in God, Voltaire really never believed in anything but the Devil; since his so-called God is nothing but a maleficent being who according to him takes pleasure only in harming. The absurdity of this doctrine, which leaps to the eyes, is revolting. . . [34]

Would Rousseau consider the destruction of Lisbon an "act of God" or an "act of man"? If anything, the Lisbon earthquake of illustrated the pitfalls of urban-living and poor urban-planning. Urban-living in crowded cities prove dangerous whenever a natural disaster occurs. A superiorly designed city might have suffered much less casualties and death. Rousseau writes in his correspondence with Voltaire:

> I do not see how one can search for the source of moral evil anywhere but in man. . . Moreover, the majority of our physical misfortunes, are also our work. Without leaving your Lisbon subject, concede, for example, that it was hardly nature that there brought together twenty-thousand houses of six or seven stories. If the residents of this large city had been more evenly dispersed and less densely housed, the losses would have been fewer or perhaps none at all. Everyone would have fled at the first shock. But many obstinately remained . . . to expose themselves to additional earth tremors because what they would have had to leave behind was worth more than what they could carry away. How many unfortunates perished in this disaster through the desire to fetch their clothing, papers, or money? . . . [35]

How Would Voltaire and Rousseau Reacted to COVID-19?

Let us wonder: How would these two French philosophers have debated about coronavirus? Would Voltaire see the pandemic as an anti-proof in the existence of a just God? Undoubtedly, Voltaire condemned the faith of those who believed in a benevolent deity. He would have also scoffed at the religious leaders of today who see the coronavirus as a divine tribulation for the city's brazen sins. As previously noted, Voltaire and Christopher Hitchens would have been in total agreement.

It is logical to presume that Rousseau would have assigned blame directly to the government of Communist China for their complete abdication of responsibility. Pandemics do not always have a divine origin; they can occur through human recklessness and moral stupidity. With greater accountability, China might have been able to better contain the coronavirus when it made its presence known in China. Similarly, Rousseau would have blasted political leaders in our country for failing to take into consideration the possibility of how a pandemic could cripple our country, along with the other countries of the world.

Rousseau's answer may be found in his writing to Voltaire, "I do not see that one can find the source of moral evil elsewhere than in man himself, because man is morally free.... with respect to physical evils, they are inevitable in any system of which man is a part of; and then the question is not why isn't man perfectly happy, but why he exists . . ."[36]Perhaps anticipating the thinking of certain modern-day 21st century environmentalists, Rousseau would have preferred that people ought to live farther apart in less congested areas—a return to nature rather than congregating in the metropolitan cities. God, for Rousseau, had nothing to do with Lisbon's destruction. The destruction unleashed by the earthquake came from man's mismanagement of his urban resources.

From Lisbon 1755 to San Francisco 1906

In keeping with Rousseau's earlier thought, during the 1906 San Francisco earthquake, up to 90% of the destruction was the result of the subsequent fires. Within three days, over 30 fires, caused by ruptured gas mains, destroyed approximately 25,000 buildings on 490 city blocks. More than 3000 people died.[37] Here too, as was the case with Lisbon 1755, much of what we consider "natural disasters" can often be attributed by the woeful and irresponsible actions of taken by people that transformed a grave situation into an epic calamity.

From Lisbon to New Orleans: Hurricane Katrina 2005

One of the most severe hurricanes of recent memory was Hurricane Katrina, Category 5 tropical cyclone that occurred in August 29, 2005; it caused $125 billion in damage, particularly in the city of New Orleans and the surrounding areas, and over 1,200 deaths. Although the weather was fierce, the onus of Katrina's damage did not come from the weather but from the systemic breakdown of government. According to the NY Times, the onus of the blame ought to go to the US Army Corps of Engineers:

> On August 29, 2005, there were over 50 failures of the levees and flood walls protecting New Orleans, Louisiana, and its suburbs following passage of Hurricane Katrina and landfall in Mississippi. The levee and flood wall failures caused

flooding in 80% of New Orleans and all of St. Bernard Parish. Tens of billions of gallons of water spilled into vast areas of New Orleans, flooding over 100,000 homes and businesses. Responsibility for the design and construction of the levee system belongs to the United States Army Corps of Engineers; the responsibility of maintenance belongs to the local levee boards. The Corps hands components of the system over to the local levee boards upon completion. When Katrina struck on August 29, 2005, the project was between 60–90% complete. Four major investigations were conducted by civil engineers and other experts in an attempt to identify the underlying reasons for the failure of the federal flood protection system. All concur that the primary cause of the flooding was inadequate design and construction by the Corps of Engineers.[38]

While it is true the US Army Corps of Engineers (USACE) bear much of the responsibility, the fact remains that after the levees were completed, local and state organizations had to see that the levees were maintained and shared. In fact, the operation and maintenance being a 100 percent local responsibility. As one study pointed out, there was a failure to inspect the levees on a regular basis and these lapses that resulted in their ultimate collapse.[39] Hurricane Katrina illustrates how the various bodies of government (e.g., the City of New Orleans, the State of Louisiana, the Federal Government, FEMA, the Mayor, the Governor, the President, the local residents, and so on) failed to make maximum use of the resources available. Local officials knew in advanced that this type of storm was possible and that the levees could break. Why was nothing done about it? Why were the monies allocated for rebuilding the levees not utilized decades after they were collected from the government? Why was there no effective evacuation plan? Why did it take so long for the relief agencies to respond? How the local inhabitants compound the problem with their disregard for the law? Human beings once again bear the responsibility for the vast majority of destruction that ensued. Assigning blame to God for natural disasters is theologically irresponsible. The same could be said about cities that are built on a known fault-line. There are safer places to live.

Improving Upon Creation

Human choices have consequences.

There is a famous Jewish story about a man who brings some very fine material to a tailor and asks him to make a pair of pants. When he comes back a week later, the pants are not ready. Two weeks later, they still are not ready. Finally, after six weeks, the pants are ready. The man tries them on. They fit perfectly. Nonetheless, when it comes time to pay, he can't resist a jibe at the tailor.

"You know," he says, "it took God only six days to make the world. And it took you six weeks to make just one pair of pants."

"Ah," the tailor says. "But look at this pair of pants, and look at the world!

The humor of this story illustrates the Jewish attitude about God and Creation. Contrary to Leibnitz, Jewish tradition teaches us that God did not create a "perfect world." God, however, did make a "good world." It is up to mortals to improve upon the flaws of Creation.

Judaism's greatest medieval philosopher, Moses Maimonides (1138-1204) accepted the fact that nature can be dangerous at times. Yet, he stresses that when disasters occur, people of good faith can improve upon Creation by imitating God's ways through justice and compassion. When God enjoined Adam to, "Fill the earth and subdue it!" (Gen. 1:28), the biblical narrator may have had this type of thought in mind. "Conquering the earth" may very well involve fixing nature's many imperfections. A mature faith in God demands that we be responsive to the various mishaps and flaws of creation through a covenantal co-relationship with the Divine.

Among other medieval theologians, Thomas Aquinas argued that all types of natural disaster derive from the fact that they are earthly phenomena, which are by their very constitution prone to corruption and dissolution.[40] A physical world based on the laws of physics has no choice but to be subject to the reverberating fluctuations of imperfection. It is up to human beings to perfect it. To summarize, it is almost certain Maimonides would have taken sharp issue with Leibnitz's view that God made this world "the best of all possible worlds." It is more likely he would have paraphrased Leibnitz's idea in more Judaic terms, namely, "God created this world to have the potential to be the best of all worlds."

We are responsible to actualize this theological possibility.

CHAPTER 5

"In February 2020, the government of China announced that it was going to conduct a massive "crackdown" on religions that do not submit to the communist regime. This, of course, includes the underground church of China. To put this plainly, one of the most hostile nations in the history of the world toward Christians has announced a new breed of hostility aimed at Christian annihilation. The new wave began in February 2020.

Why should we think it strange that a pandemic outbreak of disease has sprung up in the heart of China? How can we fail to observe the time of these two events? Is this just a coincidence, or is this a judgement of God against a nation that has systematically destroyed God's people for generations?"

Rev. Billy Prewitt
The Coronavirus In Biblical Prophecy

Dialoguing with Christian Theological Thought

Not all Christians agree with Rev. Prewitt. And among the Christian clergy I have encountered, some believe that all traces of evil, disease, and suffering would not exist in our world were it not for the Fall of Adam and Eve. By rebelling against the goodness and benevolence of God, our primal parents created an inner imbalance that continues to affect the world in countless unhealthy ways. Their act of disobedience led to the chaos we identify with the human condition. In the beginning, God made a perfect world with flawless human beings, but our primal parents' inner corruption ruined human nature for all time; consequently, our relationship with Creation suffered.

The existence of viruses and other disorders of the body and soul would not exist if not for Adam's sin. As a result of the "Fall," human history must learn to live in a world that includes the sorrow and drama of illness and suffering. The cure for a Christian is to accept Christ as his/her savior. Christians believe he alone endured all the pain of humankind. Christians believe this decision is necessary for one's entry to heaven.

In Jewish tradition, we generally do not think about being "saved" through our belief system. Judaism tends to focus on the here and now. Our actions and behavior determine our spiritual growth—in this world and in the world beyond. In terms of our faith, Jewish tradition views the whole concept of "Original Sin" differently from our Christian neighbors. From our perspective, Adam's Fall did not directly affect his posterity at all, nor did Adam and Eve's behavior result in the first sexually transmitted spiritual disease to the human race! Our primal parents' sins affected only themselves. Every child born into the world is as Adam was at creation: entirely innocent; each human being is born with the freedom to choose his or her own path in life.[41]

Early Christian Critiques of "Original Sin"

The Judaic ideas expressed in the previous section was later articulated by the great Celtic critic of Augustine, a man named Pelagius (360-420 C.E.). This scholar spent many years living in Palestine, and his thinking reflects the scholars he interacted with from the Jewish community.

> Sin is carried on only by imitation, committed by the will, denounced by reason, manifested by the law, punished by justice. . . .. If sin is natural, it is not voluntary; if it is voluntary, it is not inborn. These two definitions are as mutually contrary as are necessity and free will. Adam was created mortal and would have died whether he sinned or not sinned; the sin of Adam injured only him, not the human race; the law leads to the kingdom of Heaven, just as the gospel does; even before the coming of Christ there were men without sin; newborn infants are in the same state which Adam was before his transgression; the whole human race does not die with the death and transgression of Adam, nor does it rise again through the resurrection of Christ. . . .[42]

For Pelagius, it is morally wrong to convict the entire human race because of one person's sin. But what about illness? Jewish ethics has long taught that illness is a part of the creative order. One of my favorite illustrations for this comes from the Christian Bible. In what is arguably one of the most important teachings found anywhere in ancient Jewish wisdom. The story goes like this: Jesus once saw a man who had been blind since birth. His disciples asked him, "Rabbi, who sinned, this man or his parents, that he was born blind?" And he replied, "Neither this man nor his parents sinned," said Jesus, "but this happened so that the works of God might be displayed through him." [43]

This passage suggests Jesus did not believe in "Original Sin," this concept reflects Paul's attitude. Unfortunately, trying to determine what Jesus said, and differentiating this from what people think he said is a matter of confusion for laypeople and scholars alike. Robert Funk's historical approach to deciphering what Jesus said is instructive. Here is what he said concerning the man who was blind from birth:

> The words ascribed to Jesus in these extended dialogues are what the narrator imagines Jesus to have said on such occasions. The initial question raised by his disciples (v. 2) is based on a common assumption: all misfortune was deserved, since the calamity was the result of sin. In the case of a congenital disability, such as blindness from birth, there arose the question of whether the victim had caused it or if-perhaps because such a sin was hard to attribute to an unborn baby-the blame lay with the victim's parents. It is not difficult to imagine Jesus addressing such a question as this, since his answer here would have cut against the social grain. Nevertheless, the actual words in this exchange are the words of the evangelist and not those of Jesus. [44]

The story, in my opinion, categorically rejects the idea of a pre-natal sin. This view is especially prevalent among the Hindus, who believe the soul is tainted with the karma of a previous lifetime. But how do we account for the congenital blindness of an innocent child? The answer to this question pertains directly to how religious people ought to view the coronavirus pandemic. Terrible things occur so that the "works of God" might become manifest through us. Who knows how many futures pandemics might someday be cured because of our experience with the coronavirus?

From Jesus to Hellen Keller

Jesus' statement made me think of Hellen Keller, a woman who was stricken by illness at age two and was left blind and deaf. Beginning in 1887, Anne Sullivan tirelessly dedicated her life to helping Hellen communicate, and she went on to graduate in 1904 and accomplished many incredible things. At first, she was a problematic child and refused to cooperate with Sullivan's instructions. But Sullivan noticed that she was not making the connection between the objects and the letters spelled out in her hand. Sullivan kept working at it, forcing Keller to go through the regimen.

> Then one day, Sullivan taught her how to say the word, "water," and she helped her make the connection between the object and the letters by taking Keller out to the water pump, and placing Keller's hand under the spout. While Sullivan moved the lever to flush cool water over Keller's hand, she spelled out the word w-a-t-e-r on Keller's other hand. Keller understood and repeated the word in Sullivan's hand. She then pounded the ground, demanding to know its "letter name." Sullivan followed her, spelling out the word into her hand. Keller moved to other objects with Sullivan in tow. By nightfall, she had learned 30 words.

When a pandemic occurs, we need to realize it is one of life's challenges for us to help manifest God's compassion through our earthly attempts to solve the disease. When we will conquer it, rest assured the knowledge we will have learned will help us in combatting other diseases. Blaming people for the condition is not only wrongheaded—it is also fierce. What the world needs right now is compassion—and not hypercritical people who think they know the mind of God.

Blindness as a Psychological Metaphor

As Hellen Keller once famously observed, "The only thing worse than being blind is having sight but no vision." This applies especially to religious-minded people whose arrogance and self-righteous attitude prevents them from seeing the truth. Note how Helen Keller distinguished between having sight and having wisdom. This nexus is intriguing, for one does not necessarily suppose the other. One famous verse reads, הֶחָכָם עֵינָיו בְּרֹאשׁוֹ וְהַכְּסִיל בַּחֹשֶׁךְ הוֹלֵךְ "A wise man has his eyes in his head, whereas a fool walks in darkness" (Eccl. 2:14).

Perhaps the author of Ecclesiastes wanted to point out a similar point. People—especially scholars speaking in the name of our sacred tradition—need to have wisdom. It is not enough to merely "see" what is in front of you, you must have the insight to understand what it is that is in front of you. In life, people will often stumble and trip for failing to take into consideration what is directly in front of the walker.

Blindness need not be physical. There is another type of blindness that keeps a person enchained to ignorance and mindless behavior. In contrast, insight derives from the mind's ability to imagine and see a relational nexus in the things that occur daily in our lives. Lacking this quality, according to Hellen Keller, is worse than not having eyes at all.

A wise person must learn to see with the inner eye. Oriental religions teach that aside from the two eyes each person possesses, the most important eye one must have and use is the "eye of consciousness," which allows the individual to see beyond the *maya* (the Hindu word for "illusion"). In Buddhist theology, practitioners must learn to see the world with their eyes. Thus, the "third eye," a symbol of enlightenment. When spiritual leaders live without a vision for the future are in an endless present, through their foolishness, they create a world that is without hope; they are incapable of leading their followers without guidance. Although a blind person does not have sight, if s/he has insight, that person is far better off than those who live lives with blindness and lack wisdom. Indeed, "The only thing worse than being blind is having sight but no vision"– Helen Keller

CHAPTER 6

*"It is of the very nature of the Bible to affront, perplex
and astonish the human mind. Hence, the reader who
opens the Bible must be prepared for disorientation,
confusion, incomprehension, perhaps outrage."*

Thomas Merton

The Role of Myth in the Ancient Psyche

As we noted in the previous chapter, the scientific view of why natural disasters such as earthquakes and plagues occur differ considerably from the views advocated in the Scriptures.

But how can modern believers in the message of Scripture make sense of pandemic like the coronavirus, or the Bubonic Plague? Indeed, the Bible narrates numerous stories about plagues and other tales of divine retribution. These destructive events are invariably attributed to human sin. Look no further than the story of the Flood. Look no further than the cities of Sodom and Gomorrah. And let's not forget the Ten Plagues that befell Egypt! But as a student of the Bible and of science, I often wondered: Did these purported natural catastrophes occur spontaneously at the snap of God's finger, so to speak?

Does God react toward sinful human beings with a ferocity that has frightened sinners since millennia? Personally, I cannot believe in a God who punishes Jews for failing to observe Jewish rituals. But what I do believe is that the bible records certain natural events that did occur, but became theologically reinterpreted, recontextualized and retrojected into the narrative by the original biblical writers. They wanted their story of what happened to convey a moral meaning: God is just and He holds human beings accountable for their deeds.

Ancient people did not possess a scientific understanding of the universe. In its place, they used myth in transmitting memories about actual events that occurred millennia ago. These myths preserved valuable information about a lost world. [45] The ancestors told these stories in an idiom their peoples could easily understand—and sometimes, with the purpose of saving lives.

In a trailblazing study on myth, Elizabeth Wayland Barber and Paul T. Barber illustrate this concept by relating the creation of Crater Lake. Klamath Indian tribes maintain their ancestors witnessed its creation, some 8000 years ago. Their descendants relate an ancient story of how a beautiful maiden rejected the romantic overtures from the "Chief of the Below World." In his rage, he causes the mountain to shake. Red hot rocks and burning ash fall like rain. Local medicine men sacrifice themselves to appease the angry deity. The volcanic eruption soon ceases. Nobody ever hears from the Chief of the Below World again. After years of rainfall, eventually, water fills the hole. To this day, the Klamath Indians never visit the site. They associate it as a place of death and misery. [46]

Traces of ancestral memory persist across time. As geologists Walter Pitman and Bill Ryan theorize, the story about Noah and the Flood may be traced to a devastating flood that occurred at a time when the Ice Age was beginning to melt. Noah thus became a pseudonym for a nameless man who survived with his family and farm animals, who managed to live long enough to talk about their terrifying experience.

Does such an interpretation discredit the biblical story about the Flood? As with many mythic narratives of antiquity, the Flood story communicates something profound about the nature of human fragility and vice. Living in a dangerous world, the story of Noah reminds the generations that there will always be forces of chaos that threaten to engulf the world. Our sense of stability may ultimately prove to be an illusion for there will be always be a chaotic presence seeking to unmake our man-made world. The ancients intuited a concept that transcends their age: Humankind possesses the ability to bring about its own demise. In a paradoxical sense, the moral prescriptions drawn from these ancient tales possess a realism that makes them more credible than stories that happened in real time and space. The biological misuse of weapons of mass destruction, or unleashing a nuclear Armageddon are possibilities humankind must always be wary of. Instead of God "destroying the world," the uncreation of nature can occur through human hands—as many environmentalists have noted.

Maimonidean Theology for 2020

In his famous *Guide,* Maimonides asserted that people would often anthropomorphize tragic events to God that occur in the natural world as an expression of divine wrath. But in reality, it is not God who is lashing out against human beings, or nature, though it may on some psychological level seem so. Maimonides explains:

> EVERYTHING produced must have an immediate cause which produced it. It is logical to assume that cause was produced by yet another cause, and so on [forming a regression]—until we arrive at God as the Ultimate Cause. The reason for this is clear: It is through His will and decree all things become actualized. In their prophecy, the prophets often left out the intermediate causes and ascribed the production of an individual thing directly to God as a way of saying, "God has decreed it."[47]

In the Book of Exodus, there is a short but mysterious narrative about how one of Moses' children nearly died. The biblical narrator describes God as having "met him and tried to kill him," (Exod. 4:24). The passage is textually challenging, and the reader must somehow read in-between the lines. But Maimonides would reject such an interpretation. The biblical narrator is merely illustrating how the ancients viewed sickness and mortality. God did not make Moses' child sick, but since God is the ultimate cause for the natural laws He created, Moses' child became sick. *God is not the direct cause of Moses' son becoming ill.*

In contrast to modern thought and science which looks at the immediate physical causes for why certain things occur, the ancient Hebrew view of causation traces responsibility directly back to the Creator. The Maimonidean scholar Menachem Kellner points out in his study how Maimonides cautions his readers that there is no such thing as a direct *quid pro quo* compensation for the fulfillment of the commandments. God expects people to fulfill the commandments maturely, out of love, with no expectation of reward. This principle also works in reverse: ". . . in order that the masses stay faithful and do the commandments, it was permitted to tell them that they might hope for a reward and to warn them against the transgression out of fear of punishment, just like the child in the analogy which I cited above."

Maimonides' words may sound like he's undermining everything that we have been taught since we were small children. Part of the problem we have with understanding God's relationship with the world is that we think of God as a supernatural Daddy who is going to prevent every mishap in the world. Maimonides believed this is a childish way of viewing God. Clinging to these childish theological beliefs prevent us from developing a mature understanding of what God means, or can mean to a thinking modern person.

CHAPTER 7

*"Perhaps the problem of evil is a human problem,
one of an egotistical mind-set, an anthropocentric
bent in our thinking and perspective."*

Jacob M. Held,
Stephen King and Philosophy

A Darwinian Approach to Pandemics

Most clergy I know probably don't look for inspiration from Darwin. But I am one who does.

I have found Darwin's perspective on viruses intriguing. One could argue that Darwin's thoughts on evolution may serve to help us detach ourselves from the belief that pandemics are a punishment from God. Repeatedly, Maimonides warned us about how our species' tendency toward anthropocentrism blinds us from recognizing our true place in God's vast cosmos, a cosmos that is endowed with a transcendental purpose.

It is significant that while Darwin respected humankind as the pinnacle of the evolutionary process, he did not think that man occupied a privileged place in the grand scheme of nature. Viruses, bacteria, and parasites will remain as competitors with the human species probably for the duration of our evolutionary future.

Despite the biblical imperative to show dominance over creation, Darwin reminds us that nature is not necessarily willing to concede to our superior role over nature's other creatures. The microbial "survival of the fittest" in some ways resembles our own. Even bacteria experience viruses. Science shows that even a billion bacterial cells can be instantly wiped out by a single virus particle. As one scientist observed:

> The bacteria will be succeeded by a hundred billion viruses—whose own fate is now problematical, as they exhausted their prey (within the test tube). There may, or may not, sometimes be a few bacterial survivors, mutant

bacteria that now resist the mutant virus; if so, these can repopulate the test tube—until perhaps a second round, a mutant-mutant virus appears. Is there any reason to believe that such processes are unique to the test tube, that life in the large is exempt from them? Of course not. Only the time scale is certain to be different, by a factor or years, to minutes, of a million to one, the disparity of generation time of human to bacteria. The fundamental biological principles are the same. The numerical odds may be different by a factor too hard to estimate.[48]

Human beings, though vulnerable to the endless evolutionary threats to our existence, are not without resources. Pandemics of the past claimed much higher casualties and deaths than the pandemics seen over the last three centuries. There can be no doubt diseases afflicted prehistorical man, much the same way it afflicts us in the 21st century. Although primitive man lacked the medical technology and evolutionary improvements of his future descendants, our ancestors lived in smaller communities; there was much less opportunity to spread a virus. But as we evolved as a species, most of humanity gave up the quiet agrarian life. As urban communities grew, towns and cities lived in huddled living quarters. When a pandemic struck, the close proximity of everyone made everyone more vulnerable. The relatively sedentary lifestyle of our Cro-Magnon or Neanderthal ancestors made them less vulnerable to the spread of contagion.

The Antiquity of Epidemics and Pandemics

Epidemics, plagues, and pandemics have been around since the dawn of civilization. Indeed, they are an unintended consequence of human societies living close to one another. Disease assuredly afflicted our prehistoric ancestors, but since the earliest humans lived in small isolated bands, they had limited opportunity to share germs beyond their community. That situation changed dramatically when the agricultural revolution replaced a nomadic with a sedentary lifestyle 10,000 years ago. What used to be an epidemic affecting only a few human families, morphed into a pandemic as people began populating the planet.

The history of pandemics reveals how the absence of scientific knowledge led to the destruction of the great Byzantine Empire beginning with the Justinian Plague, which was most likely the bubonic plague transmitted by rats, transferred to a human host through fleas. This was the last of the great pandemics that destroyed the Roman Empire. Bubonic plague has occurred at other times in human history. Most notably, from 1346-1353, it decimated the entire Mediterranean and European world, killing about a hundred million people—half of the total European population.

Lest we forget, civilization has experienced other pandemics, such as the German Measles, Chickenpox, and smallpox—killing many more countless millions in its wake. The philosopher Nietzsche was fond of saying, "What doesn't kill me will make me stronger." Yet, even in the absence of modern medicine, some of our ancestors developed a resistance.

Perspectives on Natural Selection

When speaking about the evolutionary ascent to life, Darwin' borrowed a line from the English poet Tennyson, who said, "Nature, red in tooth and claw" for his theory of natural selection. Influenced by the economist Malthus, Darwin believed that as the population grew, the demand for food would ultimately surpass the supply for food, which would lead to an inevitable battle over dwindling food sources. This idea is not altogether unknown in Jewish tradition, which points out that the word for "bread" (*lechem*) is the root word of the word for "war" (*milchamah*). Thomas Huxley concurred with his teacher and proposed a gladiatorial view of natural selection where one species would inevitably survive at the expense of the weaker species. Hence, nature is a truly bloody event, according to him. Among the animals, among the creatures who fight, it is the strongest, the swiftest, and the cunningest will live to fight again. It was only a matter of time before Darwinians would apply this model to human beings and society as well.

Peter Kropotkin (1842-1921) considered Darwin's idea of "natural selection" too limited.

> In the animal world we have seen that the vast majority of species live in societies and that they find in association the best arms for the struggle for life: understood, of course, in its wide Darwinian sense—not as a struggle for the sheer means of existence, but as a struggle against all natural conditions unfavorable to the species. The animal species, in which individual struggle has been reduced to its

narrowest limits, and the practice of mutual aid has attained the greatest development, are invariably the most numerous, the most prosperous, and the most open to further progress. [...] The unsociable species, on the contrary, are doomed to decay.[49]

Kropotkin did not dispute Darwin's core concept of the "survival of the fittest," but instead expanded upon it. He attributed the survival of a species to a concept he defined as "mutual aid." For him, it is as much a law governing animal life that it favors the development of habits and characters that will promoting the survivability of the species. In Kropotkin's vision of Darwinism, the main factor of evolution is determined by the species' ability to cooperate than compete with one another for survival. Without the spirit of mutual cooperation, life on this planet might have died in its infancy. Yet, we notice throughout the animal world, those vast species who live in societies have the best arms for the struggle for life: understood, of course, in its wide Darwinian sense—not as a struggle for the sheer means of existence, but as a struggle against all natural conditions unfavorable to the species. Thus, social ecology plays a vital role in how the evolution of a species occurs. Positive interactions through cooperation in nature also play a role in natural selection.

For example, the sea-world of the shellfish and the sponge often have "uninvited guests" who benefit from the host's unconsumed food supplies. Sometimes one species allows another to benefit by utilizing what each entity needs to survive. Algae and fungi often benefit from each other. What we see is not necessarily natural selection in the competitive sense, but the natural selection in terms of how one species creates sociality with another. As Kropotkin surmised, "But if we resort to an indirect test, and ask Nature: 'Who are the fittest: those who are continually at war with each other, or those who support one another?' we at once see that those animals which acquire habits of mutual aid are undoubtedly the fittest."[50]

In terms of human evolution, this point could suggest that the human race flourishes best when it sees itself as a part of nature, rather than viewing itself as a separate entity that thrives only upon the exploitation of world habitat. Poor stewardship not only threatens himself but the world around him as well. Kropotkin believed that mutuality and sociality are pivotal for the evolution of all life. The human species might have vanished long ago in a world inhabited by ferocious creatures much more powerful than itself. Through the spirit of cooperation, human beings ensured their survival as well as their eventual mastery of nature. Indeed, in the final analysis, it is the peaceful coexistence of species that guarantees its durability and vitality in nature. This is how natural selection determines its winners from its losers. In practical terms, mutual aid served to increase the lifespan and thus the prosperity of a species.

Kropotkin's concept of "mutual aid" is also the key to defeating the coronavirus pandemic. By consolidating each of the country's greatest minds in medicine and science, human ingenuity will create a synergistic solution that will end our current pandemic. Darwin used other metaphors aside from "natural selection," e.g., "struggle for existence," "the branching tree of life" as well as the "economy of nature." Concerning "the struggle for existence," Darwin borrowed this expression from the British economist Thomas Malthus' study, "An Essay on the Principle of Population." Malthus believed as the human population expanded, the food supply would diminish, thus creating a theater of conflict, in man's struggle to survive. When factoring in epidemics, hunger, "misery and vice" would serve to keep the human population growth in check, thus ensuring the quantity of food in the world. Malthus' theory had an application in a county or city that was already overcrowded and populated, but it could not apply to sparsely populated regions of the world.

How Pandemics & Natural Catastrophes Change History

One of the most important byproducts of a natural catastrophe is how it changes a society's world and religious view. A pandemic or an asteroid crashing into this world disrupts and transforms a people's identity. Some scholars think animal sacrifice and the origin of the priesthood might have begun as a reaction to a natural catastrophe; we see this in the story of Noah, who offers God several sacrifices to ensure that God never destroys the world again. It is not at all unusual to see how natural catastrophes played a pivotal role in the formation of a people's religious identity that is mentioned in Psalm 114:1–8:

> When Israel came forth from Egypt, the house of Jacob from an alien people,
> Judah became God's holy place, Israel, God's domain.
> The sea beheld and fled; the Jordan turned back.
> The mountains skipped like rams; the hills, like lambs of the flock.
> Why was it, sea, that you fled?

Jordan, that you turned back?
You mountains, that you skipped like rams?
You hills, like lambs of the flock?
Tremble, earth, before the Lord, before the God of Jacob,
Who turned rock into pools of water, stone into flowing springs.

The study of geomythology combines the disciplines of geology and mythology based on the legends, literature depiction of natural phenomena occurring in ancient times. Poetry mainly contains rich mythical information that may well be bearing witness to important geological or astronomical events of history. Ancient people did not possess a scientific understanding of the universe. In its place, they used myth in transmitting memories about actual events that occurred millennia ago. These myths preserved valuable information about a lost world.[51] The ancestors told these stories in an idiom their peoples could easily understand—and sometimes, to save lives.

It is possible the Exodus out of Egypt might have occurred at a time when a volcanic eruption occurred on Mount Vesuvius located on the island of Thera, near Crete. The Exodus might have happened sometime in the fifteenth century B.C.E. Admittedly, biblical scholars still debate the time of the Exodus. Again, if the Psalm is accurately describing seismic activity at the time of the Exodus, there may be a hidden relationship between the fate of Minoan civilization and the Israelites.

The once-dominant and thriving Minoan culture crumbled as a result of the eruption; this great even ultimately changed the political landscape of the ancient world and of history itself. The demise of the Minoans paved the way for the city-states of Greece to become the dominant superpower of the Mediterranean world. Plato sometimes spoke of the fabled city of Atlantis, which may have been a casualty of the Thera eruption.

How Pandemics Impacted the New World

But the Indian population of the New World was not so fortunate. Europeans suffering from these pandemics, who probably develop resistance to them, inadvertently (are sometimes purposely) passed on these diseases to the Indian population, resulting perhaps in over 20 million deaths throughout the Americas.

The downfall of the Aztec nation in the early 16th century, During the siege of Tenochtitlan, one of the Spanish African slaves spread the smallpox disease to the Aztec population. That year, smallpox killed the Aztec emperor Cuitlahuac, who had rallied his people to defeat the Spaniards, just months after his accession to the throne. By the year 1521, the ranks of the Aztecs could not stand up against the conquistadors.

Before the Spanish arrival into Central Mexican, there may have been as many as 15 to 25 million people. The Spanish didn't do this on purpose; they would have gladly used the conquered Indians as slaves. They were not bent upon the Indians' extermination. But sometimes after they saw the devastation the pandemic caused, some of the European settlers made a calculus that deploying an epidemic might prove useful in eliminating an enemy. So, they did. Students of history will recall how the French and Indian War (1754–1763), pitted the colonies of British America against those of New France, each side supported by military units from the parent country and by American Indian allies. At the start of the war, the French colonies had approximately 60,000 settlers, compared with 2 million in the British colonies. The outnumbered French mainly depended on the Indians. To reduce the size of the French and Indian armies, British generals hatched an idea of how to spread smallpox to the Native Indian population in the 1760s.

The 19th-century historian Francis Parkman historian came across correspondence in which Sir Jeffery Amherst, commander in chief of the British forces in North America in the early 1760s, had discussed its use with Col. Henry Bouquet, a subordinate on the western frontier during the French and Indian War (1754–1763). In a letter, he said, "Could it not be contrived to send the smallpox among those disaffected tribes of Indians? We must, on this occasion, use every stratagem in our power to reduce them." He then passed the information to his commander.

And the rest is history.

CHAPTER 8

"An ounce of prevention is worth a pound of cure."

Benjamin Franklin

"A pandemic is a lot like a forest fire: If caught early, it might be extinguished with limited damage; if allowed to smolder undetected, it can grow to an inferno that spreads quickly beyond our ability to control it. Because of a decade of failures, we are now in the midst of that inferno, waiting for the fire to burn itself out. And there is no excuse for it."

George Bush, 2005

Wisdom from the Age of Duck & Cover

Not long after WW II, the civil defense came up with a guidance that was distributed to schoolchildren in the 1950s. This 1952 film provided a prescription how students ought to react in the event of a nuclear explosion. At the time, the Soviet Union was engaged in nuclear testing and the US was in the midst of the Korean War. The lyrics most of us recall went like this:

There was a turtle by the name of Bert
and Bert the turtle was very alert;
when danger threatened him, he never got hurt
he knew just what to do ...
He'd duck! [gasp]
And cover!
Duck! [gasp]
And cover!
(male) He did what we all must learn to do

(male) You (female) And you (male) And you (deeper male) And you!
[bang, gasp] Duck, and cover!

When we look back at this old memory, we probably chuckle. We
wonder, "Did we really think hiding under our desk would protect us from
a nuclear explosion?" Our teachers and parents realized that doing
something, however minimal, might confer a degree of calm from a
potential oncoming nuclear fireball that was likely to cause serious injury or
death.

The 2013 Noble Prize biologist Michael Leavitt served as the Secretary
of Health and Human Services during the Bush Administration. In 2004,
he urged that Americans store canned tuna and powdered milk under their
beds for when bird flu hits. But Americans did not take him very seriously,
and the comedian Jay Leno ridiculed Leavitt, who quipped, "What? …
Powdered milk and tuna? How many would rather have the bird flu?"

As a case in point, NBC news at the time of the bird flu dismissed the
doomsday predictions about the bird flu possibly becoming a pandemic.
Rather than erring on the side of caution, the skeptics criticized that
"hysteria is sapping money and attention away from more important health
threats. . . Even Dr. Anthony Fauci, the National Institutes of Health's
infectious disease recently cautioned against overreacting if the virus
surfaces in North American birds, as it is expected to do later this year."[52]
Those who worried about the bird flu were dub this psychological reaction
as Chicken Little Syndrome, who famously announced, "The sky is falling!"
The theory suggests that when an unfortunate but isolated mishap occurs,
it's easy to let your imagination run wild with all the possible causes and
eventual consequences that will lead to Doom.

Instead of thinking "Chicken Little, think, "Duck and Cover." We
ought to ask ourselves, "What would have happened had the bird-flu
morphed into a full-scale pandemic? Were we prepared for such an
eventuality?

In an answer, no.

Anthony Fauci, Alex Azar, the secretary of the Department of Health
and Human Services (HHS), Robert Redfield, MD, director of the Centers
for Disease Control and Prevention (CDC), Nancy Messonnier, MD,
director of CDC's National Center for Immunization and Respiratory
Disease, each concluded back on January 28th, 2020, "Americans should
know this is a potentially very serious public health threat, but Americans

should not worry for their own safety."[53] But the experts are not always correct—that is why we ought to take a more cautious approach.

Nobody thought of distributing facemasks or rubber gloves before we became aware of the dangers posed by COVID-19. Experts from the Centers for Disease Control suffered from the type of hubris that Aristotle characterized in his depiction of the tragic hero, who proves to be his own worst enemy. The 2013 winner of the Nobel Prize in biology Michael Leavitt wisely observed, "In advance of a pandemic, anything you say sounds alarmist," Leavitt explained. "After a pandemic starts, everything you've done is inadequate." [54]

Our political leaders would love to blame Trump for the lack of America's preparedness for the coronavirus outbreak. The pandemic revealed how the wealthiest country in the world was asleep at the wheel. Politicians, who lack foresight and wisdom, defunded monies that might have made a difference in our country's preparedness.

When we chronicle the list of pandemics, we witnessed over the last twenty-years, we recall the warning signs:

- the 2002 SARS outbreak;
- the 2003 resurgence of H5N1 avian flu;
- the 2009 H1N1 swine flu outbreak;
- the 2012 MERS outbreak;
- the 2014 Ebola outbreak.

Unfortunately, the experts of the scientific, medical, and political community failed to consider the consequences of their sightlessness.

> The story behind today's ventilator shortage is even more infuriating. The New York Times reports that in 2008, the Bush administration launched a project to stockpile ventilators for a pandemic, and in 2009 the Obama administration contracted with a California company to provide 40,000 of them. But in 2014, the company withdrew from the contract without delivering a single ventilator. So the government started over with a new contractor. It took another five years for the Food and Drug Administration to sign off on a new ventilator design, and the government did not place an order for 10,000 ventilators until December 2019 — the month

that the COVID-19 outbreak began. We lost more than a
decade due to government incompetence.[55]

Despite the warnings, we didn't take the danger seriously enough —
and were caught unprepared for COVID-19. We should have learned some
wisdom from the out cartoon, "Duck and Cover." Let us hope that we go
back to making preparedness against a potential biological threat, which
will serve to keep our country better prepared for whatever the future may
bring.

Winston Churchill once said, "You can always count on the Americans
to do the right thing after they have tried everything else." This proved true
when terrorists attacked our country on September 11, 2001, which
resulted in the deaths of 2,977 people. Now that an unparalleled pandemic
has befallen our nation, we ought to ask our leaders and ourselves: Must it
always take a tragedy to wake us up to danger?

Remember Duck and Cover.

Part 4
Pastoral Issues: God & Suffering

CHAPTER 9

*"Nothing ever goes away until it has taught us
what we need to know."*

Peme Chodron

The Problem of Suffering

Throughout history, pandemics have challenged a faith community's concept of God. How does one reconcile our faith in a personal God who loves life, but allows a natural evil to destroy everything in its path? What kind of God—if any—can allow the suffering of innocent children? Every natural catastrophe makes the belief in a personal God seem unlikely.

Most people probably associate the name Ichabod with the famous character Ichabod Crane of Washington Irving's short story, "The Legend of Sleepy Hollow." Most Jews never named their children Ichabod for a good reason; the name means, "Where was the Glory?" i.e., God. In the early chapters of 1 Samuel 4, the Israelites, after losing a battle to the Philistines decide they decide to bring in the heavy artillery—the Ark of the Covenant. Over 30,000 Israelites died in this second battle. Aside from the humiliating defeat, the Philistines captured the Ark of the Covenant.

In the ancient world, nations were not the only militants who did battle with their foes. In every campaign, the deities of a country also warred against their enemies' deities. And this time, it seemed to the Israelites that YHWH had His "clock cleaned." The loss of the Ark represented for these Israelites the loss of God's Presence. Ordinarily, the word *Kabod* means "Glory," which signifies God's immanence in the life of the nation. But after this battle, the High Priest Eli died when he heard that his two sons were killed in action. And when the daughter-in-law of the high priest Eli named her infant boy, "Ichabod," explaining, "Gone is the glory from Israel" (1 Sam. 4:22). At this time of Israelite history, God seemed as though He died or disappeared. This event probably could qualify as an example of what modern theologians and anthropologists refer to as "the death of God" in a primitive society. Once the high-deity vanishes, he is never heard from again. For all practical purposes, he is dead.

Had Sigmund Freud read this biblical story about Ichabod, he probably would have concluded the Israelites suffered defeat because God is an illusion. Freud felt the belief in a God who looks after and protects his people from harm is nothing more than wishful thinking; as humanity evolved, Freud believed society would eventually outgrow their belief in God. But Freud was hardly the first person to think this way. Among the Greeks, a philosopher named Epicurus took a similar approach. According to him, the reality of human suffering ought to be seen as anti-proof for the existence of a benevolent deity looking over mortals from afar. Epicurus asked: "Is God willing to prevent evil, but not able? Then he is not omnipotent. Is he able, but not willing? Then he is malevolent. Is he both able and willing? Then whence cometh evil? Is he neither able nor willing? Then why call him God?"

Both Freud and Epicurus' argument challenges the classical theistic tradition of Judaism, Christianity, and Islam. The question: How do we reconcile a God Who is omnipotent with the existence of evil we experience in our world? The fact God allows evil to exist in the world—whether natural or moral, suggests God is too powerless to prevent it.

But before we examine this question, let us ask a Socratic question to Epicurus: When you say, "evil exists," what do you mean? Some people might answer that evil has a real substance of its own; in terms of its ontology, it is no less real than "goodness." But Maimonides, Augustine, and others assert this understanding of "evil" is problematic. In a Platonic sense, evil is nothing more than the absence of good; its existence is parasitical—it is an apt metaphor for the coronavirus. Evil is only a contamination; it has no reality by itself. And yet, evil's effects are undeniably real in terms of its impact upon the living.

These are some of the essential questions we shall touch upon later in this book. Epicurus presupposes God cannot prevent evil, but for now, we could object: Must God prevent a catastrophe from occurring in our world—whether it be natural evil such as a pandemic, or whether it matters of moral outrage that mortals foolishly choose? Morality may not be as binary as the ancient cynic Epicurus thought; there are shades of grade. In both Judaism and Christianity, moral evil is something that human beings must take responsibility for—not God. But what about the existence of natural evil?

As stewards of God's Creation, we are responsible for that as well. How we utilize our freedom of choice, determines and shapes the kind of society we live in—not God. In addition, it is also conceivable that God creates imperfection and evil for a higher purpose that requires humanity to come to terms with its own imperfect nature. Although God considered the creation of humankind as something fundamentally "good," nowhere does it state God made man a perfect human being. This lack of perfection does not necessarily suggest a maleficence on the part of God. Still, it reflects more God's optimism that human beings will triumph over their inner demons and the reality of natural evil we experience in our world.

CHAPTER 10

"Too many religious people act passively in the face of human suffering and evil. They seek to exonerate God rather than come to the aid of the suffering community. Defending God above all else is the fundamentalist's greatest and important concern."

Albert Camus
The Plague

Camus' Wisdom for how we confront the Coronavirus

As news of the coronavirus spread, our leaders urged us to adopt social-distancing ourselves from the rest of the outside world. The time we spend sequestered from the outer world became for us an invitation to think about our life direction and journey. In quiet but worrisome times like this, I enjoy reading literature from history's most thought-provoking writers. I accidentally came across Albert Camus' 1947 short story, *The Plague.*

Camus wrote about a bubonic plague ravaging the people of a North African coastal city of Oran. Scholars and laypeople alike consider it to be a classic of twentieth-century literature. Although Camus was an atheist, some of his insights are compatible with Maimonidean theology. To his credit, Camus challenges the shallowness of facile faith. In an age where we no longer have biblical prophets, the cynics of religion often display honesty and willingness to call us upon our duplicity and hypocrisy. Too many of today's religious leaders are too reluctant to confront the complacency and moral apathy of their worshipers.

As thousands of rats infest the city, hysteria grips the population. The local papers demand swift action, but as people start falling ill with a strange fever, only then does it become evident that the illness is the bubonic plague. Only after it becomes impossible to deny that a serious epidemic is ravaging Oran, do the authorities enact strict sanitation measures. Its leaders placed the entire city under quarantine.

Tarrou is also an atheist, but his atheism is more tied in to his philosophical and moral beliefs about human responsibility. Like Rieux, he did not see any intrinsic or moral value in death and suffering. According to him (reflecting the philosophical assumptions of Camus, who uses him as his persona mouthpiece), human beings must realize they are engaged in losing but noble struggle against death and suffering. Nevertheless, by living nobly, human beings can give nobility to their efforts, perhaps reflecting the cynicism of Ecclesiastes, "Vanity of vanities, says Kohelet, vanity of vanities! All things are vanity!" (Ecc. 1:2). To his credit, Tarrou did whatever he could to alleviate the people's suffering.

The reaction of the people during the plague is instructive. Families worry about their loved ones who were confined to the city.

Hysteria grips the nation. The authorities finally arrange for the daily collection and cremation of the rats. Father Paneloux gave a scolding sermon, declaring how God is punishing Oran for its many sins. But Paneloux's attitude changes after one of his congregants excoriates the priest for suffering such a long and agonizing death from the plague. Confronted by the death of an innocent child, the priest delivers a second sermon where he admits, the inexplicable death of innocents must force the Christian to choose whether one believing everything or believing nothing about God. But the priest ultimately took ill, and as he was dying, he held fast to his crucifix. Nobody knew for certain whether he died from the plague or something else.

Paneloux's attitude is in marked contrast to Dr. Rieux, one of the main protagonists of the story who chronicles the story of the plague. In a conversation with one of his friends, Jean Tarrou engages Rieux with some scintillating questions, as Tarrou's gray eyes met the doctor's gaze serenely:

> "What did you think of Paneloux's sermon, doctor?" The question was asked in a quite ordinary tone, and Rieux answered in the same tone. "I've seen too much of hospitals to relish any idea of collective punishment. But, as you know, Christians sometimes say that sort of thing without really thinking it. They're better than they seem." However, you think, like Paneloux, that the plague has its good side; it opens men's eyes and forces them to take thought?"

The doctor tossed his head impatiently. "So does every ill that flesh is heir to. What's true of all the evils in the world is true of plague as well. It helps men to rise above themselves. All the same, when you see the misery it brings, you'd need to be a madman, or a coward, or stone blind, to give in tamely to the plague." Rieux had hardly raised his voice at all; but Tarrou made a slight gesture as if to calm him. He was smiling. "Yes." Rieux shrugged his shoulders. "But you haven't answered my question yet. Have you weighed the consequences?" Tarrou squared his shoulders against the back of the chair, then moved his head forward into the light. Rieux's response is precious. Too many religious people act passively in the face of human suffering and evil. They seek to exonerate God rather than come to the aid of the suffering community. Defending God above all else is the fundamentalist's greatest and important concern.

Tarrou ask Rieux another penetrating but personal question: "Do you believe in God, doctor?" Again, the question was put in an ordinary tone. But this time Rieux took longer to find his answer. "No—but what does that really mean? I'm fumbling in the dark, struggling to make something out. But I've long ceased finding that original." "Isn't that it—the gulf between Paneloux and you?"

"I doubt it. Paneloux is a man of learning, a scholar. He hasn't come in contact with death; that's why he can speak with such assurance of the truth—with a capital T. But every country priest who visits his parishioners and has heard a man gasping for breath on his deathbed thinks as I do. *He'd try to relieve human suffering before trying to point out its excellence.*" Rieux stood up; his face was now in shadow. "Let's drop the subject," he said, "as you won't answer." Tarrou remained seated in his chair; he was smiling again.

By the time the quarantine ends, the people of Oran lost their obsession with personal suffering. Instead, they have a new realization that the impact of the plague is everybody's concern. All the people have a new understanding of their mutual responsibility in combating the dreaded disease.

Yet, as everything returns to normal, the town returns to its old routine. They soon forget about the human suffering they endured. Despite the joy he now hears rising from the streets, Rieux felt humbled by the plague, he is mindful "that the plague bacillus never dies or disappears for good; that it can lie dormant for years and years in furniture and linen-chests; that it bides its time in bedrooms, cellars, trunks, and bookshelves; and that perhaps the day would come when, for the bane and the enlightening of men, it would rouse up its rats again and send them forth to die in a happy city."

Camus' brilliant short story contains many valuable lessons for both the religious and secular communities to take to heart. Rather than giving in to the hysteria and fear of this dreaded but new mysterious pandemic, we must work for achieving the common good and adhere to the numerous safety precautions that can reduce the plague's severity. Paradoxically, the coronavirus challenges us to confront our mortality. Perhaps it is time we realize--all of us—regardless of our race, creeds, ethnicity, and culture—are profoundly interconnected; our destinies flow together. The Reverend Dr. Martin Luther King Jr. once said, "In a real sense, all life is interrelated. All men are caught in an inescapable network of mutuality, tied in a single garment of destiny. Whatever affects one directly, affects all indirectly." Let this be the time for us to emulate God's first act of creation by creating light from the bowels of darkness; and creation from the depths of non-being and lifelessness—together as we conquer the coronavirus.

CHAPTER 11

> *"God is projected father (psychologically), and... this basis*
> *of trust is the sustaining, binding meaning that makes*
> *religion crucial to men.... It is perfectly possible that the*
> *way in which the Ground of Being makes himself known,*
> *revealed himself, was by making man biologically*
> *dependent upon his human parents and prone to such*
> *projections."*

Edward Stein,
Guilt: Theory and Therapy

Unhealthy Images of God

In our earlier chapter, we discussed Camus' short story. *The Plague* illustrates a familiar problem we see whenever natural evil occurs in the world. Whenever a pandemic occurs, it is not uncommon religious leaders often claim to know God's mind whenever an epidemic or other natural catastrophe occur. I find myself agreeing with writers and thinkers such as Camus, Sartre, and Christopher Hitchens more than I do with some of God's loyal servants. One of the severe problems the coronavirus raises is: Where is God in all of this? Many religious pietists find the biblical God of retribution a familiar theme in their personal theology. Admittedly, the Bible frequently depicts God as a dispenser of pain, a punisher of people who fail to observe God's laws and religious traditions, a producer of earthquakes and pestilence. Theologians sometimes refer to this image of God, as the "God of wrath."

Ordinary people don't have to know much about theology when it comes to the "God of Wrath" they encounter in the media, or at the churches where they worship. It is not all difficult why Jews, Christians, and Muslims across all denominational lines find it difficult—if not challenging—to relate to such an unforgiving image of the Divine. Perhaps we need a little humor when we talk about such a serious topic. Consider what Michael Shevack and Rabbi Jack Bemporad cleverly dubbed this theological view of God as the "Marquis de God."

> Wanted: Dominant deity for a submissive person. Must be into pain and bondage. Must be willing to inflict human suffering in pursuit of satisfaction. Humiliation technique a plus. Sense of humor not required. Inquire P.O. Box G.O.D... Get out the whips, the chains, the earthquakes, the pestilence. some good old-fashioned fun with a good old-fashioned god. Yes, this is the proverbial god of wrath. The Marquis de God ready to show you how much he cares by punishing you. For the Marquis de God is simply a god who hates. This is a deity who despises sins and sinners with such a passion that he'll murder to exterminate them. He forces his noblest creation to dance like a trained poodle on the brink of annihilation.[56]

According to Martin Buber thinks it is time we purge our faith of the unhealthy images of God that portray the Divine as either vindictive or abusive.

In his short but insightful autobiographical book *Meetings*, Buber described a meeting he had with a very pious and learned observant Jew. They had a conversation about the biblical story of King Saul, and the war of genocide he had waged against Israel's ancient enemy, Amalek (1 Sam. 15ff.). After Saul captured King Agag of Amalek, Saul did not kill him. The prophet Samuel became enraged and personally hacked Agag to death. Afterward, Samuel told Saul to abdicate the throne. Buber said to the man, that as a child, he always found this story horrifying. Buber recounts:

> I told him how already at that time it horrified me to read or to remember how the heathen king went to the prophet with the words on his lips, "Surely the bitterness of death is past," and was hewn to pieces by him. I said to my partner: "I have never been able to believe that this is a message of God. I do not believe it." With wrinkled forehead and contracted brows, the man sat opposite me and his glance flamed into my eyes. He remained silent, began to speak, became silent again. "So?" he broke forth at last, "so? You do not believe it?" "No, "I answered, "I

do not believe it." "So? so?" he repeated almost threateningly. "You do not believe it?" And once again: "No." "What? What?"--he thrust the words before him one after the other-- "what do you believe then?" "I believe," without reflecting, "that Samuel has misunderstood God." And he, again slowly, but more softly than before: "So? You believe that?" and I: "Yes." Then we were both silent. But now something happened the like of which I have rarely seen before or since in this my long life. The angry countenance opposite me became transformed as if a hand had passed over it soothing it. It lightened, cleared, was now turned toward me bright and clear. "Well, said the man with a positively gentle tender clarity, "I think so too." And again, we became silent, for a good while.[57]

Buber in the end of this anecdote mentioned how people often confuse the words of God with the words of man. To speak of God as "abusive," is to speak of a man-made caricature of God. Buber was well aware of the power such anti-life imagery exerts over the psyche of a people in the formation of their own personal relationships with the Divine.

Parenting Shapes the Child's Perception of God

Faith development must first begin in the home. Parenting plays a dynamic role in the formation of children's conceptions of God. But when the parents are ambivalent about their ancestral faith, young people will almost instinctively look elsewhere for religious and spiritual meaning in their lives. Just as nature abhors a vacuum, so too does a home where God is no longer a significant family value. Something will always fill the void of nothing.

Psychological studies dealing with the pathology of religion seem to confirm this truth. The psychiatrist Ann Maria Rizzuto argues the images of God tend to be patterned after the model of the parents; children who have had strongly negative experiences with their parents (such as sexual abuse) tend to develop negative concepts of God. Those children who have the lowest image of their parents reported having the diminished image of God. According to Rizzuto, by the time the child is introduced to the house of God, he or she already brings an image that is very difficult to reshape based upon perceptions the child has learned in the home. Not by word, but by deed, the child learns to cultivate a positive image of God. [58]

This kind of psychological mirroring is not limited to the home—it is also ubiquitous in the modern American center of worship. Sometimes the House of God itself serves to promote dysfunctional images and metaphors of God; the religious endorsement of God and violence is a significant reason why so many people lose faith in a personal God. Religion has demonstrated how it is capable of morphing into a death-force that is capable of omnicide. September 11, 2001, served as a wake-up call for all Americans; as Jihadists killed thousands of innocent victims, the streets of Gaza, Tehran, and elsewhere celebrated with diabolical delight. The retrograde forces of Jihadism have shown us repeatedly how religious hatreds tend to be merciless, unyielding, undying, and absolute; they are seemingly capable of spontaneous generation.

Yet, religious fanaticism is not limited to only Islam. In Judaism, we have our own religious extremists in Jerusalem who prepare rocks to be thrown over the Sabbath at motorists who are disregarding the traditional observance of the day. Secular vs. religious Jewish internecine fighting is almost a weekly spectacle. Of course, the Christian community across the spectrum have experienced similar problems.

CHAPTER 12

*"Toilet paper, disinfecting wipes and bottled water
all became COVID-19 gold."*

Steven Magee

A Potpourri of Interfaith Responses on COVID-19

The religious response to the coronavirus is a topic most inquisitive people find interesting. William James (1842-1910), America's greatest psychologist of his time, quoted a friend, "There is very little difference between one man and another, but the little there is, is very important."[59] James' remark is not limited to what the individual thinks, it applies no less to people of faith. By engaging other faiths, quite often we learn more about our own in the process.

One Muslim leader named Omar Ricci announced, "Thank God for the coronavirus. Thank God for this reminder that we are not in control and must always be dependent on God. Thank God for this reminder that we should be grateful for all things—for groceries, toilet paper, good health. Thank God for reminding us life is fragile, and we had best appreciate the miracle and blessing that God has given us in creating us as souls."[60]

At our community Passover Seder featured through ZOOM, I spoke about Imam Ricci's remark at the Seder when we got to the traditional *Dayenu* Song. This song stresses the importance of always being thankful for the little things God does for us. Most of us can probably relate to that statement—especially regarding when we consider the miracle of toilet paper. It would be hard to imagine what life would be like without it! Moses, Buddha, Jesus, and Mohammed probably would have traded gold for this useful invention. Yet, being thankful for the small things, like Ricci said, has a ring of truth. And yet, in keeping with James' earlier remark, despite the commonalities, there are interesting points of divergence. When the local markets opened for seniors in the morning, I found myself literally running with other seniors to make sure we had our toilet paper!

The Coronavirus as God's Soldier Against Non-Believers

Theological differences abound within any given faith. Religious leaders often feel the compulsion to explain why tragedies occur such as an unexpected death, or when something like a plague occurs, bringing devastation in its wake. The ancients always assumed that natural catastrophes such as an earthquake, or a tsunami (e.g., Noah's flood) had to be due to the sins of impiety to the gods, or other moral lapses on the part of the community of faith.

As soon as the COVID-19 occurred in Wuhan China, throughout the Middle East, many Muslim leaders claimed coronavirus is one of Allah's soldiers, used to bring retribution upon the Chinese for their cruel treatment and persecution of the Chinese Uighur Muslims living in Western China. When Muslims saw other Muslims experiencing an outbreak in Iran, a country that Iran has been severely affected by COVID-19, rivaling Muslim sects' leaders took a macabre delight in seeing Iran suffer for their attacks on the Sunni Muslim neighbors of Iran.

As we noted above, religions despite their basic philosophies and rituals, will often articulate a similar theological view. Rev. Billy Prewitt concurred with the Muslim viewpoint suggesting COVID-19 is God's judgement against the Communist Chinese government for their suppression of religions that do not acquiesce to the communist regime. He wrote:

> In February 2020, the government of China announced that it was going to conduct a massive "crackdown" on religions that do not submit to the communist regime. This, of course, includes the underground church of China. To put this plainly, one of the most hostile nations in the history of the world toward Christians has announced a new breed of hostility aimed at Christian annihilation. The new wave began in February 2020. Why should we think it strange that a pandemic outbreak of disease has sprung up in the heart of China? How can we fail to observe the time of these two events? Is this just a coincidence, or is this a judgement of God against a nation that has systematically destroyed God's people for generations?[61]

Religious Behavior in a Time of Pandemics

Christian and Jewish responses vary as much as the Muslim faith. While many people will flee from a pandemic, or some other imminent danger, there are those who refuse to do so. Oftentimes, the bravest people are those who refuse to abandon their flocks in the face of danger. As one scholar noted:

> Some Christians may be tempted to look back on their history of remaining physically present during times of distress. Starting around 250 A.D., A.D., a plague that at its height was said to kill 5,000 people a day ravaged the Roman empire. The Christians stood out in their service to the infirm. Because they believed that God was sovereign over death, they were willing to minister to the sick even at the cost of their lives. This witness won many to the Christian cause. Should we follow their example and gather to celebrate in word and ritual, in the sermon as well as the bread and the wine?[62]

Christian heroism during the Holocaust was no less noteworthy, and countless righteous Gentiles made similar choices and would not abandon the Jewish community, even though they would share the same fate.

Some Ultra-Orthodox rabbis in Israel blamed the LGBTQ community and Gay Pride marches were against nature and had caused the coronavirus pandemic. Yet, is it not ironic that 40-60% of COVID 19 came from the Haredi Community? One would think this alone would create some cognitive dissonance. It is odd to imagine the Ultra-Orthodox aligning themselves with Christian fundamentalists, but Pastor Steven Andrew of the USA Christian Church designated the month of March as "Repent of LGBT Sin Month," and said that "Obeying God protects the USA from diseases, such as the coronavirus." Haredi rabbis believe the Torah study in the yeshiva wards off the effect of the coronavirus. But in Israel, the Haredi (Ultra-Orthodox) community is suffering the most because of their rabbis' inability to recognize that Torah study does not avert a plague.

Some believe to prevent the spread of future diseases, China and other countries would be wise to ban live animal markets. According to the Centers for Disease Control and Prevention (CDC) warns: "… three out of every four new or emerging infectious diseases in people come from animals." The phenomena of overcrowded factory farms—even here in the United States, are breeding grounds for disease—especially as emerging pathogens become immune to antibiotic-resistant bacteria. When the "Swine Flu" (a.k.a., H1N1) pandemic broke out, it was initially to a similar disease in pigs. Dr. Julius Preuss argued that the Talmud discussed this possibility, "After Rabbi Judah heard that a pestilence was raging among the swine, he ordained a fast, because their intestines are like those of human beings.'"[63] Perhaps becoming vegetarian is an option all nations ought to reconsider. Investing in plant-based agriculture instead of farm animals would preserve the biodiversity of our planet. Besides, the animals would appreciate that very much!

Recently, Pope Francis attributed the coronavirus to the sins of climate change. He said, "We did not respond to the partial catastrophes. Who now speaks of the fires in Australia, or remembers that 18 months ago a boat could cross the North Pole because the glaciers had all melted? Who speaks now of the floods?" the Pope said. "I don't know if these are the revenge of nature, but they are certainly nature's responses," he added.[64] We must ask Pope Francis, "And what was the reason for past pandemics, such as the Black Death, cholera, measles, and small-pox?"

The Pope's view of the coronavirus plague is consistent with how the medieval Church believed the Black Death was attributed to sinfulness on the part of faith community. Their antidote to the plague: Repentance. It was not unusual to cite the story of a plague that occurred in King David's time, where God punished him carrying out a census (2 Sam. 24 ff.). Christian communities in Europe conducted penitential processions to end and ward off natural catastrophes since the ninth century, and with the arrival of the Black Death, they continued to do so, and to listen to "catastrophe sermons" given by the clergy.[65] They did so, despite the fact that within Christian circles, it was widely held that the plague was contagious, believing God's ability to intervene and protect them was greater than this risk posed by public gatherings.[66]

One is reminded of an old but familiar story: A fellow was stuck on his rooftop in a flood. He was praying to God for help. Soon a man in a rowboat came by and the fellow shouted to the man on the roof, "Jump in, I can save you." The stranded fellow shouted back, "No, it's OK, I'm praying to God and he is going to save me." So, the rowboat went on. Then a motorboat came by. "The fellow in the motorboat shouted, "Jump in, I can save you." To this the stranded man said, "No thanks, I'm praying to God and he is going to save me. I have faith." So, the motorboat went on.

Then a helicopter came by and the pilot shouted down, "Grab this rope and I will lift you to safety." To this the stranded man again replied, "No thanks, I'm praying to God and he is going to save me. I have faith." So the helicopter reluctantly flew away. Soon the water rose above the rooftop and the man drowned. He went to Heaven. He finally got his chance to discuss this whole situation with God, at which point he exclaimed, "I had faith in you but you didn't save me, you let me drown. I don't understand why!" To this God replied, "I sent you a rowboat and a motorboat and a helicopter, what more did you expect?"

Jewish tradition has long stressed that one cannot rely upon miracles. The Zohar says, "Blessings from above descend only where there is some substance, not just emptiness, below."[67] In the face of unspeakable evil—natural or moral—decent people must always make the difference. It is clear that a non-scientific approach to pandemics can only cause more misery than healing. It is a pity so many of the world faiths attribute plagues to moral lapses on the part of the religious communities. Were Maimonides alive today, it is reasonably certain he would have rejected any attempt to associate a plague with the sins of religious impiety. Maimonidean naturalism asserts God did not create a perfect world, but He did create a world that requires human stewardship in order for it to become perfect. Pandemics, tsunamis, earthquakes, and other natural catastrophes will always occur because God expects us to take responsibility and improve upon His Creation.

If anything, the coronavirus reminds us that we must work together as an international community to combat a common foe and enemy that does not distinguish between one nation and another. If anything, the coronavirus has shown us something we have long forgotten, namely, each of our lives are profoundly intertwined to one another. Even the mere act of touching another human being—even an inanimate surface—can affect the world in a potentially destructive way. One would think that if this can apply in the negative sense, how much more can this apply in positive sense. The Internet has shown that though spatiality keeps us apart, in spiritual terms, the Internet of consciousness and love shall keep our spirits healthy as we work on finding practical cures.

Hindu Insights on Pandemics

And among the Hindus, one wonders: would the belief in *ahisma* (the principle of non-violence toward all living things) apply even to a coronavirus? Mahatma Gandhi viewed ahimsa as a behavior that promotes non-injury, nonviolence, non-harm, the renunciation of the will to kill and the intention to hurt any living thing, the abstention from hostile thought, word or deed, and compassion for all living creatures. However, even Gandhi approved, "the killing of rats and insects that could carry infection in an area affected by the bubonic plague."[68]

CHAPTER 13

"The friends of Job appear on the scene as advisers and
"consolers," offering Job the fruits of their moral
scientia. But when Job insists that his sufferings have no
explanation and that he cannot discover the reason for
them through conventional ethical concepts, his friends
turn into accusers, and curse Job as a sinner. Thus,
instead of consolers, they become torturers by virtue of
their very morality, and in so doing, while claiming to
be advocates of God, they act as instruments of the
devil."

Thomas Merton

Re-reading the Book of Job

With considerable extra time on my available because of the coronavirus, I decided I would reread one of the most controversial books of the Bible, one that the ancients almost did not include in the biblical canon—the Book of Job. Whenever people wonder, "Why do bad things happen to good people?" that is why the Book of Job ought to be explored.

The name "Job" is suggestive of its story. Although there is no conclusive evidence for this ancient rabbinical theory, in Biblical Hebrew the name אִיּוֹב ('iyyôb = "Job") might be related to the verb the root אָיַב "to signifying a "personal enemy"[69] (Exod. 23:4), and it may refer to "God's enemy" (Gen. 22:17), or it might even refer to God as "the enemy" (Isa. 63:10). The noun אֵיבָה means "enmity" or someone with hostile intent (Num. 35:22). Assuming Job's name is associated with "personal enemy," we might wonder: Who is the "enemy" of this story? The answer would vary depending upon the perspective of the actors. From Job's perspective, he suspected God might be the enemy because God has hidden His face from him (Job 13:24; comp. Job 33:10). But from Job's friends' standpoint, Job is God's enemy. As Whitehead mentioned above, when terrible things happen to people, there is a popular tendency to think of God as a malevolent force that is out to "get them."

As religious leaders discuss the possible origins of the coronavirus, it is not at all uncommon for certain religious leaders to claim God is punishing those people who are derelict or religiously impious such as the LGBT communities. The irony, however, indicates that members of some of the most religious communities are more prone to be infected by the pandemic than the secular because the latter is careful to observe the protocol of social-distancing! If nothing else, this misplaced judgmental attitude ought to create a measure of cognitive dissonance pointing perhaps more toward the religiously zealous at heart.

The Book of Job is one biblical book that intelligent people ought to read and discuss at this time of our nation's history. Many of the religious attitudes Job encountered reflect the type of opinions religious leaders express concerning the coronavirus pandemic. The story of Job resonates with our contemporary experience of faith in a world where God's Presence has receded from the earth because of human thoughtlessness and lack of empathy. Camus' short story, *The Plague*, contains several themes that also resonated with the Book of Job. This point may explain why the Book of Job still speaks to all sufferers and would-be consolers.

So be forewarned:

Job is not for the theologically faint-of-heart. This story will make you question what it means to believe in a God that allows human suffering to occur. The Book of Job contradicts several biblical teachings that promise material rewards for following God's commandments (cf. Lev. 26:14-30; Deut. 27:15-28). In the beginning, Job is careful to offer sacrifices as one might expect from a pious servant of God. Job also follows God's ethics by advocating for the poor (cf. Job 29:11-20). His behavior is exemplary in every manner imaginable).[70]

Given his theological understanding of God, Job also expects God to notice his noble contributions to society, for he is convinced his God is a God of reward and retribution. Clearly, According to Job's initial understanding of the world, people get what they deserve from God. When we compare him to his critical friends, Job's behavior—in the beginning— was indistinguishable from his friends' spiritual outlook.

Centuries before the ancients composed the Book of Job, there was also a well-established biblical tradition that viewed reward and punishment in two-dimensional terms: the righteous deserve to prosper, while the evildoer deserves to suffer. Unfortunately, numerous verses in the Scriptures seem to support this facile interpretation (cf. Lev. 26:14-30; Deut. 27:15-28, *passim*).

Yes, in the beginning, Job is "blameless and upright man," one who "feared God and avoided evil" (Job 1:1). But then, God makes a bet with Satan, who torments poor Job's life, destroying his family, his possessions, and his body. Did Job really live? Maimonides thinks Job is a theological parable about the just man who suffers. Some scholars believe Job is an allegory of the Jewish people and the suffering we have endured throughout our history—past and present. Job resonates with our contemporary experience of faith in a world where God's Presence has receded from the earth because of human-generated evil and bipolar images of God that encourage gratuitous violence. It is a book that raises questions about the limitations of human suffering and its effect on the spiritual psyche of the sufferer.

Encountering the Diabolic

Before his misery, Job's community regarded his prosperity as a sign that Job must have been a holy man. Unfortunately for Job, he has one adversary—Satan. [71] Satan questions his integrity and accuses Job of being pious and obedient only because it profits him to be so. A challenge develops between God and Satan. God even grants Satan permission to do everything but destroy Job, while God passively observes.

As the story continues, one can see a striking similarity in the questions raised by Satan and the accusations made by Job's friends. Although Satan withdraws from the account after the initial prologue, his cynical voice echoes through the views of Job's friends. The entire story suggests that all self-righteous responses to those who suffer bear a sinister quality. The Hebrew word, "Satan" means "adversary." Job's friends thus became his satanic adversaries, who refuse to acknowledge his integrity and innocence. And so, it is today with the coronavirus that has infected communities everywhere in the world. Many priests, clergy, rabbis, and imams think they know the real reason why this pandemic has occurred.

The ancient Greek name for Satan is διάβολος (*Diabolos*). The English word "devil" "[72] derives from this ancient Greek etymology. Simply put: the story of Job is about a man of faith who experiences the diabolic. [73] The realm of the diabolic regard humankind and God in opposition to one another. Consequently, the domain of the diabolic produces a sense of estrangement from the Divine and weakens the bonds of interpersonal relationships affecting God and humanity alike. If Job represents every person who has ever suffered, then the sufferer's encounter with the diabolic can play an essential role in the individual's faith formation. As a parable, Job shows a challenging example of faith; one can face adversity and still rise above it.

The rapid spread of the coronavirus has claimed many great people scholars, teachers, artists, physicians, nurses, and athletes have died very quickly after getting infected. Exemplary human beings endure suffering like anyone else; spiritual mentors are no exception either. An excellent example of this type of problem is apparent in some of Mother Teresa's confessions about her sense of spiritual bewilderment. In her personal letters, she bares her soul, "I am told God loves me—and yet the reality of darkness and coldness, and emptiness is so great that nothing touches my soul."[74] Despite her ambivalence, she maintains her religious life in a state of cognitive dissonance:

> Lord, my God, who am I that You should forsake me? The Child of your Love—and now become as the most hated one—the one—You have thrown away as unwanted— unloved. I call, I cling, I want—and there is no One to answer—no One on Whom I can cling—no, No One. — Alone... Where is my Faith—even deep down right in there is nothing, but emptiness and darkness—My God— how painful is this unknown pain—I have no Faith—I dare not utter the words & thoughts that crowd in my heart—and make me suffer untold agony.

> So many unanswered questions live within me afraid to uncover them— because of the blasphemy—If there be God—please forgive me—When I try to raise my thoughts to Heaven—there is such convicting emptiness that those very thoughts return like sharp knives & hurt my very soul.—I am told God loves me—and yet the reality of darkness, coldness, and emptiness is so great that nothing touches my soul. Did I make a mistake in surrendering blindly to the Call of the Sacred Heart?[iv]

The gospel that many of these self-righteous preachers consistently stress how human beings are fallen creatures, sinful to the core, and worthy of Divine retribution. This type of faith often depicts God as a capricious and alienating force that is out to get us if we do something wrong. But when pious people believe this way, they inadvertently reduce the stature of humanity; their self-righteous attitude sees human beings and their existence in the worst possible light. And for the simple of heart, many imagine that God is out to "get" His prized creation in the event the worshiper commits the smallest infraction.

When we experience the diabolic in our lives, it cuts through the bond that links humanity with her Maker and focuses on the polarity and tension that exists between God and the Creation. The gospel that many of these self-righteous preachers consistently stress how human beings are fallen creatures, sinful to the core and worthy of Divine retribution. This faith often depicts God as a capricious and alienating force that is out to get us whenever we do something wrong. But when pious people believe this way, they inadvertently reduce the stature of humanity; their self-righteous attitude sees human beings and their existence in the worst possible light. And for the simple of heart, many imagine that God is out to punish His prized creation in the event the worshiper commits the smallest infraction.

Why Did Job Suffer?

Since Late Antiquity, many commentators—both Christian and Jewish—attributed Job's suffering to all sorts of divine, satanic, karmic, and physical causes.[75]

Modern commentaries rarely attribute Job's plight to a *human origin*. However. However, an examination of Job's complaints will show that much of his pain was directed at a community that failed to show compassion toward him when he needed it the most. Based on how we define the term "community," we could say that Job had no community for support.

A healthy community has a synergistic nature. When people work together with a communitarian attitude, they create something greater than the sum of all their parts because every person is committed to the care, nurture, growth, and well-being of each other's body, soul and mind. However, Job does not live in such a community. He lives in a city whose citizens practiced the rugged ethic of individualism—every person lived for himself. The people who inhabit Job's world measure God's blessings solely concerning wealth and property.

Job's experiences point to a natural source of his trouble and distress—his friends. God never judges Job for expressing his feelings of ambivalence and protest—and God later criticizes Job's friends for misrepresenting His views in their disputes with Job (Job 42:7). This approach was first expressed by the most famous of medieval Jewish exegetes—Rashi (twelfth century). [76]

A computerized search conducted on the text seems to confirm Rashi's intuition The word חֶסֶד (*ḥesed*, "loving-kindness") appears only three times in the Book of Job. Likewise, the Hebrew word for "comfort," נֶחָמָה (*neḥāmâ*) appears only seven times in the entire Book of Job. Only twice, does Job ever receive *neḥāmâ* from his friends—the first time was at the very beginning, in Job 2:11. At this stage, Job's friends did not criticize him. The second instance is at the very end of the book (Job 42:11), after God vindicates Job. Strangely, the entire book seems to be bereft of metaphors depicting human and divine compassion. This substantiates Rashi's view that the whole book is a parable about pastoral care.

Rashi's asserted that empathy and tenderness are essential ingredients in when it comes to healing the heart of a sufferer. Conversely, the story of Job shows how pious-minded people often compound human suffering; in Job's case, his community treated him like a pariah. People often experience angst when they see a friend experience a personal hardship; on some psychological level, one fears that what is happening to a neighbor could be contagious and might happen to them (to quote from Bob Dylan's song, "Isis"). If the righteous Job could undergo such pain and torment, how much more so could they! On a psychological level, the friends responded to Job out of fear that a similar fate could await them. The friends tried to justify their own righteousness by castigating Job, using him as an emotional scapegoat to cover up their own securities.

Job's friends feared a truth later expressed in rabbinical tradition, "Woe to the wicked, and woe to his neighbors!" Or, "Stay away from an evil person; otherwise, you will end up like him." Job's life became full of loneliness, and he felt disconnected from God and those around him. He wondered: What did I do to deserve such miserable friends like these?!" Yet, the Talmud notes that human beings need friendship to live. Death itself is preferable to not having any friends at all—even if they are like the friends of Job. [77]

Schadenfreude: The Hidden Cause of Job's Suffering

The Book of Job serendipitously challenges you—the reader—with an unsettling theological realization: Not all suffering necessarily derives from God but from human actors who routinely misrepresent God. Their confused idea of God fails to heal the suffering soul. Rabbi Harold Kushner's moving book, *When Bad Things Happen to Good People,* touched upon a visceral note when he raised serious questions about the nature of human suffering. Indeed, this issue has haunted the imagination of humankind since the beginning of recorded history. Job raises another equally important question—one that typically gets ignored: How do we respond when bad things happen to other people?

Let us expand on this point. On the surface, Job's arguments with his friends seem very intellectual, almost the kind of debate one would expect to find in a Socratic dialogue of Plato. Yet, we can easily discern from their carefully worded arguments a measure of emotional detachment. Job's friends exhibit no doubt about their success in life, but they view Job's suffering as something that he deserves. They almost seem to take perverse pleasure in seeing cosmic justice destroy Job's life. We can easily coax ourselves that "we are righteous," or "just in God's eyes" while assuming our friends, neighbors, and colleagues are lowly sinners.

If this interpretation is correct, then feeling self-righteous about our neighbor's suffering is one of the primary causes of human pain. The way one responds to someone else's suffering speaks volumes about the community's character. Offering platitudes of sympathy mean very little unless the words are heartfelt and sincere. Indeed, nothing undermines human kindness and solidarity like one who secretly and vicariously rejoices in the pain of another. In his examination of schadenfreude, the German etymologist Richard Trench observed,

> What a fearful thing is it that any language should have a word expressive of the pleasure which men feel at the calamities of others; for the existence of the word bears testimony to the existence of the thing. And yet, in more than one such a word is found.... In the Greek *epikhairekakia,* in the German, "Schadenfreude." [78]

Schadenfreude means "malicious joy in the misfortunes of others," and it derives from "damage-joy," from *schaden* "damage, harm, injury" and *freude* ("joy"). The concept of *schadenfreude*, as Trench observes is hardly new for Aristotle, where he examines this trait in his Nicomachean Ethics. In contrast to Νέμεσις ("nemesis") where a person feels that the object's good fortune is undeserved, ἐπιχαιρεκακία (*epikhairekakia*, "spite") is the exact opposite. Spite involves feeling pleasure at the deserved misfortune of others. [79]

Some people we know experience discomfort or emotional at the good fortune of others, a point that Jewish ethics has long recognized. [80] Based on Aristotle's keen insight, one may infer from the friends of Job, a quality that is not obvious in the story. Perhaps Job's friends resented his previous success. Job's suffering enables them to feel morally and spiritually superior to him; his suffering justifies their unspoken animus toward Job erstwhile prosperity.

Renée Girard's Theory: Job as Scapegoat

It is interesting to compare Rashi's interpretive approach with that of the French literary critic, Renée Girard, who also views Job's suffering within the context of his community. [81] In both of their expositions of the Jobian narrative, they argue that his particular community is responsible for exacerbating Job's suffering. Girard asserted that primitive societies learned to develop a means of controlling such outbursts of collective violence by choosing a surrogate victim; the community agrees on an object that will serve to channel and redirect such violent forces raging in the soul of their society. At first, the mob directed its violence to a hapless human victim. But eventually, the animal sacrifice became practically universal in all cultures and times because it served to create order out of chaos and civility out of social unrest. Animal sacrifice plays a significant role in sublimating these violent impulses. Once the scapegoat is removed, the social order became restored as it was in the beginning; the people become content once more until the cycle begins again. In the case of Job, Girard argues that his friends insist that Job accept his role as the community scapegoat.

Girard compares Job's suffering to Sophocles' famous tragedy, *Oedipus Rex*, where Oedipus, like Job, goes from being the most blessed of gods and mortals to being the most accursed by them as well. But unlike Oedipus, who accepts the criticism and judgment of his peers, Job refuses to be the victim; he defends his personal integrity and stands against the *vox populi* that also claims to be the *vox Dei* (Psa. 31:11-13). According to the Greek myth, Oedipus became genuinely guilty for killing his father and marrying his mother. Ergo, Oedipus, therefore, deserved to be banished and shunned; in the case of Job, the friends make many accusations about him, but it is the voice of Job that has the last word. Ultimately, Oedipus is a "successful scapegoat," while Job is an example of a failed scapegoat because he stands up for his integrity whenever he confronts the mob mentality of his community.

Girard might have considered comparing Job's ordeal with his friends to another source for his theory other than Sophocles. The British anthropologist Sir James Frazer describes a shadowy side of Greek civilization that is seldom ever discussed by it many admirers:

> But in civilized Greece the custom of the scapegoat took darker forms than the innocent rite over which the amiable and pious Plutarch presided. Whenever Marseilles, one of the busiest and most brilliant of Greek colonies, was ravaged by a plague, a man of the poorer classes used to offer himself as a scapegoat. For a whole year he was maintained at the public expense, being fed on choice and pure food. At the expiry of the year he was dressed in sacred garments, decked with holy branches, and led through the whole city, while prayers were uttered that all the evils of the people might fall on his head. He was then cast out of the city or stoned to death by the people outside of the walls.
>
> The Athenians regularly maintained a number of degraded and useless beings at the public expense; and when any calamity, such as plague, drought, or famine, befell the city, they sacrificed two of these outcast scapegoats. One of the victims was sacrificed for the men and the other for the women. The former wore round his neck a string of black, the latter a string of white figs. Sometimes, it seems, the victim slain on behalf of the women was a woman. They were led about the city and then sacrificed, apparently by being stoned to death outside the city. But such sacrifices were not confined to extraordinary occasions of public calamity; it appears that every year, at the festival of the Thargelia in May, two victims, one for

the men and one for the women, were led out of Athens and stoned to death. The city of Abdera in Thrace was publicly purified once a year, and one of the burghers, set apart for the purpose, was stoned to death as a scapegoat or vicarious sacrifice for the life of all the others; six days before his execution he was excommunicated, "in order that he alone might bear the sins of all the people."[34]

It is intriguing to compare the Job's story to a depiction that is found in the writings of Plutarch. Although these Greek stories and traditions were written millennia ago, there exists a resonance to what we are hearing from devout religious leaders today concerning the coronavirus pandemic. Pious people today would love nothing more than for the "sinners" afflicted with the coronavirus to own up to their religious waywardness.

One minister named Rev. Ralph Drollinger, leads a weekly Bible study group for the White House, released a new interpretation of the coronavirus pandemic this week, arguing that the crisis represents an act of God's judgment. Drollinger claimed in two of his blog postings that the pandemic is a form of God's wrath upon the nations, but not one as severe as the floods described in the Old Testament or the destruction of Sodom and Gomorrah. He added:

> According to him, the coronavirus is a form of God's wrath upon nations, but not one as severe as the floods described in the Old Testament or the destruction of Sodom and Gomorrah. "Relative to the coronavirus pandemic crisis, this is not God's abandonment wrath nor His cataclysmic wrath, rather it is sowing and reaping wrath," wrote Drollinger. [82]

Some people find it comfortable to sit in judgment of others from a safe distance like Rev. Drollinger. But how would he feel it this virus affected his children or family members he loves dearly? He probably would recant his harsh words. This writer suggests he read Camus' *The Plague*. Perhaps he will walk away with a new understanding. It is always easy to scapegoat the Other. Anti-Semites will always blame the Jew or the State of Israel for everything that is wrong in the world. The Book of Job illustrates how the human community scapegoat will weaker members of society who in turn bear the burden of their denied violent impulses. As the pandemic rages, it is surprising to see the anti-Semites blame the Jew, or the white nationalist and religious fundamentalist from Iran to the United States and every place in between, blame members of the LGBT (lesbian, gay, bisexual and transgender) community. Drollinger is no different than Father Paneloux of Camus' story mentioned above.

But what is the psychological mechanism that leads a person to view the non-believer as an "enemy" of God? The psychologist Carl G. Jung argued forcefully that the "enemy" is constructed from the denied aspects of the self; we love and hate others according to the degree that we love or hate ourselves. In the face of the enemy, we paradoxically see a distorted image of ourselves staring back at us, and this would explain why Job's friends respond with such vitriolic hatred of him. The philosopher Sam Keen alerts us about the "enemy." According to him, the hostile imagination possesses a complete repertoire of images it uses to dehumanize the enemy. This darker region of the soul will more often look outwardly at what is wrong rather than turn inwardly and seriously self-examine one's own self-righteous conduct. [83]

The healing of our society requires we recognize these dark forces exist within ourselves. It is no small wonder why one could argue that self-righteousness is the oldest and perhaps the most severe sin of the Bible. The healing of our society requires we recognize these dark forces exist within ourselves. It is no small wonder why one could argue that self-righteousness is the oldest and perhaps serious sin of the Bible.

In William Blake's famous illustrations of Job, the viewer cannot help but see how Job's face resembles the Divine face of God. Blake wanted to draw attention to how the caregiver ultimately reflects God's Face; the visitor mirrors God's "Presence." As the philosopher Emmanuel Lévinas, the human face points to something vital for all relationships—the respect of the Other. As such, the entrance to the face is ethical at the very start."[84] The face functions as the locus of human interaction. It conveys or betrays our intentions and frames of mind. Consciously or unconsciously, the human face reveals our emotions and feelings. Caregiving must always begin with gazing at the human face. Levinas explains:

> Thus, our face is the most important identity mark of who we are, both physically and socially. By gazing into the face, the face summons me to have a relationship with you. It is weak and powerful—all at the same time. It is weak in that it is naked and vulnerable to attack; it is easily

injured as well. Yet, the face can conquer the strongest power through its gentleness of spirit. The face commands and forbids us to kill; it demands an ethical obligation upon all who look upon it.

At First, Job's Friends Get It Right ....

Sometimes the best kind of support a person can give a friend or loved one is by just being there. Loneliness makes painful moments seem more intense. The gift of a compassionate presence that each person possesses offers solace that is more powerful and eloquent than words alone. Job's friends are oddly at their best when they say absolutely nothing. The biblical narrator relates:

> Now when three of Job's friends heard of all the misfortune that had come upon him, they set out each one from his own place: Eliphaz from Teman, Bildad from Shuh, and Zophar from Naamath. They met and journeyed together to give him sympathy and comfort. But when, at a distance, they lifted up their eyes and did not recognize him, they began to weep aloud; they tore their cloaks and threw dust upon their heads. Then they sat down upon the ground with him seven days and seven nights, but none of them spoke a word to him; for they saw how great was his suffering.
>
> Job 2:11-13

At first, the mere sight of Job produces intense sadness in his friends. Job's bleeding ulcers, his general disfigurement, and his body odor had a powerful impact on the way Job's friends regarded him. Their loss of composure indeed was of no help to Job and his condition. But then again, for seven full days, they sat next to him; they were stunned into silence. At this point, Job's friends honestly acted in a kindly, sympathetic, and supportive manner. Their body language and silence probably meant more to Job than his friends could have imagined.

The language of tears might have sufficed. It is only when they open their mouths and speak as 'professional theologians' that they lash out at Job with one insensitive comment after another. A comforter would do well to remember that sometimes the best way to comfort a grieving person is by simply saying nothing. One can acknowledge the sufferer's questioning with sympathy and understanding. What the griever is experiencing is the loss of a relationship, the anxiety that comes with separation. The language of touch, the language of caring eyes, the effectiveness of a listening ear always provides a salve for the griever's wounds.

Job's Miserable Friends exacerbate his Suffering

But the moment Job began expressing his anger and pain; his friends suddenly start to attack him. A reader of this story might wonder: Job's friends react so harshly because they feel personally threatened by Job's words; he single-handed endangered the social system of the wealthy and the powerful. In the silence of their thoughts, Job's friends wonder: What if Job is right? What could this mean for the rest of us? The wealthy want to believe that their prosperity is a sign of blessedness by God; the poor, on the other hand— by their misery—deserve to be cursed! Job's loss of fortune could happen to anyone of them. The social realities of their world reflected God's justice and the maintenance of the social order. Job's bold words could create a social upheaval among the poorer classes. The friends knew that silencing Job would mean that life would continue to be good for the wealthy and the powerful.

Job's friends parrot the conventional wisdom of their day; they are determined to keep him silent and make him wallow in self-remorse and culpability. As far as they were concerned, Job is not as "righteous" as he claimed to be. His suffering could only mean that either Job or his children must have committed concealed crimes that have provoked God's punitive response. They fear if they refrain from criticizing Job, God will implicate each of them—ironically, each of Job's friends suffers in the end (Job. 42:7-9)—but not for the reason they imagined! God holds them accountable for not being supportive of Job!

To persuade Job, the friends even try to intimidate Job with homilies about philosophy, morality and theological discourses about the carrot and the stick. They insist that Job beseech God for forgiveness because he spoke heresy! They try to "force-feed" Job with the perennial wisdom of the day. Job's friends found scriptural support in the old doctrine of retribution. Cleverly, the friends mask their true intentions by speaking in the name of God's righteousness. Eliphaz, the first of Job's fair-weather friends, attempts to persuade Job.

Think now, who that was innocent ever perished?
Or where were the upright cut off?
As I have seen, those who plow iniquity and sow trouble reap
the same.
By the breath of God, they perish,
and by the blast of his anger they are consumed.

Job 4:7-9

See, God will not reject a blameless person,
nor take the hand of evildoers.

Job 8:20

According to Eliphaz, everything that happens to man is determined by his own deeds. He tries to make Job responsible for his own misfortune. Rather than showing solidarity with the sufferer, he stands and criticizes Job's religious attitude and behavior. Eliphaz is convinced that Job can experience a complete reversal of fortune if he sincerely repents. Bildad, another friend, echoed the same view:

Bildad proclaims there could be no such thing as innocent suffering, nor was there anything such as divine injustice. He extols God's justice so much (cf. Job 25ff.) but acts indifferently toward, nor does he care about Job's suffering, which he sees as justified. Bildad views Job's fall from grace as empirical proof that Job was not as perfect as everybody thought he was. Had Job been righteous, how could God have allowed Job to suffer so intensely? Job's children deserved to die since they were hopelessly wicked (Job 8:4). Conversely, Bildad argues in v. 6, that if Job is convinced that he is truly innocent, then it stands to reason that he ought to maintain his trust in God that He would free him from his troubles and restore him. If on the other hand he does not, then it is evident that Job is not as "innocent" as he claims to be! It is instructive that it is Job's friends ultimately live to see God vindicate Job (Job 42:7).

Job refuses to accept such a simplistic view of God. He regarded Bildad's belief as a misrepresentation of God's justice. He refuses to believe in a God that was vindictive and insecure. Such an evil deity was incompatible with the God of mercy in the Bible. The God of retribution, as portrayed by his friends to Job, is an idol fashioned after the depths of human depravity.

What you know, I also know;
I am not inferior to you.
But I would speak to the Almighty,
and I desire to argue my case with God.
As for you, you whitewash with lies;
all of you are worthless physicians.
If you would only keep silent,
that would be your wisdom!
Hear now my reasoning,
and listen to the pleadings of my lips.
Will you speak falsely for God,
and speak deceitfully for him?

Job 13:2-7

Job Gets Impatient with Theological Platitudes

Job grew impatient and refused to take part in thoughtless clichés and rhetoric. Job yearns for healing. Job's friends did not allow him to heal and mend but exacerbated his wounds, instilling guilt and alienation. They kept Job's wounds open, keeping his pain ever fresh. Job rejects such an idolatrous depiction of God; their imago Dei was so distorted that they misconstrued their role as friends and healers. They would have been far wiser to remain quiet. Outraged by such a capricious image of God, Job yearns for his friends to reveal a God who delights in compassion and mercy. Zophar, a third friend of Job, expresses the same argument against Job, that the others have shown, albeit somewhat differently. According to him, the wages of sin is suffering; there can be no other explanation. He insists that Job acknowledges that he is a sinner and that Job has failed to act piously. Remarkably, in the first round of their discussion with Job, Zophar does not ever acknowledge the depth of Job's pain. His approach is academic and emotionally detached. Job must suffer, because God's justice has finally caught up with him—there can be no escape.

By refusing to take responsibility for his sinfulness, Job's community perceives him as both a hypocrite and a scoffer. They scoffed at Job's claim to piety. Job tells his friends, "Miserable comforters are you all" (Job 16:2), and says of their words, "You comfort me with empty nothings" (Job 21:34). He urges them to comfort by listening instead of speaking (Job 21:2). Yet, as the debate rages on, the friends try to corner Job, but Job still refuses to comply with their demands of silence and submission. He will not consent to the charges that he was a sinner who brought on his suffering from previous misdeeds. In one of his essential disclosures, Job recalls how the community used to treat him with respect:

> *I wish I were as in the old days, back in the times when God watched over me; when his lamp shone over my head, and I walked through the dark by its light; as I was when I was young, and God's counsel graced my tent. Then Shaddai was still with me, my children were around me; my steps were awash in butter, and the rocks poured out for me streams of olive oil. When I went out to the gate of the city, when I took my seat in the square, the young men saw me and withdrew, and the aged rose up and stood; the nobles refrained from talking, and laid their hands on their mouths; the voices of princes were hushed, and their tongues stuck to the roof of their mouths. When the ear heard, it commended me, and when the eye saw, it approved; because I delivered the poor who cried, and the orphan who had no helper. The blessing of the wretched came upon me, and I caused the widow's heart to sing for joy. I put on righteousness, and it clothed me; my justice was like a robe and a turban. I was eyes to the blind, and feet to the lame.*

> Job 29:2-15

Subsequently, at Job's home, even his own family does not want to have anything to do with him. Job's own wife wishes for him to die, "Then his wife said to him, 'Do you still persist in your integrity? Curse God, and die'" (Job 2:9). Perhaps she too blames the death of her children on Job's lack of piety. He had become a social outcast; people gossip behind him. Job's former friends do not want to know of him. Following their parents' example, even the community's children treat Job with utter scorn and contempt.

> *He has put my family far from me, and my acquaintances are wholly estranged from me. My relatives and my close friends have failed me; the guests in my house have forgotten me; my serving girls count me as a stranger; I have become an alien in their eyes. I call to my servant, but he gives me no answer; I must myself plead with him. My breath is repulsive to my*

> *wife; I am loathsome to my own family. Even young children despise me; when I rise, they talk against me. All my intimate friends abhor me, and those whom I loved have turned against me.*
>
> Job 19:13-19

Job's suffering reaches new heights; everyone has expelled him from the community; they no longer regard him as a holy man. Everyone sees Job as a man who has fallen from grace; he is the recipient of taunts and torments and insults. Those who saw Job as the embodiment of evil, as one condemned by God, may have even physically harassed him. Victimized by a society that treated him as if he did not exist, Job's call for justice (19:7) go unnoticed. Job's suffering meant nothing to those around him. He feels cut off, isolated, and "fenced in" much as the leper was in the days of Moses. It was as though he had no self-worth as a human being whatsoever.

> *He has walled up my way so that I cannot pass, and he has set darkness upon my paths.*
>
> Job 19:8

Anyone suffering from the loss of a loved one can easily relate to the apathy and callousness of Job experiences from his community. Job's reaction is familiar to all who have suffered and received little or no support from the community. Those who experience the pain, and the shame, often feel that God and their community hate them for their "sins."

Spiritual writers of the medieval era describe the Jobian experience in their mystical writings as, "The Dark Night of the Soul." This is a psychological place where the sufferer feels as if he is totally cut off from a relationship. Defined: the experience of intense suffering brings us to a realm of darkness. We feel here we feel as though our last link of hope—our relationship with God—has been lost or severed; A part of us wonders whether God is more an enemy than a companion, who is out to punish us for wrongdoing. Illness and pain have a demoralizing effect on a sufferer's ability to feel God's love and concern. Job's reaction is indeed understandable as it is honest. Intimidated by this emerging dissident who freely speaks his mind, the friends become increasingly frustrated with Job's refusal to admit that he is a miserable sinner, whom God is justly punishing for the crimes he committed.

Of all of Job's friends, Elihu, the youngest of Job's friends, attempts to put the entire debate from a different perspective. He lashes out at the friends for trying to find fault in Job, instead of trying to see Job's innocence. He accuses the friends pretending to know what was on God's mind. However, to his credit, Elihu rejected Job's other friends' arguments. Also, Elihu attempts to get Job and his friends away from viewing the justice of God from an anthropocentric perspective. It was not necessarily what Elihu said that was different; it was how he said it. Elihu spoke out of love and a genuine concern for Job in contrast to the other friends who saw Job as an adversary to be conquered in verbal battle.

The Real Source of Suffering: Ignorance

The great twelfth-century Jewish philosopher Maimonides observed that although Job is described in the beginning of this narrative as being an upright and decent individual, the one characteristic he lacks was the quality of insight.[85] Although Job lived a pious life, but he was not wise. Maimonides' words suggest the absence of wisdom in our lives makes the experience of suffering all the worse.

> These great evils that come about between the human individuals who inflict them upon one another because of purposes, desires, opinions, and beliefs, are all of them likewise consequent upon privation. For all of them derive from ignorance, I mean from a lack of insight. Analogically, a blind person can cause considerable harm to himself and others because he has nobody to guide him. A person afflicted with ignorance is no different; it is one of the principle reasons why the human race suffers. If people possessed moral and spiritual clarity, they would refrain from harming themselves and others. A realization of this truth would put an end to hostility and hatred in a civil society. The Scripture teaches us:

> > *Then the wolf shall be a guest of the lamb,*
> > *and the leopard shall lie down with the kid;*
> > *The calf and the young lion shall browse together,*
> > *with a little child to guide them.*
> > *The cow and the bear shall be neighbors,*
> > *together their young shall rest;*

> *the lion shall eat hay like the ox.*
> *The baby shall play by the cobra's den,*
>   *and the child lay his hand on the adder's lair.*
> *There shall be no harm or ruin on all my holy mountain;*
>   *for the earth shall be filled with knowledge of the LORD,*
>   *as water covers the sea.*
>
> Isaiah 11:6-9

Knowledge of the Divine produces a mindful awareness that brings an end to hostility, disagreement, and tyrannies. Once human beings attain this mindful awareness, the world will change for the better, for "the earth shall be filled with knowledge of the LORD, as water covers the sea" ...."[86]

At the beginning of the narrative, Job "fears God," but he does not serve God out of love; nor does he serve God out of wisdom. His worship was predicated upon the principle of *quid quo pro*. By living a pious lifestyle, Job remains convinced he will be blessed with material prosperity. He is at the beginning of his story someone who is following the kind of philosophy in Deuteronomy that promises material abundance and goods. But God shows Job the theology of the carrot and the stick does not really work. Pious and righteous people suffer like everyone else. Job's inability to think outside of what he was taught concerning God's governance of the world produced much of his suffering. His spiritual expectation was a disappointment waiting to happen.

The first Chief Rabbi of Palestine, Rabbi Abraham Isaac Kook, arrived at a similar conclusion. Like Maimonides, Kook believed the lack of insight exacerbates our perception of the Divine:

> All the ideological arguments among people and all the inner conflicts that every individual suffers in his own world outlook are caused by a confused conception of God. One must always cleanse one's thoughts about God to make sure they are free of the dross of deceptive fantasies, of groundless fear, of evil inclinations, of wants and inadequacies. Faith in God must enhance human happiness. When the duty to honor God is conceived of in an enlightened manner, it raises human worth and the worth of all creatures, filling them with largeness of spirit, combined with genuine humility. But a crude conception of God tends toward the idolatrous, and degrades the dignity of man and of other beings.[87]

Kook's message may serve as a sharp rebuke toward the plethora of voices we hear today from the ministers who do not know how to console and shepherd the victims of the coronavirus.

Job's Life Lessons for an Age of Pandemics

What does it mean to be a human being? In the theophany Job experiences, he comes to realize that the human vocation sets humanity apart from the rest of Creation. Rather than complaining about the inequities of the world, God teaches Job that human stewardship ultimately brings healing to oneself and the world. Creation finds its completion through tenderness and care. Given the fragility of life, God beckons Job to combat the experience of pain with a loving response. Life deserves to be treated with reverence and respect. God encourages Job to take a pro-activist stand in eradicating evil and suffering. Most of the wickedness that we see in the world comes from human cruelty or indifference. Unlike natural evil, human-generated evil (also called "moral evil") is a stubborn and determined force; it never voluntarily relinquishes its short hold of power, even at the expense of its own wellbeing.

The attempt to justify why evil exists (a.k.a., theodicy) produces canned theological answers that only legitimize human suffering by silencing the sufferer's endless cry from the dust and ashes of the world. In Job's religious experience, he receives an awakening. God encouraged Job to open up to the plight of others and make their suffering his concern. Job discovered that without his participation, the world remains a place of irredeemable suffering—this world is as Keats once poetically described the soul's purpose on earth as the "the vale of soul-making." By eliminating pain, our souls become genuinely human.

Although God's power is not coercive, it is limited only by human freedom and choice. God's love gives humanity the space to develop its own spiritual potential. Human suffering can just end when human beings decide to eradicate it from the face of the planet. Cognitive faith and the conventional "Wrath of God" theology that was in currency in his day kept Job suffering and entrenched in his misery. Such a misguided theology could not solve Job's problems but only exacerbate them. Hasdai Crescas, (1340-1410) the great arch-critic of Aristotelian philosophy, felt convinced that all theological discussions about the nature of God were of little value unless they inspired deeds of love and compassion. God's love is the Power that is behind the creative processes unfolding throughout the world and universe.

> It is the joy of *giving*; it is the joy of the good that is lavished unto His creatures. He makes them act by His will and intention. He makes them persist by the emanation of His good. God loves to spread Goodness and Perfection. The joy He feels is due to this constant gift of being that spreads throughout creation, in the most perfect manner possible. *The joy that God experiences in an infinite and an essential way is through the act of giving.*[88] (Emphasis added).

We become God-like only when we share and disperse love. By spreading this gift, we participate in unfolding God's own love to the world. This alone is where human salvation can be found. Our concern for justice must emanate out of the desire to promote God's goodness in the world. It is both human thoughtlessness and the withholding of this gift that creates evil and suffering. For human beings, Crescas maintained, the mere possession of intellectual knowledge per se does not represent the highest good attainable by humankind. Nor is the love of God measured by paying lip-service to dogmas, creeds, and other forms of mindless orthodoxies as the friends of Job erroneously and arrogantly thought.

The love of God is engendered by our capacity to experience communion with our fellow human beings—especially those who suffer. The stronger our sense of fellowship, the stronger our love for God will become. Once Job realized this elemental truth, his life will change forever. Job indeed has not found a simplistic answer to all his penetrating questions, but he did receive that one revelation that could enable him with the wisdom to face his pain and suffering. In Job's vision, he discovers that it is not the pain which has meaning, but on the contrary—it is what Job would later bring to his pain that gives pain its redemptive purpose. It is this discovery that paradoxically enables Job to walk away and begin his whole life anew.

Job Becomes a Wounded Healer

The epilogue states that "After the LORD had said these things to Job, he said to Eliphaz the Temanite, 'I am angry with you and your two friends because you have not spoken of me what is right, as my servant Job has...'"

(Job 42:7). Professor Marvin Pope raises an interesting question, "How could Job's friends be condemned for such valiant defense of traditional dogma as they make in the Dialogue, and how could Job be commended for his vehement attacks on their doctrine and the God they presumed to defend?" He cites, the view of F. Delitzsch, who observed:

> [T]he correct elements of Job's speeches were his denying that sin is always punished with affliction and his holding fast to his innocence despite his friends' attack. God approved this sort of truthfulness rather than the dissembling of the friends who could not admit Job's innocence without upsetting their neat system of doctrine. Job had indeed accused his miserable comforters of lying to defend and flatter God; and he suggested that an honest God would certainly reject and punish the pious sycophants, 13:4, 7–11. If this verse refers to the arguments of the Dialogue, it is as magnificent a vindication as Job could have hoped for, proving that God values the integrity of the impatient protester and abhors pious hypocrites who would heap accusations on a tormented soul to uphold their theological position; cf. 6:14–30.[89]

Did something seriously wrong befall Job's friends? The verse could suggest that they too experienced heavenly retribution for castigating Job. Sometimes we cannot understand the pain of another until we walk in that person's shoes. Yet, the real issue is not so much the friends' dilemma, but Job's reaction to their suffering. There is much said in these few words. The biblical narrator implies that something terrible unexpectedly befell Job's three friends. Perhaps God simultaneously wanted to teach these men a valuable lesson, for now, they have become the victims hated by society. In effect, they ironically have a Job-like experience. Would Job sit and enjoy his restored fortune and slavishly adhere once more to the "God of Wrath" theology—especially in light of the shabby way his friends tormented him? Would Job, perhaps, bask in the euphoria of his newly gained spiritual consciousness while being oblivious to the rest of the world? Would Job forget about his new religious experience and act as he did previously? Would he remain emotionally aloof from those who suffer? Here is where real test now begins.

Job's new theology finds its realization in showing compassion for those who grieve and suffer. It is not Job's place to castigate, blame, or heap criticism upon his friends—even though he might feel justified for doing so. Instead, Job thus becomes a shepherd of hope. Moreover, by doing so, he gives purpose and redemption to his own suffering by reaching out to those who had oppressed him. Whereas the old Job acted no differently from his friends, in adopting a "holier-than-thou" type of attitude, the "new" Job is different. The manner and alacrity Job shows toward his friends is revealing. he now brings comfort, mercy, healing, compassion, prayer—and most importantly—personal forgiveness. He does not offer pious platitudes as his friends did with him. Job becomes a wounded-healer who was sensitive and responsive to the pain of others. The suffering Job experienced made it impossible for him to go back to the way things once were. Like Jacob's encounter with the angel, his life is altered forever. Job's woundedness thus becomes his own source of inner strength. Any person who has experienced and lived to survive suffering knows this odyssey all too well.

Also, Job's suffering sensitizes him to the plight of all beings, and as a result, he will not stand passively by when it comes to the suffering of others. Job's firsthand experience of the "Dark Night of the Soul" changes him into a new kind of human being, radically different from when he was at the outset of our story. Suffering made him even more determined to counter its presence by shouldering the yoke of his neighbor's pain. This biblical motif is not necessarily unique to the Book of Job; it is a reoccurring theme in much of the Tanakh—especially concerning the role of the "Suffering Servant of God" mentioned in Isaiah 53.

Improving upon God's Creation

Yet, every aspect of Creation, from the most majestic galaxies to the most infinitesimal particle, functions as God intended it to.[90] From the horns of the mighty oxen to the bacteria that creates dangerous viruses and plagues. Nature's capacity for self-destructiveness is part of the chaos we must learn to master—beginning first with ourselves. Although the term "good" טוֹב appears six times earlier[91] in the creation narrative, here it appears for the seventh time to symbolize completeness. The *peshat* reveals that it is only after God has created humankind—after His image and likeness—that Creation graduates from being merely "good" to now becoming "very good." Some Jewish mystics observed that the letters of the word מְאֹד (*mĕ'ōd* = "very") may also be read as an anagram for אָדָם ('*ādām* = "human being").[92]

A different perspective is offered in Ecclesiastes 7:29, "Behold, this only have I found, that God made humankind upright; but they have sought out many contrivances." People can choose to be upright and honest; the fact that they are not can only be attributed to the willful misuse of their God-given freedom. The text raises an important theological question: Can the existence of natural evil: tsunamis, cyclones, earthquakes, pandemics, and the like, be considered "good"?

Human intervention in the places where these catastrophes occur reveal how humankind possesses the capacity to act upon nature's defects and transform Creation from being merely "good," to becoming that which is "very good." While evil is a pervasive part of the human experience, the upshot is that evil does not exist as an ultimate principle of reality. Although nature is far from perfect, humankind's ability and willingness to correct its flaws brings an added excellence and completion to the Creator's handiwork. Human solidarity, transcending geographical boundaries when the world falls apart.

Our attitude matters whenever something tragic happen in the world.

William James was fond of saying, "The greatest discovery of my generation is that a human being can alter his life by altering his attitude." James' wisdom certainly applies to the painful wisdom we have gained from the COVID-19 coronavirus. Although it has killed thousands of people around the world, the pandemic does offer some valuable benefits. For one thing, it shows us how inextricably linked we are with other people scattered across the Earth. We occupy the same planet and breathe the same air; what happens in one part of the world affects all other parts. Human destiny demands we work together if we are to survive this pandemic or future pandemics. Nature is far more complicated than we probably realized. Now, with our burgeoning human population and global economy, rest assured the human race will face new threats from a wider distribution of diseases like this new strain of coronavirus. But if we learn to communicate correctly, we will overcome this disease, as we have conquered polio, cholera, and other pandemics.

Part 5
The Poetics of Space Social Distancing & Pastoral Issues

CHAPTER 14

"The one who bears the sore of leprosy shall keep his garments rent and his head bare, and shall muffle his beard; he shall cry out, 'Unclean, unclean!'"

Leviticus 14:35

Social-Distancing in the Bible

These days we continuously hear a phrase that did not exist just a few weeks ago – "social distancing." What precisely does this social distancing mean? By having fewer interactions individuals have with one another, this withdrawal from society will help slow down the rushing force of a dangerous pandemic. As a result, all sporting events have come to a grinding halt; social gatherings have been postponed. Creating physical space between ourselves and our friends or associates protects everybody involved.

The effects of the coronavirus are evident everywhere. We have seen a cessation of all public-school and college activities. Local parks and tennis courts are padlocked. Malls, theaters, houses of worship, theaters, parades— even mass transit have been temporarily closed or be used only for essential travel. Interestingly, the social interaction has gone to the Internet; Web-based learning and video conferencing have become the new normalcy—at least for the time being. Another phrase that is similar to "social distancing" is "self-quarantine."

As I began thinking about social distancing, I wondered: What does Jewish tradition have to say about the new phenomena of "social distancing"? Surprisingly, our religious traditions have a lot to say about this matter. The most obvious example pertains to those individuals who were stricken with leprosy. Leprosy has afflicted humans for thousands of years. The Scriptures tell us that a leper, "shall remain unclean as long as the disease is on him. Being unclean, he shall dwell apart; his dwelling shall be outside the camp" (Lev. 13:46). [93] In an age when the ancients knew nothing about how leprosy was spread, separating the afflicted from the rest of society was the only way the ancients felt they could "contain" the plague.

Such behavior is not restricted to how human beings respond to a mysterious disease. Many species of animals also avoid fellow-creatures if they perceive there is something sickly about them, which they may discern through the power of scent. Yet, bear in mind the leper was not completely abandoned. The local priests healed the body as well as the soul of their patients; their task was to help provide healing and support for the leper and ultimately reintegrate him back to his family and society. The biblical priesthood worked at "Ground Zero" with the lepers. They refused to abandon them. In ancient terms, think of the priests as first-responders. They knew that a spiritual approach to disease could facilitate the healing of a disease. Their approach was holistic.

More Thoughts on Social Distancing in the Bible

The second place where social distancing is also discussed is in the Talmud concerning the night of the Exodus when the angel of death struck Egypt's firstborn. The Sages taught: If there is plague in the city, gather your feet, i.e., limit the time you spend out of the house, as it is stated in the verse: "And none of you shall go out of the opening of his house until the morning." And it says in another verse: "Come, my people, enter into your chambers, and shut your doors behind you; hide yourself for a little moment, until the anger has passed by" (Isa. 26:20). And it says: "Outside the sword will bereave, and in the chambers terror" (Deut. 32:25). [94]

During the medieval era, some scholars pointed to a scriptural verse from Jeremiah, "Whoever remains in this city shall die by the sword or famine or pestilence. But whoever leaves and surrenders to the Chaldeans who are besieging you shall live and escape with his life" (Jer. 21:9). In other words: remaining in a place of danger is foolish. A prudent person must always seek to avoid danger and not rely upon miracles per se. From this passage, it is clear Jeremiah endorsed a kind of social distancing when it came to the threat of an oncoming plague. But as simple as this might seem for us in the 21st century, the medievalists lived with a different set of values.

CHAPTER 15

"The most beautiful and most profound experience is the sensation of the mystical. It is the sower of all true science. He to whom this emotion is a stranger, who can no longer wonder and stand rapt in awe, is as good as dead. To know that what is impenetrable to us really exists, manifesting itself as the highest wisdom and the most radiant beauty which our dull faculties can comprehend only in their primitive forms - this knowledge, this feeling is at the center of true religiousness."

Albert Einstein
The Merging of Spirit and Science)

Social Distancing in Jewish Law: The Cholera Pandemic of 1831

The concept of social-distancing at a time of pandemics is discussed in the Responsa literature. The term "responsa" refers to questions people have asked rabbis for almost 1500 years in matters of Judaic law, traditions, and values.

There were six cholera outbreaks in the 19th century. The first cholera outbreak spread widely beyond India began in 1817, and spread by both ship and overland route to Syria and the Crimean region. Within a short span of ten years, it became rampant in both Persia and southeastern Russia. By 1831, the second cholera pandemic spread throughout Western Europe. It affected Europe from 1829-1837.

How did the rabbis of that era respond?

In this chapter, we will look at one of the great rabbis of the 19th century—R Akiba Eiger (1761-1837) Each of these scholars took practical measures to ensure there would be social-distancing during the Great Cholera Pandemic of the 19th century. R. Akiba Eiger was a distinguished rabbinical scholar who lived during the second great cholera pandemic that affected Europe from 1829-1837. R. Eiger's responsa contains much valuable material is found on the social, economic, and religious situation of the Jews of his region. This information provides the historian with the tools to study the living conditions of a period.

During this time, R. Eiger kept close contact with the local authorities. Entire sections of the Jewish quarter were quarantined and forbidden to enter. But he took it upon himself to personally ensure that the poorer members of the Jewish community received the necessary supplies of food and medical care. Rabbi Akiba Eiger disregarded the danger and went into the stricken sections of the city to care for the sick.

He also established social-distance guidelines for the synagogues that would prevent larger numbers of worshipers from perishing. He limited the number of people who could participate at a religious service. Together with his lieutenants, he managed to reduce the number of people infected by the disease.

When King Frederick III of Prussia heard about his heroism, he honored the rabbi with a special commendation. He recalls:

> His Honor's letter has reached me, regarding prayer in the synagogue during the pandemic. It is my view that gathering in a small space is inappropriate. However, praying in smaller groups consisting of fifteen people is apropos. The same process ought to be done with the Afternoon Service. Each group consisting no more than fifteen people. This manner can be applied to other groups of fifteen, who will have a designated time when to appear and pray. This method also applies to the Afternoon Service. After the prayer quorum, let each group recite the appropriate Psalms of healing, as selected by the King. In addition, the prayers concerning the incense should also be recited.

> And they should be careful that more people than the quota of fifteen people should not push their way into the synagogue, perhaps by using a guard from the police to oversee this. Once they have reached the maximum prescribed] number, nobody else must be allowed to enter the synagogue until the first group has finished. Set this request before the magistrate, and let the magistrate know that I have written this instruction for you.

In the event of noncompliance, then the local authorities must be immediately notified. You will certainly succeed if you mention my name, and that I have instructed you not to have large gatherings in the synagogue, which is a small space. I have advised you of these arrangements. Continue reciting the Psalms and pray for the King as well. May God protect him! Collect from each person a tax of six large coins—from the youngest to the oldest. You must use this money to help save the lives of those suffering from the disease. In the event the King sends me more money, this too will be distributed to help the needy.

In terms of practical matters, dressing warm is essential; preferably, each person ought to wear flannel, and wear a belt around the waists. Avoid eating bad foods, especially pickles, and to reduce consumption of fruit and fish, and imbibe less alcohol. Don't overeat! Actually, it would be better for you to eat smaller portions to avoid overeating a lot of food.

- Keep your living quarters clean at all times.
- Wear clean clothing each week.
- Try not to worry and avoid getting depressed.
- Do not take nightly strolls.
- Take your strolls outside during the sunlight hours. Or, alternatively, take a walk in the open-fields.
- Make sure there is adequate sunshine in your rooms.
- Avoid going outside on an empty-stomach.
- Eat some mustard seeds and oak bark.
- Making washing your face and hands a part of your daily routine.
- Wash the floors with a pungent vinegar, and if you can, mix it with some rose water.
- Be clean. Don't leave any filth or dirt in the home. This includes changing into clean clothing regularly each week. Do not worry. Distance yourself from any kind of sadness. Don't walk about the city at night. During the middle of the day, when the sun is shining, it is good to stroll in the fields for air, and to open the

windows in the morning so that air will enter the rooms of your home.[95]

One of R. Eiger's most significant rulings that would change how Ashkenazi recite the Kaddish in synagogues pertaining to the recitation of the Kaddish Prayer. Prior to the cholera pandemic, the recitation of the Kaddish was said by the person who was a mourner, and it was not chanted by everyone else as we do today. However, the pandemic produced so many mourners, he established that each person could recite the Kaddish simultaneously. Throughout the duration of the cholera pandemic, R. Akiba Eiger proved to be a courageous shepherd to his people.

Perhaps the Haredi community ought to consider emulating R. Akiba Eiger, one of the great Talmudic stalwarts of the early 19th century. But it the measure of this man's greatness was not because of his vast encyclopedic.

CHAPTER 16

"Every leaf before it falls must think itself immortal."

Mart Rubin

*"I died as a mineral and became a plant, I died
as a plant and rose to animal, I died as an
animal and I was Man. Why should I fear?
When was I less by dying?"*

Rumi

Coming to Terms with Our Mortality

Gov. Andrew Cuomo said something that recently caught my attention. He recently remarked, "I did everything we could do. ... This is about saving lives. If everything we do saves just one life, I'll be happy."[96]

Jewish tradition might seem to concur. "God created the first human being alone to teach us that whosoever kills a single soul is considered as though he has destroyed an entire world. Anyone who preserves a single human soul, it is as if that person sustained a whole world." So, admittedly, on the surface, Cuomo's remark sounds reasonable, but we could argue that his statement reflects an unrealistic view of the world and of life. The "one life" argument has some practical limitations.

But here is an alternative approach I would like you to consider. Approximately 16,438 car crashes occur per day in the US. And 37,461 people get killed in car crashes each year in the United States. On average, that's 90 deaths a day. Besides, there are about three million people are injured or disabled. More than half of all road traffic deaths occur among young adults ages 15-44.[97]

Based on Cuomo's advice, perhaps he should consider banning all motorists from using their cars. This approach would undoubtedly save the world a substantial amount of lives, not to mention those who have been injured.

Part of living involves taking a measured chance in the decisions we make. Obviously, at a time of this pandemic, particular caution and effort must be made to minimize the potential spread of the contagion. Washing our hands, wearing facemasks, and maintaining a distance of six feet is prudent as it is practical. But I do not believe confining people to their home is necessarily the best approach to this problem. In Sweden, the Swedish people have been advised to adopt several safety precautions. For example, these are the following guidelines enacted: no gatherings of more than 50 people (revised down from 500 last Friday), avoid social contact if over 70 or ill, try to work from home, table service only in bars and restaurants.

This approach seems more adultlike than the guidelines many states have enforced. It also helps the Swedish people make a gradual transition to normalcy—something we will also have to do at some point. Dennis Prager also took issue with Cuomo's significant remark:

> It is hard to imagine a more morally absurd sentiment. Anyone who thinks rationally knows it is not worth depriving millions of people of their incomes, forcing thousands of companies to go out of business, causing recovering addicts to lapse back into addiction and much more economic and social damage to 'save one life.' As we are fighting a "war" against the virus, I used a war analogy to make my point. I noted that if we had fought World War II with the attitude that we cannot lose one life, we would never have fought the Nazis or the Japanese. I further noted that we do not make any social policy based on saving one life. For example, every time we raise the speed limit, we know thousands more people will die.[98]

As Prager observed, death is a part of our human experience in this world. Nobody wants to die, and we must do everything we can to avoid dying for naught. We take a chance on dying the moment we go outside of our homes; we take a chance whenever our country sends its young people to fight for the preservation of our freedom. Our country needs to find a way to reengage normalcy. We cannot allow a virus to destroy everything that reduces our nation to a state of paralysis—not without first destroying our economy. The coronavirus pandemic has become for all countries of the world—a new world war, or WWIII, except the enemy here is no nation, it is a disease that all humanity must work together to conquer. And with any conflict, people die.

But the good news is once we succeed in conquering the disease, the international relationships between nations—especially nations that war with one another—will take a positive and more meaningful step. If Israel were to find the cure for COVID-19, perhaps this could confer a heroic status to the Jewish nation as one of the Saviors of the Islamic world.

But again, perhaps not. The forces of social entropy are always at work deconstructing a society. The pandemic has exposed our insecurity about mortality. Since the fear of death is so devastating, we try not to think too much about it; our conscious psyche buries this feeling in our unconscious. Our inner child imagines that we will never die—or we hope we won't be there when it happens (Woody Allen); our psychological armor enables us to feel safe and make believe that the world is a manageable place. Our inquisitive curiosity about the nature of our being in this world is both a source of awareness and also a source of our creaturely anxiety.

When a forest fire destroys herds of wild animals in Africa, surviving zebras and lions do not ask, "Why do bad things happen to good zebras or lions?" Due to our intelligence, we ask the question because in our cleverness, we have figured out how to cheat death or at least postpone it from happening in our lives. Yes, other animals recognize they can die; their instincts serve as a warning system to flee from danger. But even these beautiful creatures are oblivious to the reality that they will inevitably die. Human beings are unique in this sense.

Marcus Aurelius, writes in his *Meditations*, "If you are distressed by anything external, the pain is not due to the thing itself, but to your estimate of it; and this you have the power to revoke at any moment." He also said, "You have power over your mind — not outside events. Realize this, and you will find strength." In other words, we cannot always control the events that intersect in our lives; we can only control how we react. Rabbinical wisdom concurred with Marcus Aurelius, Ben Zoma asked, "Who is mighty? He who conquers his inclinations." If my understanding is correct, I believe he is telling us the same thing. We must not let our insecurities and phantasms get the better of us. Ultimately, we are responsible for each of our souls. Had Marcus Aurelius been familiar with Ecclesiastes, he might have concurred with its proto-Stoic wisdom:

There is an appointed time for everything,
  and a time for every affair under the heavens.
A time to be born, and a time to die;
  a time to plant, and a time to uproot the plant.
A time to kill, and a time to heal;
  a time to tear down, and a time to build.
A time to weep, and a time to laugh;
  a time to mourn, and a time to dance.
A time to scatter stones, and a time to gather them;
  a time to embrace, and a time to be far from embraces.
A time to seek, and a time to lose;
  a time to keep, and a time to cast away.
A time to rend, and a time to sew;
  a time to be silent, and a time to speak.
A time to love, and a time to hate;
  a time of war, and a time of peace.[99]

The Buddhist say, "Death is unavoidable. It might seem morbid to contemplate this truth, but doing so can fill our day-to-day life with more meaning and joy." As we are sequestered in our homes, we ought to use the time to contemplate our earthly journey. Finding or rediscovering the inner peace with our own soul is the perfect recipe for conquering and transforming the chaos of the outer world into something meaningful and purposeful. Should we lose that ability, we will succumb to darker forces of our being that yearn to find expression. Conversely, when we survive a dangerous ordeal, we can better savor the beauty of life that God has given us. And be thankful that we have made it to see yet another beautiful day of creation.

CHAPTER 17

"In order to understand this role, we must penetrate to the core of the Shabbat institution. It is not rest per se, in the sense of not making an effort, physically or mentally. It is rest in the sense of the re-establishment of complete harmony between human beings and between them and nature. Nothing must be destroyed and nothing be built: the Shabbat is a day of truce in the human battle with the world. Neither must social change occur. Even tearing up a blade of grass is looked upon as a breach of this harmony, as is lighting a match. On the Shabbat one lives as if one has nothing, pursuing no aim except being, that is, expressing one's essential powers: praying, studying, eating, drinking, singing, making love."

Erich Fromm
To Have or to Be?

Henri Nouwen: The Importance of Finding Solitude

For the past month, every day seems like a Sabbath. Home time is often underappreciated. Sometimes work can be overrated. And during this pandemic, there is something to be said about having a decent night's sleep. As Fromm observed concerning the Sabbath, it is a day where we can realign our souls and find inner peace. The human conquest to control the world ceases. As Fromm observed, "On the Shabbat one lives as if one has nothing, pursuing no aim except being, that is, expressing one's essential powers: praying, studying, eating, drinking, singing, making love."

But during our solitude on the Sabbath, God gives us an invitation to explore an unchartered part of our personality that remains somewhat hidden to us because we are trying to put bread on the table. In all my years, I have never seen an entire country come to a screeching halt.

Many of us tend to identify with our outer lives more than we do with our inner lives—the undiscovered realm of spirit that exists within us. R. Avraham Ibn Maimon differed from his father in many respects. For one, he had a great admiration for the Sufis, who lived in Egypt at that time. One of the things he liked about them was their penchant for isolating themselves in the wilderness, mountains, and wastelands. They would utilize their surroundings to be alone with God. According to him, the biblical prophets also practiced seclusion before achieving a state of prophetic inspiration.

Many of us tend to identify with our outer lives more than we do with our inner lives—the undiscovered realm of spirit that exists within us. R. Avraham Ibn Maimon differed from his father in many respects. For one, he had a great admiration for the Sufis, who lived in Egypt at that time. One of the things he liked about them was their penchant for isolating themselves in the wilderness, mountains, and wastelands. They would utilize their surroundings to be alone with God. According to him, the biblical prophets also practiced seclusion before achieving a state of prophetic inspiration.

Through the reflective contemplation of nature, the initiate would attain an appreciation of God's immanence in the world. In the Book of Genesis, Isaac is described as "going out in the evening to take a walk in the field" (Gen. 24:63). Isaac cherished that time for connecting himself to God through prayer and meditation.

Solitude is a good thing, especially when it comes to prayer. But while most people tend to think about prayer as "speaking to God," prayer is also a way we can learn how to listen to God. And yet, when we pray—we cannot pray only for ourselves.

Every crisis bears inside it an opportunity. Aloneness should not be confused with creative solitude. Henri Nouwen explains there exists three movements in the spiritual life. The first movement is when we move from loneliness to solitude. The cure for loneliness is to create solitude. Solitude does not mean one is necessarily alone, but it involves something else. Nouwen elaborates how solitude differs from aloneness and loneliness.

> All human beings are alone. No other person will completely feel like we do, think like we do, act like we do. Each of us is unique, and our aloneness is the other side of our uniqueness. The question is whether we let our aloneness become loneliness or whether we allow it to lead

us into solitude. Loneliness is painful; solitude is peaceful. Loneliness makes us cling to others in desperation; solitude allows us to respect others in their uniqueness and create community. Letting our aloneness grow into solitude and not into loneliness is a lifelong struggle. It requires conscious choices about whom to be with, what to study, how to pray, and when we ask for counsel. But wise choices will help us to find the solitude where our hearts can grow in love."[100]

Nouwen acknowledges even relationships need space.

When we feel lonely, we keep looking for a person or persons who can take our loneliness away. Our lonely hearts cry out, "Please hold me, touch me, speak to me, pay attention to me." But soon we discover that the person we expect to take our loneliness away cannot give us what we ask for. Often that person feels oppressed by our demands and runs away, leaving us in despair. As long as we approach another person from our loneliness, no mature human relationship can develop. Clinging to one another in loneliness is suffocating and eventually becomes destructive. For love to be possible we need the courage to create space between us and to trust that this space allows us to dance together, [101]

The coronavirus presents us with an unexpected windfall. Perhaps this time is more than something fortuitous. Human aloneness, when converted into solitude, can enable people to renew their relationship with God. The challenge is for us to create our spatiality with a new sense of meaning, creativity, and spirituality. By committing one hour a day for personal reflection, we may discover strength we never knew we possessed.

In addition, for many of us who subsist on five to six hours of sleep, having eight hours of sleep has felt like a healing experience for my body and soul. More importantly, a good night's sleep help builds up our immune system. In a peculiar sense, the coronavirus created a new opportunity for individuals and families to rediscover the joys of homelife.

Lastly, in our moments of solitude, it is always important to ask: What is it we wish to fill in our lives? The coronavirus occurred this year close to

Passover time, a period where many people do their "spring-cleanings." Perhaps it is time to this as a spiritual metaphor and turn it into a reality.

The Coronavirus as a Chrysalis

The coronavirus not only threatens the physical health of millions of people across the globe—regardless of race, ethnicity, and faith, it has devastated world economies; we are only now beginning to feel its rippling effects. The psychological violence on our collective and individual psyches has left everyone feeling more depressed, anxious, and helpless as each of us gaze ahead at tomorrow.

The subject of suffering is central in the writings of the great psychologist Victor Frankl, whose book, "Man's Search for Meaning," remains a perennial best seller. When my father Leo Israel Samuel was in the Auschwitz concentration camp, one of the problems he faced was anxiety; would he survive the next day? Would there be enough food? Frankl told my father to portion out his food; he should save a portion for the evening; it would give him something positive to look forward to in an environment pervasive with death.

Frankl believed in a meaning-based therapy with the goal of helping the patient discover meaning in one's life. The search for meaning is for him, the primary motivational force of the human psyche—and it is each person's responsibility to actualize this potentiality. The most important lesson in Frankl's psychological system, is that finding meaning enables one to, "Say yes to life." In Frankl practice as a clinical psychologist, he typically used people's current difficulty to help them find future meaning in either work, relations or their capacity to deal with suffering.

Nature illustrates this idea in a poignant way. Caterpillars are not commonly regarded as nature's "beautiful" creatures, yet its metamorphosis from a tree clinging, twelve-legged into the regal flying butterfly is a frequent metaphor in all religious traditions as a symbol of rebirth and transformations. As amazing as it is to us staring from the outside, the caterpillar's transformation is what science calls a chrysalis. But for a caterpillar to turn into a butterfly, it must digest itself using enzymes triggered by hormones. Then, its sleeping cells (similar to stem cells) grow into the body parts of the future butterfly. Ultimately, the emergence of the butterfly is a stunning illustration how evolution transforms a species commonly regarded as a pest, into an entity of pure beauty that subsists upon nectar.

Suffering through these times can have the same impact upon us as well. There is always a potential for discovering meaning even in the most barren wastelands of life. "What matters," noted Frankl, "is to make the best of any given situation." Our challenge is to make the best of pain and transform a personal tragedy into a triumph by facing it with dignity and integrity. "In some way, suffering ceases to be suffering at the moment it finds a meaning."[102]

To some degree we can already see this among our fellow American citizens. Many people look for simple ways to help keep restaurants in business by ordering more take-out food. Others make it a point to stay in contact with loved-ones and friends, encouraging them to find something positive in their day. This is a time where people are taking stock about the life-directions they have taken thus far.

Like the caterpillar, let us hope our personal chrysalis to create a newer and more resplendent identity as we look and move forward with our lives with a greater serenity and sense of purpose.

CHAPTER 18

"Our material eye cannot see that a stupid chauvinism is driving us from one noisy, destructive, futile agitation to another."

Anne Sullivan

A Parable About Dealing with Noise in Your Home

This morning I had an appealing thought I would like to share with you. I call it the "poetics of space." Most of you have probably heard the famous line from the beginning of the Star Trek show, "Space—the Final Frontier." Let us change that statement to: Inner space the final frontier.

When I walked through the synagogue this morning, I experienced an emptiness in the building; perhaps its symptomatic of the emptiness so many of us feel in our lives, as we feel stranded from the places of worship. But the synagogue is not the only place where we see this. Restaurants owners experience this same sense of loss; American cities resemble ghost towns. The emptiness confronts us, as are forced to flee like refugees. Who can recall ever living such a pariah like existence?

How we utilize space that we share—now that's a real challenge! As we noted in the past article, social distancing provides a practical approach to a community faced with a growing pandemic. Many of us are afraid to go outside and interact with others—without wearing a face mask and protective gloves. Many have complained about the social distancing guidelines. Yet, it has, to some degree, created some problems with close couples and their families who must share the same space for unusual periods of time. It's easy to get on your significant other's nerves because we feel spatially "confined." Everyone seems to be stepping on each other's toes.

Jewish folklore speaks about a farmer who complained there was too much noise in his house. Wherever room he entered, everyone spoke too loudly. He felt as though he was going crazy. To find a solution to his problem, he went to the local town rabbi, a man known for his wisdom.

The prescription the Rabbi gave him made no sense to him at all! At first, he tells him to bring in the chickens, goats, and sheep (Note that Jewish farmers had no pigs!). Well, if the situation was bad before, it got even worse with all the farm animals contributing their noise to the house.

Feeling upset and angry at the Rabbi, he stormed into his office and blamed him for making the situation worse! The Rabbi closed his eyes and thought for a moment. He instructed the following advice "This is what you do. Take your sheep back to the barn. Take your goats back to the barn. Take your chickens back to their coop and come back and see me in a few days."

The farmer carried out the Rabbi's instructions. As he took the animals out of the house, everyone did their part to clean the place up; the house finally had a neatness and gave everyone a comfortable feeling that "there's no place like home." A few days later, the farmer felt a remarkable difference. His home became quieter and more peaceful than what it was before. He thanked the Rabbi profusely for solving his dilemma.

As I thought about this story, the message seemed obvious. Although we are stepping on each other's toes, something good may come from this. The good news is this: we will find a vaccine; life will return to normal—and none of us will have to feel as though we are like lepers forced to live in a special shelter reserved for lepers.

Yet, spending more time at home need not be a psychological burden. It is an opportunity for families actually to listen to one another. Many parents seldom sit down to talk with their children and fail to engage them in a meaningful way. It's one thing when you have a parent living in a different part of the country; it's quite different when you talk with your parent inside your own home. Most young people and adults prefer to speak to their virtual friends on the Internet than to each other. But it doesn't have to be that way. While we are worried about the spread of this virus, and we must talk about it with our families.

And afterward, take out the Scrabble or chess game and have some good old-fashioned fun! Sometimes an illness can help us gain perspective on what is important; let's use this time together to nurture the ties that bind us as a family.

CHAPTER 19

"In how many ways does the Holy Blessed One show His lovingkindness to His people! A man builds a house; says the Holy Blessed One to him: "Write My Name and put it upon your doorpost (mezuzah), and thou wilt sit inside your house and I will sit outside your door and protect you!"

Zohar 2:35b

The Mezuzah and the Coronavirus

The coronavirus is changing Jewish behavior across society. In Israel, the Chief Ashkenazi Rabbi asked Jews to stop kissing mezuzahs because of the coronavirus. At the same time, a major European rabbinical group published its directives on how to contain the spread of the illness. For those who are unfamiliar with what a mezuzah is, a mezuzah is a small parchment that contains some of the most sacred Jewish prayers, most notably, the Shema that is placed on the doorpost of one's home. Jews are instructed not to touch the mezuzah or a Torah scroll with their hands.[103]

One of my Orthodox colleagues and friends in Israel related how someone asked him to lend a Torah scroll to his son having a Bar Mitzvah. Given the circumstances, the Bar Mitzvah could not take place at the synagogue. He told him that he would make up the missing Torah portions, and his son would read and celebrate with him—but not at this time. Furthermore, he told him that he should not even practice from reading the Torah at this time. In the absence of a Torah scroll, it is enough for a person to read the Torah portion in a printed Pentateuch, a view that many medieval scholars sanctioned.

These kinds of responses are what a responsible rabbinical leader should promote. However, some Ultra-Orthodox groups' (e.g., Chabad and Aish HaTorah) rabbis urge their followers to have their mezuzahs checked to see if they are kosher or not. They argue not having a "kosher" mezuzah makes one physically vulnerable to all sorts of possible maladies, such as the coronavirus.[104] Several of their website articles surveyed neglected to mention that nobody should even touch their mezuzahs or a Torah scroll at this time—especially considering how kissing the mezuzah on the door is a common way of spreading the coronavirus.

Despite the good work Chabad and Aish do, they are not the only groups of Ultra-Orthodox Jews who believe in the inherent efficacy of the mezuzah in preventing tragedy. Still, they are probably the most vocal concerning the protective power of the mezuzah. And for some, the creation of talismans such as the Kabbalah Center's famous "red string" has proven to be a lucrative business. Their "Kabbalah" bracelet is made out of braided red string to protect them from "the unfriendly stare and unkind glances," as the Kabbalah Centre--where the red string sells for a paltry $26! [105]

The wonders of Kabbalistic Capitalism never ceases to amaze me!

It is hard to imagine how such retrograde beliefs remain embedded in the human psyche, but buried inside each one of us is a primitive, screaming to come out!

In Judaism, there is something seriously wrong when the mezuzah is transformed into an amulet or talisman intended to ward off the effects of the "Evil Eye." The mezuzah is not an amulet designed to protect us from evil. Moses Maimonides excoriated people in his time who believed the mezuzah had curative properties. Maimonides warn us not transform religious traditions into a superstitious practice:

> Anyone who whispers an incantation over a wound and reads a verse from the Torah, or one who recites a biblical verse over a child so he won't be frightened, or one who places a Torah scroll or *tefillin* (phylacteries) over an infant to enable him to sleep, are not only included in the category of sorcerers and charmers, but such persons are also included among those who reject the Torah. By doing so, they use the words of the Torah as a physical cure, whereas they are exclusively a cure for the soul, as it is written, 'they will be life to your soul.' On the other hand, one who is enjoying good health is permitted to recite biblical verses, or a psalm, that he may be shielded and saved from affliction and damage by virtue of the reading."[106]

One of Carl Sagan's most notable books was "The Demon-Haunted World: Science as a Candle in the Dark." In his book, Sagan talks about how we tend to fill our world with demons and other imaginary monsters. When we don't understand something, as children, we fill our darkened bedrooms with all sorts of fanciful creatures that are hellbent upon harming us. Despite the centuries of our species' scientific evolution, on some primitive level, we still hold on to archaic superstitions that should have been discarded millennia ago. Sagan encouraged each of us to develop our own "baloney-detection kits."

That's a great idea—especially today.

Had Maimonides read Sagan's book, he would have found a kindred spirit across the centuries of time. Not all the ancients were "primitive" or "backward" Hippocrates and Galen argued the poor quality of air contributed much toward the spread of contagion. They stated that there is nothing "sacred" (ἰερῆς = hierēs) about a disease; all diseases originate with a natural cause; the fact that men believe the condition has a "divine" origin, is due to the inexperience of the physician who fails to understand the etiology of the disease.

Conclusion:

In short, this writer recommends that no responsible Jewish person should have one's mezuzahs or Torah scroll inspected at this time —and if anyone wishes to have them checked, it should be done while wearing protective plastic gloves. Some rabbis would be wise to start accepting a more scientific view of the world as to how diseases spread. Knowledge of science is, as Sagan stated, a candle intended to dispel the darkness of human ignorance. And the rest is commentary.

Part 6
Wisdom from the Bible, Mishnah & Talmud

CHAPTER 20

"When one hand washes another, both become clean."

Yiddish Proverb

The Importance of Handwashing

This scriptural verse teaches us that any service conducted by a priest whose hands and feet are unwashed is invalid. The חָק־עוֹלָם "perpetual ordinance" also reappears in the laws regarding the priestly garments, וְהָיוּ עַל־אַהֲרֹן וְעַל־בָּנָיו בְּבֹאָם אֶל־אֹהֶל מוֹעֵד אוֹ בְגִשְׁתָּם אֶל־הַמִּזְבֵּחַ לְשָׁרֵת בַּקֹּדֶשׁ וְלֹא־יִשְׂאוּ עָוֹן וָמֵתוּ חֻקַּת עוֹלָם לוֹ וּלְזַרְעוֹ אַחֲרָיו "Aaron and his sons shall wear them whenever they go into the Tent of Meeting or approach the altar to minister in the Sanctuary, lest they incur guilt and die.

This shall be a perpetual ordinance for him and for his descendants" (Exodus 28:43). From the similarity of expressions, the wording conveys a mutual point. Just as a priest who lacks the priestly garments invalidates the priestly service, so too the priest who has neglected to sanctify himself through the ritual washing of hands and feet as noted earlier. Handwashing is a daily ritual that begins from the moment we wake up in the morning and thank God for returning our souls to our bodies.

Jews have long been accustomed to washing their hands whenever food is served, or whenever leaving a cemetery—the act of handwashing serves to remind us that we must always conduct our affairs with complete integrity and holiness. Before eating bread or a meal, it has long been considered a mitzvah to wash our hands. Before we pray, we wash our hands. After leaving the bathroom, we always wash our hands. Whenever we touch hidden parts of our body, we wash our hands.

Rabbinical tradition even considered this act to be one of the most important rituals in the daily life of a Jew. Rabbi Abraham Isaac Kook once explained that the physical act of eating has the potential to diminish our sense of holiness. But to counteract this influence, we wash our hands before and after a meal. One of my favorite verses from the Psalms reads:

The act of handwashing is not just a health requirement, it is an act that reminds us that we must sanctify our lives to God in all of our relationships and actions. Historically, even when Jews lived in the filthy ghettos, Jews continued to wash their hands as prescribed by our tradition. During the period of history when the world suffered from the Bubonic Plague, which has occurred several times over the last 2000 years or more.

- The first documented case of the Bubonic Plague occurred in 542 C.E., where it was known as the Plague of Justinian. This pandemic killed almost 10,000 people in Constantinople.
- In the 700s, almost half the European population perished; estimates of almost 100 million deaths were recorded by the time the pandemic subsided.
- In the 14th century, China lost over 25 million people.
- Between 1346 and 1353, over 75 million people perished from the plague.
- The "Black Death" of London killed 70,000 people.[107]

In such dangerous times, the Jew has often been accused of being the agent that caused these plagues in Europe. Fortunately, Jews were often able to avoid the effects of the plague—by a ratio of 50% less than their Christian neighbors. When the Christian anti-Semites noticed this, citizens often banded to kill the Jew. In Strasbourg, Austria, in 1349, nearly 2000 Jews were killed. The Jewish communities of Mainz and Cologne were exterminated at this time. Interestingly, Jews stopped observing the Tashlich ceremony on Rosh Hashanah, lest they be accused of poisoning the water.

A personal note: My father Leo Israel Samuel was a Holocaust survivor who had served as a tailor in several concentration camps. He told me that one of the hardest problems he faced was keeping himself clean in the camps; disease was everywhere. He was determined to do his best to keep his body clean and healthy. What did he do? He would bathe naked in the winter snows. The Nazis found it amusing, but he persevered. As a child, sometimes anti-Semitic kids would call us "you dirty Jew!" but Father would have us say, "No, I am not a dirty Jew. I bathe twice a day!" His tongue-and-cheek humor always proved endearing—but in retrospect, I think he was speaking from his actual experience at the Auschwitz camp! The famous biblical commentator Abraham Ibn Ezra wrote that if someone was suffering from gonorrhea, he recommended that he had to be scrupulous in thoroughly washing his hands. Once he does so, if his hands touch the food of another, the food will not become ritually impure (Commentary on Leviticus 15:2). Ibn Ezra's insight is valuable in terms of the history of medical science history. Most people seldom realize the importance of handwashing is from the perspective of medical hygiene.

The Story of Dr. Ignaz Phillips Semmelweis

Here is a brief article I shall quote which tells the remarkable and tragic story about a Hungarian obstetrician-gynecologist, Ignaz Phillips Semmelweis (1818–1865), a Jewish immigrant whose serendipitous medical discovery in a Vienna hospital changed the practice of medicine forever.

The medical world was a radically different place from what it is today. Back in 1846, Dr. Ignaz Phillips Semmelweis joined one of the most prestigious medical staffs in the European world. When he arrived, he discovered at the time that hospital virulent infections which ensued after surgeries led to an astounding 45% mortality rate. New mothers were faced with a 25% death rate.

Bear in mind, this was before Louis Pasteur would eventually discover the Streptococcus bacteria responsible for childbed fever back in 1878. Nor would penicillin be discovered until 1928. Within a month of his arrival at the famous Viennese hospital, to Dr. Semmelweis's chagrin, he discovered that 36 out of 208 women died following the delivery of a baby, a mortality rate of 17 percent. One maternity ward in particular, suffered from 451 infectious-related deaths, while a second maternity ward lost only 90 women. He wondered about why was there such a discrepancy.

One day, he came across an expectant mother, who was crying because the Hospital administration assigned her to the medical students' ward, instead of the midwives' ward. Everyone knew that the students' ward had a much higher mortality rate, and to be assigned was tantamount to a death sentence. The woman later died. But one day in 1847, a friend of Dr. Semmelweis's friend accidentally cut himself with a scalpel while performing an autopsy of a woman who had died from the disease physicians back then called "childbed fever." Semmelweis's friend soon died himself. After personally attending his friend's autopsy, to Semmelweis's surprise, he observed that the lesions on his friend's body were exactly the same as the lesions seen on the women dying from childbed fever.

The pieces of the puzzle finally came together, as Semmelweis realized that the same poisonous substance which had come from the diseased cadaver, must have entered his friend's cut finger resulting in death. This same substance was apparently being introduced into women after childbirth by the hospital physicians and students who came to examine them with unwashed hands immediately after performing autopsies on the victims of childbed fever. Before then, many causes of the malady were sought, including mother's milk, foreign doctors, fear, and medical student incompetence.

Something clicked inside him; he intuited that maybe the reason the death rate was so high on the students' ward was that they were participating in autopsies, not because they were incompetent. The midwives were not studying medicine, so they did not attend the autopsies. Semmelweis excitedly ordered all the students and doctors to wash their hands thoroughly with a calcium chloride solution and clean sand after each autopsy. The death rate fell from one out of six to one out of 100 within a year.

Shortly thereafter, an outbreak of sepsis occurred on the ward, killing 11 out of 12 women. This outbreak began after a pregnant woman with infected cervical cancer was assigned to the first bed in the row. Realizing that the infective material must have spread from this woman, Semmelweis insisted that all the physicians and students not only wash their hands after autopsies, but between patients on the ward. Later he also isolated the badly infected cases. By 1848 the mortality rate was so low on these wards that during one month no death from childbed fever was reported. Throughout all these events, Semmelweis made a number of enemies. People found his personality to be difficult; he was also moody, unstable, and arrogant. Furthermore, other physicians complained he often ordered them to perform novel, burdensome sanitary techniques, and he often met great opposition. He bluntly called his opponents to these hand-washing techniques "murderers." His conflicts with supervisors and peers ultimately led to his dismissal in 1850.

And when handwashing ceased at the Vienna hospital, and the death rate again soared. He wrote his classic book concerning his findings in 1861, unfortunately while in a manic state. The words rambled and were difficult to comprehend. The book was a failure, and his mental health deteriorated. In 1865, at 47 years of age, he entered a mental institution. On admission he had a wounded finger on his right hand, probably inflicted during his most recent obstetrical operation. A few days later he died, ironically, of childbed fever.[108] The moral of this anecdote is to highlight, that one of the most brilliant intuitions of the Torah, is the laws governing bodily hygiene. Let us now return to our original subject: the current pandemic. To prevent the spread of the coronavirus, remember:

- Wash your hands frequently.
- Regularly and thoroughly clean your hands with an alcohol-based hand rub or wash them with soap and water.

Let us do our part in minimizing the effects of this dangerous pandemic.

When the Israelites were being chased by the Egyptians, our ancestors found themselves surrounded by the Red Sea, the wilderness and an army of Egyptians closing in on them. Remarkably, God told Moses to go through the sea, and so they did. Sometimes we find ourselves in a similar situation where the only thing we can do is wade through the danger together and find strength from each other until we make it to the other side of the shore.

CHAPTER 21

*"In every aspect of life, purity and holiness, cleanliness and
refinement, exalt the human condition . . . Even in the
physical realm, cleanliness will conduce to spirituality."*

Abdu'l-Baha'

Ritual Purity & the Coronavirus

When I was a young yeshiva student, I would get up every day and
bathe in the hot mikveh (similar to a jacuzzi) around 5:00 in the morning.
Then I would walk to the yeshiva hall and study the entire Mishnah while
observing the sunrise. By my second year, I had completed the study of the
Mishnah with its commentaries. This experience afforded me the
opportunity to study the laws of animal sacrifices; most people might be
surprised to see how the sacrificial cult influenced the origins of Jewish
prayer—especially with respect to the role of intentionality, for one stray
thought, could invalidate a sacrifice.

But when I came to the section regarding ritual purity, the laws
pertaining to the mikveh seemed fairly straightforward. But the laws
regarding ritual contamination left me wondering about the practical
application of the ritual contamination laws. I wondered: Did the rabbis
think of ritual impurity as a spiritual or as a physical phenomenon? This
question bothered me for many years and decades. The rituals of
handwashing originated from these Levitical laws and historically,
handwashing helped prevent the spread of contagions. To this day, the
pious Jew almost instinctively washes his/her hands several times in the
course of the day.

In this week's Parsha Tazria and Metzorah, considerable space is
dedicated to the theme of the problem of ritual uncleanness with respect to
the ancient dreaded disease of leprosy—a disease that does not kill but
disfigures the victim. The ancients practiced social-distancing because they
did not know how to deal with a threatening disease that might spread upon
close contact with others.

In Levitical literature, uncleanness describes ritual uncleanness as a substance that can cling to a person or thing and may be transmitted to others in a variety of ways. The Mishnah creates a hierarchy of ritual contamination. The "grandfather" of all uncleanness is the human corpse. Ritual uncleanness can be transmitted in a variety of ways. The Mishnah distinguishes between the primary source of impurity, commonly referred to as (אַב הַטֻּמְאָה), and from there it imparts uncleanness to the object that is infected. The latter is what is sometimes called, a "child of uncleanness (וְלַד הַטֻּמְאָה).[109]

Examples of the former include anyone who has been in contact with the dead—either directly or indirectly, e.g., sharing space under the same roof with a corpse. An animal carcass, the blood of couches, beds, foods, and drinks; it includes being in touch with lepers, or human bones—each of which is considered primary transmitter of ritual uncleanness.[110] Thus, we have primary sources of ritual contamination, along with second, third, and fourth degrees of uncleanness. Men, hands, vessels, and clothes are infected only directly through contact with the dead, or with a leper.[111]

Secular or non-sacrificial meats and drinks (חֻלִּין,) are susceptible to second-degree infection. First-fruits, priestly tithes, are affected only to the third degree, and sacrifices to the fourth. The intensity of infection weakens a stage with each transmission. The ancient Greeks were no stranger to the concept of ritual pollution, a term they called μίασμα(miasma), believed to be a physical contagion that is airborne. This pollution especially occurs when there is a murder or any kind of heinous crime, thus leaving those responsible of taint pollution. These laws probably make little sense to a modern Jew. If the most Orthodox Jew were to travel in a time machine to the time of the Second Temple, odds are s/he would feel completely out of place in a Jewish society that took the purity laws seriously.

As with the Mishnaic laws of uncleanness, the parameters concerning how the COVID-19 virus can live in the air and on the surfaces. One study from the John Hopkins School of Medicine found the virus is viable for up to 72 hours on plastics, 48 hours on stainless steel, 24 hours on cardboard, and 4 hours on copper. The virus has also detectable in the air for three hours. The virus is purported capable of lasting on plastic for 72 hours. According to the New England Journal of Medicine, COVID-19 can be detected in the air for 3 hours. Nevertheless, one is more likely to catch the infection through the air than to someone infecting them off of a surface. Cleaning the surfaces with disinfectant or soap is very effective because once the oily surface coat of the virus is disabled, there is no way the virus can infect a host cell.

Objects to be concerned about include tables, doorknobs, light switches, countertops, handles, desks, phones, keyboards, toilets, faucets, and sinks. Avoid touching high-contact surfaces in public. Handwashing with a strong disinfectant soap and water for at least 20 seconds upon returning home, or from public places such as a bank or grocery store. Social distancing requires there be a distance of six feet between people standing in a line.[112]

Although these laws have not played a dominant role in Jewish life for over 2000 years, the guidelines bear a striking resemblance to the precautions we now observe in stemming from this pandemic. Note that in the days of the Temple, rabbinic tradition imposed social distancing in preventing people who were ritually unclean from entering the Temple.

According to Maimonides, the laws governing ceremonial uncleanness are designed to help heighten the faith community's respect when entering the Temple. But today, these ancient rules of uncleanness take on an altogether new meaning in the age of the COVID-19 pandemic.

CHAPTER 22

"Most people do not really want freedom, because freedom involves responsibility, and most people are frightened of responsibility."

Sigmund Freud
Sayings of Freud

Mishnaic Wisdom: Man is Always Responsible for His Actions

The question whether the coronavirus is an "act of God," takes on new meaning if we examine the problem through the lens of rabbinical tradition. The ancients debated the limits of practical liability in cases where one party injures another. The Mishnah discusses an interesting case concerning an individual assumes personal liability for damages that one inadvertently causes to another. The text reads: "A human being is always considered 'forewarned' and is responsible in all situations where he inadvertently or purposely caused damage to another—whether he was awake, or even if he was asleep. If someone blinded another person's eye, or broke his vessels, he must pay full damages.[113]

The philosopher Jean Paul Sartre was fond of saying, "Man is condemned to be free; because once thrown into the world, he is responsible for everything he does . . , Condemned, because he did not create himself, yet is nevertheless at liberty, and from the moment that he is thrown into this world he is responsible for everything he does,[114]

Who would imagine Sartre and the Mishnah concurring on a matter of vital importance—personal responsibility? Let us suggest this legal principle not only applies to the individual, it ought to be apply no less to sovereign states. As human beings, we cannot evade the negative consequences of our deeds. And this takes us to the question concerning China's role in the coronavirus pandemic.

According to one writer:

> On New Year's Eve, December 31st, China first informed
> the World Health Organization (WHO)...a full three

weeks after it was almost certainly aware of the severity of this new disease. On the same day, however, the government issues a statement downplaying the risk by indicating that "the investigation so far has not found any obvious human-to-human transmission and no medical staff infection."

This was flat-out lie and the Chinese government knew it.

The same day, health officials in Taiwan reported to the WHO evidence of human-to-human transmission of the virus, its warnings apparently went unheeded. Two weeks later, using information supplied only by the Chinese, the WHO tweeted "Preliminary investigations conducted by the Chinese authorities have found no clear evidence of human-to-human transmission of the novel coronavirus (2019-nCoV) identified in Wuhan, China."[115]

Some would argue the coronavirus began as a biological weapon, conceived in a secret laboratory outside Wuhan, China, a city that is approximately the size of Chicago. Without the emergence of concrete and irrefutable evidence, we must dismiss such theories. Nevertheless, one of the outcomes of the COVID-19 will lead to greater preparedness on the part of our country and other Western countries to the possibility of biological weapons in the future. If the COVID-19 can create so much social and economic havoc by accident, imagine what a purposely deployed biological weapon can accomplish? Given China's penchant for totalitarian behavior anything is possible.

One of the reasons I doubt it is a biological weapon that went awry is because this pandemic has decimated the Chinese economy far more than President Trump's sanctions, not to mention the global economy as well. Factories came almost to a halt, because migrant workers who left for New Year celebrations could not return to their workplaces, thus impeding production and China's trade capacity. The current export outlook of China remains under the shadow of the continuing spread of the virus. No sane leader would deliberately inflict such a mortal blow to one's own country.

Or so we nervously hope.

But this much we know.

The Chinese claimed there have been only 3,299 coronavirus-related deaths, with most taking place in Wuhan, the epicenter of the global pandemic. However, Chinese media outlet Caixin reveals that in some funeral homes, there has been as many as 5,000 urns. This would suggest the numbers could vastly greater than admitted by the government. In the last quarter alone, there were 40000 cremations in Wuhan according to data from the city's civil affairs agency.[116] The numbers could be vastly greater.

Let us assume the pandemic has a natural origin, nevertheless, the Beijing government still bears the responsibility for trying to cover it up. Its mishandling of the virus contributed to the hundreds of thousands of deaths seen across the globe. The Chinese Communist leadership must not be given a free pass. According to the New York Times, since the time the Chinese officials disclosed the danger of the coronavirus on New Year's Eve. In the interim, over 430,000 people arrived to the United States on direct flights from China. This included approximately 40,000 in the two months President Trump imposed travel restrictions for flights coming out of China. These flights came directly from Wuhan, the epicenter of the virus.[117]

When the courageous Chinese physician Li Wenliang tried to warn his fellow medical practitioners about the situation in Wuhan. One day before Dr Li's death, lawyer Chen Qiushi released videos describing chaotic scenes in Wuhan hospitals with coronavirus victims lying in corridors were shared with an audience of more than 400,000 YouTube and 250,000 Twitter followers. He too went missing. His family was told the following day he was being held in medical quarantine at an undisclosed location. And not surprisingly, he was soon dead of the very plague he tried to warn about. Other physicians have also mysteriously disappeared or died because they tried to warn their people about the danger of this pandemic.[118]

Let me tell you another story about unknown hero named Fang Bin, a forty-year-old businessman who felt compelled to speak out against the government's attempt to suppress what really happened.

What did Fang Bin do? He had the audacity to expose the truth about the coronavirus outbreak, but refused to remain silent. To get his message out to the Chinese people, he posted a video of people dying of the virus, along with scenes of body bags piling up outside the hospital. Over 200,000 saw this video before it was taken down. In another video he had posted, he urged the people, "Citizens resist, Hand back power to the people."

And then Fang Bin received an unexpected visit from the state police, dressed in hazmat suits took him away to medical quarantine.

Voices of conscience exist in China, who fight valiantly against a rogue and totalitarian regime, determined to suppress the truth no matter what the cost. Normally, Fang Bin is a shy person, but he could not believe what was happening in his city. He felt compelled to do something and protest. It is believed he and other dissidents are being tortured and forced to sign a confession that they were guilty of making mischief.[119]

The Chinese Communists fear whistleblowers and people brave enough to challenge the status quo. They fear it more than they do the coronavirus.

The fearsome knock on the door came after nightfall. Outside were two men in hazmat suits who told businessman Fang Bin they had come to take him into medical quarantine. But the textile trader, a gangly man in his early 40s, wasn't ill and the men outside his Wuhan apartment weren't doctors. They were police officers confronting a menace the Chinese Communist Party had been grappling with as ferociously as the coronavirus itself – ordinary people who bravely expose the truth about the outbreak and refuse to keep quiet.

Mr. Fang's 'crime' was to post a video he had filmed of people dying of the virus and the body bags piled up outside a hospital clearly overwhelmed by casualties at a time when China insisted that the virus was under control. It was seen 200,000 times before censors took it down.

It would be bad enough if this was all there is to the problem the world is facing. But the Chinese communist government's apparent penchant for corruption, greed, and cowardice made matters far worse. And even the New York Times admitted that as hospitals around the world are desperately looking for respirators and surgical masks to protect doctors and nurses from the coronavirus pandemic, the Chinese government has been less than cordial in supplying the countries with these necessary tools to battle the coronavirus. Interestingly, over half the world's surgical masks are made in China. Such a selfish policy is only compounding the suffering we see on a global scale.[120] In another new story, Spain has returned "defective" coronavirus testing kits but from China.[121] Price gouging is yet another example China's misbehavior. In China, it costs only five cents to make a facemask at their factories, but they sell these masks to countries suffering from the coronavirus for anywhere between $1.30 to in one case $4.[122]

My father used to say only a guilty man runs away from the police. If one has not done anything wrong, one need not flee but rely on the one's personal integrity and hold fast to the conviction that one is innocent of wrongdoing. As of April 12, 2020, China has imposed restrictions on the publication of academic research on the origins of the novel coronavirus, according to a central government directive and online notices published by two Chinese universities, that have since been removed from the web. According to this new policy, "all academic papers on Covid-19 will be subject to extra vetting before being submitted for publication. Studies on the origin of the virus will receive extra scrutiny and must be approved by central government officials, according to the now-deleted posts."[123]

This writer would argue based on rabbinical tradition that the lessons learned from the Mishnah apply not only to people who inadvertently cause injury to others, it applies no less to countries who act irresponsibly in allowing a contagion to spread. Our own government must also be held accountable for allowing the pandemic to spread. One can only come to the inevitable conclusion that while China is to blame for much of what has happened here, the businesses of the West have allowed all this to occur under their watch.

There is plenty of blame for everybody!

When the coronavirus pandemic eventually subsides, it is my hope the international community will confront Beijing's moral cowardice and irresponsibility, and dishonesty in the early days of the outbreak. The pandemic in one sense has morphed into a new World War, but this time it is humanity that is fighting for its life. Let us pray that every nation will emerge humbler and wiser to the lessons we have learned, namely, each of us is our brother's keeper. On May 13th, 2020, the Chinese authorities on Sunday arrested Zhang Xuezhong, 43, a constitutional lawyer for posting an open letter on social media that criticized the government's handling of the coronavirus pandemic and its suppression of free speech, according to reports. He courageously said, "The best way to fight for freedom of expression is for everyone to speak as if we already have freedom of speech," Zhang wrote on his WeChat post alongside the letter. Zhang is merely one of hundreds of people, including doctors, journalists and lawyers, have been arrested in China for merely speaking out about the virus, according to reports from human rights activists.[124]

Misguided Political Decisions Exacerbate COVID-19

It has been said, "The road to Hell is paved with the best intentions." States have committed a terrible injustice toward the elderly of our communities who are confined to a nursing home. New York state require nursing homes to accept those recovering from COVID-19—even though their condition remains highly contagious. One Long Island nursing home had only a single resident who had COVID-19, but one month later, over twenty-four residents died.

One could almost get the impression the lives of our elderly are expendable, but for now I must give the benefit of the doubt and attribute this awful decision to political incompetence from the Governor on down. If you—the reader—are blessed with common sense and a critical mind, you must wonder: Why would anybody in a position of responsibility mandate such a foolish policy? We are told the purpose is to clear the beds in hospitals for patients who are much more seriously ill.

David Grabowski is a professor of health policy at the Harvard Medical School. He proposed that COVID-19 positive patients be kept at an exclusive COVID-19 facility after they are released from the hospital.

Does one have to be a professor at Harvard Medical School to arrive at such a common-sense solution?

Probably not!

To President Trump's credit (note we praise him when he does something right, and criticize him when he does not), he commissioned a 1000 bed Naval hospital ship to help relieve the New York City's overburdened hospitals. To date, only 2% of these beds have been used. If the media were truly interested in featuring a story on this topic, someone ought to ask: Why haven't these hospitals been used?

Somebody dropped the ball.

I hope families who lost loved ones at the nursing homes will seek justice after this pandemic is over. Their lives are not less important because they are aged and frail.

CHAPTER 23

Ben Azzai used to say, "It is easier to be a King and rule the entire world, all of it, than to sit and teach in the presence of men who cloak themselves hypocritically in Sages' linen."

BT Sotah 23b

Religious persecution may shield itself under the guise of a mistaken and over-zealous piety.

Edmund Burke

The Talmud Warns Against False Piety

In ancient times, the rabbis worried about the excesses of piety. The Sages believed piety should not transform people into religious automatons. Nor should it make people neurotic and incapable of functioning in a sane world. Did not Freud warn us, "Religion is comparable to a childhood neurosis, and he is optimistic enough to suppose that mankind will surmount this neurotic phase, just as so many children grow out of their similar neurosis."[125] Unfortunately for Freud, he could not imagine religion creating healthy people and values; but he did understand the nature of religious pathology, which produces unhealthy and maladjusted people.

And the Talmud also concurred with Freud.

The Jerusalem Talmud records a remarkable teaching that could certainly apply to today's time:

> Who is a foolish man of piety? Take the case of a man who sees a woman is drowning, but says, "It is unseemly for me to look at her, and therefore, I cannot rescue her." Some say a pious fool is someone who sees a child struggling in the water, and says, "When I have taken off my phylacteries, I will go

and save him" because he does not wish to get them wet. By
the time he arrives to rescue him, the child has already died.
Who is the "crafty scoundrel"? R. Huna says, "He is the man
who behaves leniently toward himself while teaching others
only the strictest rules." 126

Piety—when alloyed with common sense, can prove useful in creating
a well-balanced individual who takes his/her relationship with God and
humanity seriously. However, excessive piety can easily be misplaced; the
attitude of extreme stringency may even convey—such as religious
arrogance, which is arguably the exact antithesis of piety. Herein is the
problem of today's Haredi communities in Israel. One of the best examples
of seeing this is evident in Israel among the Haredi (God "Tremblers") who
make up only 12% of the total Israeli population, and yet they make up for
about 40-50% of the coronavirus patients at four major hospitals,

These statistics beg the obvious question in the spirit of a Passover
question: How are these Haredim different from all other Jews in Israel
when it comes to the coronavirus pandemic? There are many ways we may
answer this question. For one thing, the Haredi tend to have large families
and live in an overcrowded environment. Secondly, they tend to be
unfamiliar and illiterate when it comes to practical knowledge of science
and matters of health. Although we take the Internet for granted, the Haredi
rabbis take great pride in discouraging—even forbidding the use of
computers when it comes to the lives of their followers.

The Haredi not only live in the physical ghetto; in many ways, they still
live in a psychological ghetto as well.

If you talk to them about "social-distancing," odds are they will ignore
you; or they will tell you that God is protecting them because they study
Torah. Jewish prayer rituals among the Haredim demand they all show up
to services. Weddings are much too important to call off because of some
virus. In their world, they have complete trust that God will always protect
them, but they neglect to observe one of the most important precepts of the
Torah——one that Jewish survival depends upon: רַק הִשָּׁמֶר לְךָ וּשְׁמֹר
נַפְשְׁךָ מְאֹד "But be on guard and watch yourselves closely" (Deut. 4:9).

Creating barriers to help protect people from harm is a theme that
occurs repeatedly throughout the Pentateuch. One could just as easily cite
four other biblical precepts that deal with the same problem: (1) A person
must cover a pit that is exposed to the public (Exod. 21:33); (2) you must

not place an obstacle in the way of the blind (Lev. 19:14); (3) Nor shall you stand idly by the blood of your neighbor (Lev. 19:16); (4) and lastly: one must make a parapet upon one's flat roof so that nobody will fall (Deut. 22:8). Boundaries serve to protect people from harm. Some of the Haredi rabbis have violated some of the most important precepts of the Torah by carelessly and recklessly disregarding the dangers that they are allowing to be unleashed in their communities.

The Haredi communities believe they are fighting for the preservation of Judaism as they understand it. Its leaders realize the outside world is full of seductive temptations. To combat this threat, they constructed Halakhic walls around their community. Televisions, computers--even cellphones are forbidden because the owner might choose to "surf the Internet." Unfortunately, this social group also remains distrustful of the State.

But such isolation inevitably leads to the ignorance of the health risks among its religious leaders. They perceive social-distancing rules as an intrusion into their religious community. These rules threaten fundamental activities for the ultra-Orthodox, including worship, religious study, and the observance of life-cycle events like funerals and weddings. This may account for why many of the schools in the Haredi neighborhood are remaining opened. But given the mutation capabilities of the coronavirus, the rabbinical leaders are taking a big risk.

The rabbis who have governed their communities have a talent for coming up with new ideas. If the study of Torah does not stop the spread of a pandemic, some of the leading Haredim urge their followers to make larger than usual donations to their Vaad HaRabbonim (Rabbinical Center). Givers receive a promise that by giving charity, none of their loved ones will be affected by the pandemic! How much exactly should be given? Three-thousand Israeli shekels ($849).

The rationale for this behavior derives from the Rosh Hashanah prayer, "And repentance, and prayer and charity shall remove the evil decree." This passage is unambiguously clear—all evil decrees will cease in the believer's life. In the Middle Ages, priests used to sell indulgences for people who were sinners. One wonders whether this might be next in the Haredi community. Now, if they were collecting monies to buy food for the hungry families who are out of work, there would at least be some merit to this enterprise. [127]

Anthropologists point out that when a community feels threatened by the outside world, they create barriers to keep the dangerous Other away. These force fields serve to protect the community of faith by limiting their exposure to threatening ideas based on the current cultural climate of a society. This mentality often creates an "us" vs. "them" attitude and in Israel, the religiously devout tend to disregard the rules of the secular realm that exists outside their religious sphere of influence. Martin Buber described such impersonal relations as predicated upon the "I and It" relationship. Unfortunately, there is not much personal interaction between these segments of Israeli society. This is a chronic problem that many Israelis must come to terms with understanding. Nevertheless, it is worth noting the Haredi community has now finally realized the importance of social-distancing.

Still, it is a pity it came at such a high price!

CHAPTER 24

*"If you have a fruit-tree in your hands and someone
says to you, 'Here is the 'Here is the Messiah.' Go
and finish planting your fruit-tree just the same,
and afterwards go out and welcome the Messiah."*

Avoth D'rabbi Nathan 31

Will the Messiah Come This Year?

Ever since the coronavirus started, many of my congregants asked me whether this year might be the year of the Messiah's arrival. A couple of days ago, I came across an earlier article, the Israeli Health Ministry Rabbi Yaakov Litzman, who has struggled to manage the coronavirus crisis among the Haredi (Ultra-Orthodox) community in Israel. Still, Litzman is an optimistic person. In a recent interview, he indicated that while he is trying to take the pandemic seriously, he looks forward to a more supernatural deliverance—the arrival of the Messiah.

He candidly admitted, "We are praying and hoping that Messiah will arrive before Passover as it is a time of our redemption. I am sure that the Messiah will come by Passover and save us the same way God saved us during the Exodus, and we were freed. The Messiah will come and save us all." One rabbi claimed that since "corona" means "crown", the pandemic is an obvious sign that the Messiah will soon arrive![128] In our long history of pandemics, many faith traditions thought the same, but the Messiah has yet to appear.

Most of our readers probably know the ancient rabbis generally took a skeptical view of people announcing when the Messiah will arrive. Consider the following citations from rabbinical literature. The Talmud records a statement Rabbi Zera once made concerning the Messiah: "Three things occur when you least expect it—the Messiah, a found article, and a scorpion."[129] I have often thought about this passage. Most people don't expect to find a lost object, typically finding something that occurs when you least expect it. The same principle applies to someone who is bitten by a scorpion; frequently, these things happen when you expect it the least.

Concerning the Messiah, the Talmud teaches that we are far better off not to speculate when the Messiah is going to come. R. Zera's remark ought to make us pause and wonder: Why did he express such ambivalence toward the arrival of the Messiah? Aren't pious Jews supposed to believe in his appearance?

The Jews of the early centuries learned the hard way that those claiming to be the Messiah are more often mentally unbalanced, or they are charlatans, or more likely—a combination of both!

Yet, this did not stop the Jews of Late Antiquity from attempting to predict his arrival. In every instance where this occurred, the rabbi predicting the Messianic arrival was always proven wrong to his discredit. Josephus mentions that before the destruction of the Temple, several men claimed to be "the Messiah." One famous figure was a certain charlatan named Theudas; he claimed to be a prophet and insisted that his people follow him with their belongings to the Jordan, where he would make the river split for them. The Roman authorities did not find him amusing. The Roman governor Cuspius Fadus[ii] sent his soldiers after him and his band, slew many of them, and took captive others, together with their leader, beheading the latter. [130]

Then again, there was an Egyptian Jew who claimed to be the Messiah. This mysterious individual commanded an impressive following and gathered about 30,000 followers that met on the Mount of Olives, opposite Jerusalem. A Roman procurator of Judea Province named Marcus Antonius Felix told his followers that God commanded them to come to the Temple. Upon arriving there, they would receive miraculous signs of their deliverance. Felix did not find this "Messianic" personality amusing either. Many people were killed and taken captive, and the Romans beheaded their leader. [131]

Josephus mentions yet another zealot leader named Menachem b. Hezekiah, whose name later appears in the Talmud. [132] He was the leader of a faction called the Sicarii, who carried out assassinations of Romans and collaborators in the Holy Land. Menahem was the son of Judas of Galilee and was the grandson of Hezekiah, the leader of the Zealot faction who proved difficult to Herod; he was a fine warrior. When the war broke out with Rome, he and his followers attacked Masada and stored his weaponry there. Afterward, he proceeded to Jerusalem, where he captured the fortress of Antonia. After defeating King Agrippa's soldiers, he claimed to be the king. But Elazar, the Zealot leader, conspired against him and assassinated Menahem. [133]

Perhaps the most famous of the pseudo-Messiahs apart from Jesus of Nazareth, a topic we must approach at another time, was Shimon ben Kosiba, better known to us as Bar Kokhba. He led a revolt against the Roman Empire in 132 CE. And for three years, he managed to establish a three-year-long independent Jewish state in which Bar Kokhba ruled as Nasi. The most famous rabbinical leader of his time, R. Akiba, saw Bar Kokhba as fulfilling the scriptural verse, Num. xxiv. 17: "A star shall advance from Jacob, and a scepter shall rise from Israel, and shall smite through the corners of Moab," (Num. 24:17). I will shake the heavens and the earth; and I will overthrow the thrones of kingdoms. . . ." [134] The second-century sage, R. Johanan b. Torta opposed Akiba's acceptance of Bar Kokhba as the Messiah, saying to him, "Akiba! Grass shall grow from your jaws before the son of David appears."[135]

The list of other aspirants, such as Shabtai Tzvi, Jacob Frank, (and, more recently, R. Menachem Mendel Schneerson, a.k.a. the Lubavitcher Rebbe) failed to realize their ambition, and in the process created some disillusionment among their followers. Is it not any wonder why the Talmud offers practical advice on this matter, "Rabbi Yohanan ben Zakkai taught: If you have a fruit-tree in your hands and someone says to you, 'Here is the Messiah.' Go and finish planting your fruit-tree just the same, and afterward go out and welcome the Messiah."[136]

There have been many worse pandemics than the coronavirus that have decimated thousands of our people. The Israeli Health Minister Yaakov Litzman would be wise to stay focused and do his job in protecting the people he meant to serve.

The prophet Isaiah offers a postmodern message for those who think they know the mind of the Divine, "for my thoughts are not your thoughts and your ways are not my ways, declares the LORD (Isa. 55:8 NJB). And in another notable passage, "The hidden things belong to the LORD our God, but the revealed things are for us and for our children forever, to observe all the words of this Torah" (Deut. 29:28),

Many years ago, R. Avraham Levitankski, one of my favorite teachers and friends, was accosted by some missionaries in Los Angeles. They asked him, "What would you do if an atom-bomb exploded in the city of Los Angeles?" He stroked his beard and smiled, "I don't know and I could care less." They retorted, "How could you not be concerned about where your soul would be in such an eventuality?" The rabbi retorted in a Talmudic chime, "I worry what God expects of me in this world, and what will happen to me in the next world is God's problem to worry about!"

Martin Luther King Jr. said it best, "We can't pray for God to do what we are unwilling to do ourselves." God expects all of us to do our part in bettering the world. A friend of mine once said, "I have two things to tell you about the Messiah. But first let me tell you the bad news: There is no such thing as the Messiah! Now for the good news: You're it!" Perhaps each of us needs to get in touch with our own inner Messiah and make the decision to make this world worthy of the Messiah.

May we all be blessed with a beautiful Passover.

CHAPTER 25

*"The true creator is necessity, who is
the mother of our invention."*

Benjamin Jowett's Translation of
Plato's Republic, Book 2: 369c

2020: The Year of the Virtual Seder

One of the more remarkable changes brought about by the coronavirus this year is the absence of Passover celebrations at synagogues. Passover is traditionally a time when families get together to celebrate the holiday with one another, often traveling from one end of the country to the other. But this year, only immediate families celebrate the Passover. The social distancing and the quarantines required to minimize social contact poses a particularly significant challenge for Jews living in Israel. Israel can ill-afford to lose any of its citizens to a pandemic.

Given the number of Jewish adults—young and especially the old—living by themselves, the coronavirus pandemic has led various Jews across the world to find a new way to connect with their loved ones: through Zoom or Facebook Live. Many Modern Orthodox rabbis in Israel and across the globe permitted the use of a video-conferencing program to connect for the Passover Seder.

In general, the Orthodox community has long maintained the attitude, "novelty is forbidden in the Torah," but this year is different. Based upon the responsa of the first Sephardic Rabbi of Israel, Rabbi Ben-Zion Meir Hai Uziel, who ruled that the use of electricity on the Yom Tov Holiday is permitted.[137] And while many rabbis cheered and supported this ruling, Chief Rabbi David Lau and his supporters rejected the leniency. But other than their willingness to embrace a little bit of halachic innovation, most of the rabbis criticizing the idea of a virtual Seder had no real concrete objection, other than the fact that it has been done before.

Sadly, no sooner had scores of rabbis permitted the virtual Seder, many of them later recanted their previous decisions to support Rabbi Lau. The

Haredi rabbis refuse to stand apart from the rabbinical status quo when it comes to accepting halakhic innovation. Most people do not realize that it is permitted to make use of fire on the Yom Tov holiday, so long as one does not start a wholly new fire. One of my teachers taught me over 50 years ago, "The only thing that is etched in stone are the Ten Commandments, and everything else is negotiable." One of the most remarkable aspects of rabbinic Judaism was its willingness to bend the law when necessary.

The Sages often circumvented the law to make biblical law more humane. Most of the Sages interpreted the biblical law of *lex talionis* (Exod. 21:24-2) in terms of compensation—contrary to Rabbi Eliezer, who insisted on a more literal interpretation of the 'eye for an eye" law. [138] The Torah prescribed death to the wayward and rebellious son (Deut. 21:18-21), which the Sages effectively abolished, along with the biblical laws regarding the apostate city found in Deuteronomy 12:12-18. [139]

R. Jacob ben Wolf Kranz (1741-1804), known as the Dubna Maggid, once gave a charming analogy. One of his most famous stories, is where he recalled how he once walked in the forest, and saw tree after tree with a target drawn on it, and at the center of each target an arrow. He went to a young child with a bow in his hand. He asked, "Are you the one who shot all these arrows?", I asked. "Yes!" he replied. "Then how did you always hit the center of the target?" I asked. "Simple," said the boy, "first I shoot the arrow, then I draw the target."

The moral of the parable is clear: Wherever there is a Halakhic will, there will always be a halakhic way to do something or solving a problem. Jews have never been fundamentalists when it comes to interpreting the canons of their traditions. The orality of Torah stresses the importance of oral interpretation over the primacy of scriptural literalism. This logic can undoubtedly apply this year to using a video-conferencing software for this years' Passover celebration.

Part 7
Practical Questions Concerning Jewish Law & Other Assorted Queries Concerning the Coronavirus

CHAPTER 26

Humpty Dumpty sat on a wall,
Humpty Dumpty had a great fall.
All the king's horses and all the king's men
Couldn't put Humpty back together again.

Mother Goose

When the Haredim met Humpty Dumpty

Jews and non-Jews find the Haredi Jewish world peculiar and interesting. When non-Jews see the Haredim, they think they must be related to the Amish, sometimes known as the "Chaimish Amish!" ("the friendly Amish") in Yiddish. When the coronavirus broke out in centers of "Haredi" Judaism and many people in my community wanted to know how COVID-19 changed the way they look at their faith.

For those unfamiliar with the term "Haredi," it comes from the Hebrew verb "tremblers," although the verb "quaking" is equally descriptive; they see themselves as the vanguard of Jewish piety and they practice a strict adherence to Halacha and traditions as opposed to modern values and practices. Most of my friends who identify as "Haredi," do not like being labeled ultra-Orthodox, a description they find pejorative and judgmental. Haredi Jews believe they represent the purest form of Orthodox Judaism.

In a past life, I used to believe that way.

Some scholars have suggested that Haredi Judaism is a reaction to societal changes, including emancipation, the Haskalah movement derived from the Enlightenment, acculturation, secularization, religious reform in all its forms from mild to extreme, the rise of the Jewish national movements, etc. In contrast to Modern Orthodox Judaism, followers of Haredi Judaism are usually uncompromising in their adherence to Jewish Law and custom, and, as a result, they segregate themselves from other parts of society to an extent. However, many Haredi communities encourage their young people to get a professional degree or establish a business.

Furthermore, some Haredi sects, like Chabad-Lubavitch, encourage outreach to less-observant and unaffiliated Jews as well as to non-Jews. Chabad's emissaries in places like India, Africa, or Thailand provide a very valuable contribution in keeping Jewish life vital in these remote communities. Among the Haredi and the non-Jews, they often develop professional and social relationships

Israel is a remarkable place; the personalities that inhabit the country are an endless array of unique characters. The religious parties governed by the Haredi community have long adopted a strident attitude toward modernity and science. To the Haredi community's immense credit, after the Holocaust, its spiritual leaders managed to establish one of the most pious and learned Judaic societies in many centuries, if not millennia. Its birth rate is the highest in Israel, and they have always considered themselves apart from everyone else. Thus far, their model seemed to work.

But did it?

In March 26th, 2020 edition of the JPOST, featured an article about the Health Minister Yaakov Litzman, who tested positive for coronavirus. He did not obey the guidelines as defined by his ministry before contracting the illness. Unfortunately, Prime Minister Benjamin supported Litzman's desire to enforce harsher guidelines in the ultra-Orthodox neighborhoods to be delayed by a week.

In Bnei B'rak, one of Israel's oldest cities since early rabbinical times, the coronavirus has spread exponentially more than it has in the rest of the country. And the epicenter of the problem: the synagogue. The centers of Haredi piety in Israel are not alone; In Europe, cities like Antwerp, Belgium; London; Strasbourg, France; as well as in Borough Park, N.Y., the coronavirus pandemic has produced an unusually high number of deaths of Haredim living in the Diaspora.

Although the Ultra-Orthodox makes up only 12 percent of Israel's population, the ultra-Orthodox account for 40 to 60 percent of the coronavirus patients at four major hospitals, hospital officials told Israeli news media. The true dimensions of the epidemic among the ultra-Orthodox can only be estimated because testing is rare. All of this has occurred under Rabbi Litzman's watch. And to make the situation even worse, he contracted the virus. Obeying the social-distancing rules might have prevented the spread of COVID-19. [140]

Usually, the Haredi can always point to the secular Israeli state for being at the root cause of their social problems. Still, this time the average Haredi Jew knows that the problem here is not the secular Other, but the way of life they have long embraced. In their effort to create a Jewish ghetto to protect themselves from the problems of the outer community, the pandemic has shaken the confidence of their followers in their rabbis, whom they believe are incapable of making errors. The Israeli writer David Landau calls it, "the logic of implied infallibility."

And yes, Catholics are not the only ones who believe the Pope is infallible (except for the theologian Hans Kung, who later got excommunicated from the Church for contesting this doctrine), the Haredi rabbis hold their rabbinical leaders with similar esteem. To their followers, their Haredi rabbis have almost a rock-star status; they appear larger than real life.

Among the Haredi followers, their rabbis prohibit their followers from watching television, radio, or newspapers. The rabbis discourage the use of the Internet on their Android, or Apple phones are discouraged—this absence of communication prevents their communities from ascertaining the problem of a pandemic.

It is interesting to contrast the Haredim with the Amish, another religious community that keeps its distance from modernity. Once informed, the Amish immediately observed the social-distancing guidelines. They canceled large gatherings, weddings and services.[141]

But the Haredi communities' isolation is compounded by the population density of their cities. The largest city is *Bnei Brak,* which is packed with over 27,000 residents on average in one square kilometer. It is hardly any wonder why the ultra-Orthodox community has emerged as the nation's most vulnerable community. Since the founding of the State, the Haredim believed it is their study of Torah and prayers, rather than soldiers' maneuvers in the field, that provide the last line of defense for the Jewish people.

The Haredi attitude is not without historical parallels. Carl G. Jung writes in his book *Memories, Dreams, and Reflections* about his encounter with the Pueblo Indians in the Southwestern section of the United States. Jung asked them about their religious beliefs:

> I could observe from his excitement that he was alluding to some essential element of his religion. I, therefore, asked him: "You think, then, that what you do in your religion benefits the whole world?" He replied with great animation, "Of course. If we did not do it, what would become of the world?' And with a significant gesture, he

pointed to the sun. I felt that we were approaching extremely delicate ground here, verging on the mysteries of the tribe. "After all," he said, "we are a people who live on the roof of the world; we are the sons of Father Sun, and with our religion, we daily help our father to go across the sky. We do this not only for ourselves, but for the whole world. If we were to cease practicing our religion, in ten years the sun would no longer rise. Then it would be night forever.[142]

Elsewhere Jung elaborated on some of the important insights he received from his meeting with the Pueblo Indians:

It is the role of religious symbols to give a meaning to the life of man. The Pueblo Indians believe that they are the sons of Father Sun, and this belief endows their life with a perspective (and a goal) that goes far beyond their limited existence. It gives them ample space for the unfolding of personality and permits them a full life as complete persons. Their plight is infinitely more satisfactory than that of a man in our own civilization who knows that he is (and will remain) nothing more than an underdog with no inner meaning to his life.[143]

Perhaps based on Jung's observation, the same may be said of the Haredi communities. They believe their worship serves to protect the State of Israel from those plotting to destroy her. But there comes a time when the community needs to think in terms of its immediate physical survival. Utilizing modern medical science holds the best cure for this community to survive the coronavirus pandemic. Will life ever return to normalcy after the pandemic is over? Perhaps. But one thing is relatively certain: it is doubtful the Haredi community will ever believe that their leaders are infallible. If nothing else, the pandemic has laid this belief bare; for all the Torah study they have done, it is powerless against a virus that is indifferent to their religious piety and fear of Heaven. Since their teachers instilled in them the belief that Torah is the best medicine, and that the Torah protects and saves—now they tangibly see that "this is not so at all."

To use the Humpty Dumpty nursery rhyme as an analogy, the Haredi community can now see the collapse of a religious world-view they never thought would possibly fall. It is difficult to imagine how they are going to put their communities back together again. Their leaders' hubris produced the suffering their families must now endure.

Despite protestations from their spiritual leaders, even before the pandemic began, the Haredi communities had already crossed the Rubicon; Not long ago, the share of Haredim connecting to the web crossed the 50% mark. After this crisis is over, one can almost guarantee the Haredim will fully embrace the Internet—and when this happens, their insular community will begin to waver as its people perhaps begin to clamor for some genuine social and religious change.

CHAPTER 27

When it's a question of money, everybody is of the same religion.

Voltaire

Amulets, Coronavirus, & Election Day in Israel

Whenever Election Day comes to Israel, you can always count upon the ultra-Orthodox political parties to boost voter turnout in their cities. The religious politicians will often offer amulets and blessings to ensure their people will be blessed. This year in particular, some of the Shas and United Torah Judaism political parties handed out amulets with prayers and excerpts from the Jewish liturgy, promising that their reelection would guarantee that the coronavirus would not affect the voters' families.

But it does not stop there. Representatives of the Shas political party were reported handing out "protective" charms and Shabbat candles at polling stations across the country. Fortunately, the State of Israel is not a theocracy. Israeli election laws fined the Shas party about $2150. This fine is barely a slap on the wrist. Incidentally, the Shas Party is one of the backers of Benjamin Netanyahu's voting bloc. And while I am certain Netanyahu does not believe in this cynical use of religion, I have yet to hear him condemn this practice.

But it hardly ends here. Some Haredi charitable institutions such as the *Kupat Ha-Ir* of the town of Bnai Brak, promise immunity from the coronavirus to anyone who donates no less than 3000 shekels, which amounts to $836.[144] In the 2016, they promised their donors, "you can win the jackpot: *Parnassah*, children, nachas, Torah, wealth, *shidduchim*, good health and happiness! Don't wait another 28 years for a *yeshuah!*" ("salvation") [145]

This is not chickenfeed.

If Christopher Hitchens were alive today, I wonder what would he say about the pecuniary exploitation of the coronavirus? He would probably ask that if the pious rabbis possess the power to banish the coronavirus away, why don't they do it for everyone—regardless whether they pay or not? And what happens if they cannot deliver upon their promises? Are they prepared to offer a refund? The truth is that rabbis are not spiritual supermen; nor are they psychics or prophets. Tragically, so many religious leaders pander to people's superstitions. Jewish tradition has since the days of the Talmud taught us that we must not rely upon miracles.

Concerning those Haredi Jews who believe in the efficacy of amulets, their behavior may lead to them contracting the disease since they are apt to disregard the social-distancing protocols. This would expose them to the virus. And despite their belief in amulets, they will get sick and die.

When rabbis endorse this kind superstition, they are putting a stumbling block for the blind. They will have to answer before God's Heavenly Court for causing the death of innocents. And while one may believe in the power of prayer, we still have to do everything humanly possible if we wish to secure God's blessings.

Orthodox Jews cannot afford to ignore this problem. They must hold their rabbis morally accountable. To see a crime being committed and failing to respond to it—either directly or indirectly—makes the observer complicit and ethically guilty.

The Israeli government must impose greater financial penalties that the religious perpetrators will feel in their pocketbooks.

In my opinion, these rabbis are doing a disservice to their followers; they behave like amoral atheists. The great Protestant theologian Paul Tillich in his book, "Dynamics of Faith" once defined religion as, "man's ultimate concern." For Tillich, people's "religion" centers upon what people consider to be the meaning of life. Every individual has some concern that he considers "ultimate." And it is in this sense, each person can be said to be "religious." For some individuals, their "ultimate concern" might consist of things like success, money, political power, sexual pleasure, fame, or social concern. Whatever concerns a human being the most, that object becomes his god and religion. And while God ought to be the focus of one's religious passion and devotion, some people have replaced God with mammon and political power.

Our money says, "In God we trust."

As a child, I used to enjoy watching the Jack Benny Show. He was a brilliant comic, blessed with a sharp wit. In one comedy routine, a bandit with a gun came up to him and said, "This is a stickup! Your money or your life!" When Benny doesn't immediately answer, the bandit repeats:

"Look, buddy, I said, 'Your money or your life!" Benny says, "Hang on, I'm thinking it over. I'm thinking it over."

For certain people, the accumulation of wealth is the sole focus of their existence. That is why Voltaire cleverly said, "When it comes to money, everybody is of the same religion."

And the rest is commentary.

CHAPTER 28

Prophecy is an intercept from the mind of an all-knowing and all-seeing and all-powerful God.

Joel C. Rosenberg

The Eye of Prophecy?

Great writers of science fiction literature often display a keen intuition of what the future might bring. Whether you read H.P. Lovecraft or H. G. Wells, science-fiction writings make the impossible seem almost believable. H.G. Wells' is probably best known for his classical story, *The Time Machine*, which he published in 1895. His insights into the future were prescient in many ways. Wells anticipated many technological changes, e.g., airplane battles conducted in the air; the sexual revolution; motorized vehicles, world-wars, a federalized Europe (think: European Union), the emergence of the atomic bomb. Wells also anticipated the dystopian genre. The same could be said about Gene Rodenberry's *Star Trek Series.*

The coronavirus we have experienced, appears to have been anticipated by an Israeli writer named Hamutal Shabatai's 1997 novel entitled, "2020." In her dystopian story, she foresaw a time when a pandemic would cause people to turn against one another in fear. Amazingly, the writer had a clear vision how our world would change. He tells the story about a virus that threatened to doom the human race. In her story, the pandemic began in New York, and from there it spread throughout the world. The virus was so contagious, it made any human intimate encounter deadly.

Shabatai's psychological depiction resonates with our experience of the coronavirus. She explained in an interview, "The dynamic of a pandemic, which requires constant testing and separations, arouses the feelings that really do appear in the book in us all. The anxiety that someone you want to be close to, or whom you are close to, could end up among the ill, gives rise to a paranoia. It's like in vampire stories, where the victim who is infected and afflicted is also the one who could infect you, as if he already belongs to the forces of evil. This is what the illness does. The victim is also the demon, and fear grips all of us."

And yet, Shabatai's concept may have an earlier antecedent in the science-fiction writer's Dean Koontz's novel, "The Eyes of Darkness," written in 1981. This book became a best-seller on the New York Times. In his novel, Koontz wrote about a fictional biological weapon known as "Wuhan-400," which had a 100% fatality rate. Anyone reading this book will discover that its similarities to the coronavirus end here. Unlike "Wuhan-400," the incubation period occurred only in four hours. The coronavirus has an incubation period anywhere between two and fourteen days. Oddly, in his 2008 edition, he referred to the "Wuhan-400," even though in his 1981 edition he called it "Gorki-400" after the Russian city, where the virus was engineered.

In our third example, let us turn to the psychic Sylvia Browne (1936-2013) wrote something interesting in her book, "End of Days," a book that was published in 2008. She wrote, "In around 2020 a severe pneumonia-like illness will spread throughout the globe, attacking the lungs and the bronchial tubes and resisting all known treatments. Almost more baffling than the illness itself will be the fact that it will suddenly vanish as quickly as it arrived, attack again ten years later, and then disappear completely."

What does Jewish tradition have to say about these things? The Arabic theologian Avicenna of the 8th century believed prophecy could be best understood as a paranormal phenomenon that enables an individual to see beyond the present. Perhaps the same can be said about "genius," some people are endowed with gifts of the imagination that may give that person a glimpse of the future. Such a notion is evident in the dreams of Joseph in the Bible. It is not something that is beyond the realm of the possible.

The British physicist David Bohm in many of his writings discusses the idea that everything that exists is composed of energy and that this energy runs throughout the cosmos concurrently. He calls this energy as a level of consciousness that interconnects everything—from the macro, to the micro; it includes an unseen (which he terms, "implicate") and visible (an "explicate") order. To use a more modern idiom, think of consciousness as kind of spiritual or ethereal "Internet" that binds all beings together. Such a concept has mind-bending implications about the power of prayer, or healing in general. Ultimately, the only thing that separates one human being from another is the illusion of space. Bohn calls this, "nonlocal reality." This would suggest some events are far removed from our conscious field of awareness that can have an effect on how we see and experience the world. To use another analogy, think of the radio. Radio waves are everywhere, but to tune in we must have a receiver. For the prophet, this "receiver" is his imagination and intuition.

Writers, psychics, yogis, and biblical prophets, as well as true geniuses have something in common: an ability to get in touch with intuition. These gifts of the human psyche can sometimes enable people to see beyond the immediate present. It is one of those many gifts God has given us truly outlines our uniqueness in the cosmic order.

As a people deeply rooted in the prophetic experience of its past, the Jewish imagination possesses a genius for anticipating the future.

Though Jews often forget who they are, anti-Semites have an unusual (but unpleasant) way of reminding us, that as Jews, we stand for something. If the Jewish people stood for nothing, it is doubtful our enemies would ever be bothered to take notice of us. I believe this gift of imagination and creativity will help the Israeli scientists and medical experts be among the first to find a cure for the coronavirus.

CHAPTER 29

"The Rum Tum Tugger is a Curious Cat:
If you offer him pheasant he would rather have grouse.
If you put him in a house he would much prefer a flat,
If you put him in a flat then he'd rather have a house.
If you set him on a mouse then he only wants a rat,
If you set him on a rat then he'd rather chase a mouse.
Yes the Rum Tum Tugger is a Curious Cat -
And there isn't any call for me to shout it:
For he will do
As he do do
And there's no doing anything about it!"

T.S. ELLIOT,
Old Possum's Book of Practical Cats

The Hutzpah of the Contrarian Child

When we read in the Haggadah about the Four Children, one wise, one "wicked," one simple, and one who is too young to ask questions, it is the "wicked," son, whom I preferably identify as "the contrarian child." His question cuts to the essence of the holiday: "What does this holiday mean to you?"

Yes, all the contrarian children of the world have a place in God's community. It is a pity the Hagadah considered him as a "wicked child." His questions are not less inquisitive than his brothers. The contrarian son's honesty is refreshingly different from the other sons at the seder. One could argue the contrarian child asks the best question of the Passover Seder—and obviously the most important.

The Passover Seder teaches us that it is not enough to merely read the Passover story on the night of Passover. Parents must dialectically engage their children in a thoughtful discussion about the relevance of the Passover story and how it corresponds to contemporary society. The inability of a parent to personally relate to the Passover message is bound to come across as a mechanical rite, devoid of value.

What do we teach our contrarian child? How do we answer his questions about the significance of the Exodus? First of all, the thoughtful parent needs to spiritually process the message of Passover for oneself. Ask: As a parent, what does the Exodus mean to me? If we can be honest with ourselves, our rebellious children will respect honesty and authenticity. Perhaps our answer will prod the young man or woman to seriously investigate the meaning of one's faith. Admitting that we are constantly searching for truth is the best way to make a religious tradition meaningful to the age of rebellion.

And this year, this seder was very different from previous Seders. Asked in a more contemporary tone, your children could consider this relevant question: "What does the Exodus mean to us living in post-coronavirus world?" Whenever bad things happen to good people, we find our faith in a personal God challenged. As the deaths of thousands occur with the spread of the coronavirus pandemic, people of faith find themselves scrambling for answers.

Are we not like the Israelites who huddled in their homes, practicing social-distancing, not knowing if the coronavirus might strike us or someone we know and love? That interpretation will stir the religious consciousness of your children. As the holiday of Passover nears completion, we find ourselves struck by the incongruity of it all. It is one thing to read about the ten plagues. It is quite another to personally experience them.

CHAPTER 30

"Can cyberspace be considered sacred space for prayer?"

Anonymous

Is an Internet Minyan Permitted?

The question has come up: May one may participate in a virtual minyan on the Internet? Many of my colleagues tend to rule against such a possibility for a variety of reasons.

> Judaic law specifies the importance of ten people (we count women in the Conservative Movement) must be clustered in one central place. Even if they are in another room, but within hearing distance of the place where people are praying, they may not be counted as part of the minyan. [146]

> In one respect, the question whether our rabbinical scholars would have approved of an internet minyan seems almost a silly proposition to consider. How can one compare the world of pre-modernity to our postmodern and technological world that has so little in common with the social reality of our ancestors? Yet, rabbinical tradition was not completely unaware of such a situation arising. The Sages said, "Jephthah in his generation is like Samuel in his generation"[147] in order to teach us that even an unworthy person, when appointed to a position of importance has to be regarded as one of the greatest," [148]

In my opinion, the Sages wished to teach us that no future generation of Jewish leaders can afford the luxury to wonder how the previous generation of Jewish leadership would respond to a crisis or situation in their time. In the final analysis, that decision belongs exclusively with the

173

leadership of the future—even if the quality and caliber of the leadership pales in comparison. Readers may recall how Jephthah made a rash and boneheaded decision to offer the first thing out of his house as a burnt-offering to God (Judges 11:30-31), and in the end, his daughter:

> When Jephthah arrived at his home in Mizpah, there was his daughter coming out to meet him, with timbrel and dance! She was an only child; he had no other son or daughter. On seeing her, he rent his clothes and said, "Alas, daughter! You have brought me low; you have become my troubler! For I have uttered a vow to the LORD and I cannot retract." [149]

Had the Talmudic rabbis been familiar with Winnie-the-Pooh, they would have declared, Jephthah was a leader who was "of very little brain," As it was, the Rabbis exclaimed, "What would he have done had a pig left his house?" Would he have offered it as a burnt-offering to God? Therefore, Jephthah is considered to be a classical example of a "pious ignoramus."

The point of this digression is that today's rabbinical leaders must make decisions based upon the exigencies defined by today's problems—not necessarily those of the past. When we take into consideration how the most pious synagogues across the world have closed their doors to enable social distancing, the idea of a virtual minyan is not such an implausible idea at all.

In Los Angeles, the Kabbalah Center streams it Shabbat services every week for people across the country to participate. I am certain this is done through the help of non-Jews, but it is still a permitted way to reach out to those who cannot attend the services.

Now, an examination of the relevant Halakhic texts from the *Shulchan Aruch* (*Code of Jewish Law*) will show how the rabbis often applied an elastic principle of what I call "flexidoxity" when determining practical Jewish law. I added the relevant footnotes from the *Mishnah Berurah*.

> **OH 55:13:** Those constituting a minyan must be in one specific place with the prayer leader being amongst them. In the event, someone is standing in the doorway from the threshold and outward, i.e., where the door is closed, from the point where the interior of the door's face rests and is outward, it is treated as the outside. [*which according to*

certain authorities may still be considered part of the minyan—MB. [150]

OH 55:14: In the event someone was standing outside the synagogue and there was a window looking downward several stories below, but could still see the individuals below—that person(s) may still be counted. However, this does not apply to someone standing upon a roof or an upper floor. Such persons may not be counted. [even though there is a partition separating them, if one can see their face(s), they may be counted as a part of the minyan] [151]

OH 55:15: If some of the potential participants were inside and a few were outside, and the prayer leader is standing at the entrance; his visual gaze is sufficient to help him form the minyan. But if part of the ten worshipers stood in the courtyard, while others were in the synagogue—they do not constitute a minyan.

As the reader may see, an Internet minyan could conceivably be put together; the concept of "place" is not as rigid as some scholars think; especially since the halakhot cited above does not even take into consideration whether those people who are within visual range are aware that they are participating in a minyan. The problem with the halakhah is the rabbis did not consider the anthropological concept of a participation mystique, where everyone is conscious that one is participating with the collective (minyan).

With online participants, the faces of the participants are not a two-dimensional image; they reflect living and willing participants. This in my view should not be considered inferior to the cases in OH 55:13 and OH 55:14.

With respect to the use of a computer on the Sabbath, this is a whole different subject. Rav Shlomo Auerbach, arguably one of Haredi Judaism's most original halakhic scholars of the 21st century ruled that there is no prohibition to turning solid state appliances on the Shabbat since any creation of "sparks" should not be considered as "fire," and does not even qualify as a rabbinical prohibition in the unintentional creation of sparks."

Rabbi Michael Broyde & Rabbi Howard Jachter are two Modern Orthodox rabbis who wrote in their online responsa:

> Rabbi Auerbach (Minchat Shlomo 74, 84), after rejecting all the potential sources discussed above for prohibiting the use of electricity when no light or heat is generated, concludes that, at least in theory, electrical appliances that use no heat or light (e.g., a fan) are permitted on Shabbat and Yom Tov. However, he declines actually to permit their use absent urgent need. He states, "In my opinion there is no prohibition [to use electricity] on Shabbat or Yom Tov... There is no prohibition of *ma'keh bepatish or molid*... (However, I [Rabbi Auerbach] am afraid that the masses will err and turn on incandescent lights on Shabbat, and thus I do not permit electricity absent great need...) ... This matter requires further analysis. [152]

While one may disagree with the use of solid-state computer technology on the Sabbath, this writer is of the view that the halakhah—when interpreted beyond a classical literalist perspective–can allow for a flexidox interpretation. By the way, the human brain runs on electricity and it is every bit as complicated as a solid-state computer.

I suppose cryogenic stasis will always be an option for those not wishing to utilize electricity on Shabbat, but I do not recommend

According to the Mishnah, one more factor should be mentioned. The Mishnah, (as ruled by the later authorities)[153] even people who eat their meals apart from the others may participate in the leading the Grace after Meals with respect to counting a quorum of people for leading *zimun*—so long as they can visually see one another. [154]

Again, let us reiterate the guiding principle here: "The Sages said, "Jephthah in his generation is like Samuel in his generation" We can only rule in accordance with our understanding of how a halakhah might apply here. No scholarly rabbi is any worse than Jephthah was in his time. Although the ancient and medieval rabbis did not anticipate of the modern reality of a "Virtual Presence," the principles discussed above allow for a new postmodern idea of the minyan in cyberspace. The concept of "space" and especially "cyberspace" can arguably be incorporated into the traditional understanding of "space." Visual consciousness of other participants is far more compelling than the examples we cited earlier.

Technology and the Changing World of Jewish Law

Lastly, I will add one last caveat to our discussion based upon one of my favorite stories. Once a congregant went to his rabbi on the Eve of *Yom Kippur* and said, "Rabbi: I have a dilemma; tonight, is *Kol Nidrei* and it is also the first night of the World Series. What should I do?" The rabbi did not look amused; he replied, "Have you ever heard of the VCR?" The congregant thanked the rabbi profusely, "Thank you Rabbi, thank you! I did not know I could record *Kol Nidre*! I must go back to the game!"

Obviously, due to the seriousness of the coronavirus, we must not use the Internet to excuse ourselves from participating in a real minyan with real people you can touch and interact with. This responsa of mine only applies to our present emergency such as a pandemic or a severe snowstorm that has made attending services an impossibility. Once normalcy is established, minyans will occur in real time with real people. For people who are shut in their homes for whatever the reason, the new technology of live-streaming has made it possible for people to participate in a minyan outside the synagogue. The spirit of Halakhah in Judaism's greatest strength is its ability to adapt itself to ever new changing circumstances.

CHAPTER 31

"We are all our own bodies' visitors."

Mokokoma Morkhonoana

Cremation and the Coronavirus

Jewish tradition has long frowned upon the practice of cremation—especially given the history of the Holocaust, where millions of Jews met their fate in the crematoria, such as my grandparents and their families. The ancient worship of Moloch, the Canaanite deity associated with death, who was the Semitic version of Hades. The Scriptures warns, "No one shall be found among you who makes a son or daughter pass through fire" (Deut. 18:10),

The horrific imagery of such child sacrifices found in the Midrashic literature that is cited by R. David Kimchi (14th century), who describes how the ritual occurred: An image of Moloch was made out of brass and was hollow. A fire was kindled within the idol. When the extended hands became hot, Moloch's priest taking the infant from its father's hand, placed it in the deities' hands to the accompaniment of drums to prevent the father from hearing the screams of his dying offspring. [155]

Archeological evidence revealing the skeletons of infants near pagan shrines, suggest that human sacrifice may have been transplanted to Canaan from Carthage, Sardinia, Sicily, and the Greek islands, and later spread to Canaan via the Phoenicians. [156] Not all scholars agree on this point.

So, it is with surprise, one of Israel's leading Modern Orthodox Rabbis, Kenneth Brander, who is the dean of the Israeli Ohr Torah Stone network of institutions came out with an unexpected ruling: bodies infected by the coronavirus ought to be cremated in order to save the life of the living. One such person in Buenos Aires was cremated despite protests from his community. This ruling applies only when the government demands that cremations take place for the health of the public. In places like Italy or Britain, the governments there have made an exception to the faith communities. [157]

Ever since the pandemic started, most Jewish communities temporarily discontinued the traditional *taharah* (ritual bathing of the corpse). Physicians point out that the virus lives on in the infected person's blood and bodily fluids. However, many communities that continue to prepare the body in accordance with Judaic tradition, do so with wearing protecting clothing and operate in smaller groups, utilizing a disinfectant when washing the bodies.

Given the seriousness and potential for contagion, there is good reason in my opinion to cremate. One scriptural antecedent derives from the Book of Amos 6:10, which reads:

> And if a relative, one who burns the dead, shall take up the body to bring it out of the house, and shall say to someone in the innermost parts of the house, "Is anyone else with you?" the answer will come, "No." Then the relative shall say, "Hush! We must not mention the name of the LORD!

According to R. David Kimchi's interpretation, this case might have been due to exceptional circumstances, as in the case of a pandemic. Cremation would have been the most sanitary way to keep disease from spreading. [158]But it is also possible that in Amos' time, cremation did not have a negative stigma, the burning of the body was considered a sacred duty—one that fell upon the closest of kin, either the uncle, or the mother's brother who was called the מסרף "one who burns" (Shalom Paul).

However, not translations concur here. However, not all translations concur here. The NJPS translation renders the text differently:

> And if someone's kinsman -- who is to burn incense for him -- comes to carry the remains out of a house, and he calls to the one at the rear of the house, "Are there any alive besides you?" he will answer, "No, none." And he will say, "Hush!" -- so that no one may utter the name of the LORD.

Based on this reading, Amos might have been referring to the custom of burning aromatic spices in honor of the dead or to the practice of burning corpses at the time of a plague in order to restrict the danger of infection. Therefore, some Halakhic scholars ruled that an alternative to burial is to use quicklime to hasten decomposition of the body after death to prevent contagion.[159]

Parenthetically let us add:

As far as the burial of ashes from a cremation, even when a pandemic is not a factor, some traditional Jewish communities permitted the ashes of a person to be buried in a Jewish cemetery. Since the 19th century, other traditional cemeteries might decline accepting the ashes as a deterrent to would be violators of Jewish law. However, there is nothing in the Halakhah that prohibits burying Jewish ashes in a cemetery.

Curiously, nowhere in the Talmud is cremation even discussed. It is interesting to add that among the ancient Jewish ossuaries, urns with ashes have been found. But we cannot tell whether the ashes might have merely been the remains of someone who died in a fire, or not. There is an interesting Midrash that is suggestive. It reads, "When Isaac pleaded with his father on Mount Moriah, he said, 'Burn me completely, and bring my ashes to my mother that she place them in an urn in her own room, and that whenever she enters the room she may remember me with tears.'" [160] Although Chief Rabbi Herman Adler (1839-1911), of Great Britain considers cremation a violation of Jewish law and custom; he permits the "levayah" at the burying of the remains.[161] This is a policy that should adhered to everywhere. For those determined to conduct the taharah in any event, they would be wise to wear protective clothing and use disinfectants as much as is necessary.

Funerals in the Age of the Corona Virus

The rules of social-distancing have posed a serious problem for those who have lost ones. For funeral homes, there are no longer large funeral homes filled with mourners. The funeral has been limited to only the immediate families of ten people or less. Funeral directors are faced with a daunting task: They have to figure out how to comfort mourning families from a distance.

One of the most important ways of showing respect is to attend the funeral of a loved one or a friend. It is a way of showing appreciation for everything a loved one has done for the living while alive. The ritual of saying farewell to a loved one transcends social and cultural differences. But these traditions are being temporarily suspended as governments across the globe impose strict social distancing orders. This situation as in effect, forcing people to discover new ways of expressing grief. During the week of *Shiva*, a time Jews dedicate to mourning for a loved one, it is customary for everyone in the community to come, bring food, and show solidarity and concern to the relatives. When meeting, people hug one another and cry together. But the coronavirus has prevented that possibility.

In one story I heard, a survivor drove a considerable distance to comfort his sister, while standing in the front yard of her home, a few feet away from the window. One of the remarkable changes the pandemic has produced is the live-streaming of funeral and other lifecycle events—from the ritual of circumcision to those who are holding a Zoom wedding. Even Bar and Bat Mitzvahs are now being conducted online. With the technology of the Internet, families can still stay together in solidarity. I suspect that even after life resumes back to normal after the pandemic has ended, I am convinced the live-streaming of Jewish, Christian, and Muslim lifecycle events will continue well into the future. Our congregation is discussing the possibility of starting a weekday Zoom Minyan. Such an idea would never have been considered a year ago.

With social-distancing law slowly loosening, more funerals are being held at the graveside.

I am confident life will eventually resume its normal course.

Part 8
Jewish Issues & Concerns

CHAPTER 32

"History doesn't repeat itself but it often rhymes."

Mark Twain

The Coronavirus and the Jewish Problem

Scientists gathered at a conference to present their research projects on the life of elephants. The Englishman wrote a paper on, "Hunting the Elephant." The Frenchman wrote about, "The Love Life of the Elephant." The Jewish scientist submitted a study on, 'The Elephant and the Jewish Problem." Most American Jews no longer consider themselves like outsiders standing on the peripheral of society. Today's Jews occupy the highest echelons of American life. Jewish professors are on the faculties of the most prestigious colleges.

Our joke dates back to the time when the European and American Jew felt insecure living in a country that merely tolerated their presence. At the whim of a ruler, Jews often were expelled by their host county. The Diaspora Jew felt like Tevye, playing the fiddle on a shaky roof—one that could collapse at any time. The fiddler is in many ways a metaphor for Jewish survival in a world that is characterized by uncertainty and danger.

It is intriguing to compare the Diaspora Jew to the Jew raised in the Modern State of Israel. To Prime Minister Ben-Gurion's immense credit, today's Jew living in Israel refuses to act passively in the face of anti-Semitism. The Israeli Jew is strong, active and determined to survive. As an autonomous nation, Israel does not permit other nations to impose their will upon their citizens. Israeli Jews believe that their destiny is literally in their hands; they know they can both act and impact history around them.

Israeli Jews do not see themselves as inferior underlings, but they know they can stand toe-to-toe, eye-to eye with the most powerful leaders of the world. On June 22 1982, when Joe Biden was a Senator from Delaware, he confronted the Israeli Prime Minister Menachem Begin during his Senate Foreign Relations Committee. Biden threatened to cut off aid to Israel. Begin forcefully responded, "Don't threaten us with cutting off your aid. It will not work. I am not a Jew with trembling knees. I am a proud Jew with 3,700 years of civilized history. Nobody came to our aid when we were dying in the gas chambers and ovens. Nobody came to our aid when we were striving to create our country. We paid for it. We fought for it. We died for it. We will stand by our principles. We will defend them. And, when necessary, we will die for them again, with or without your aid." It is difficult to imagine American Jewish leaders confronting President Roosevelt during the Holocaust. In modern times, rarely did American Jewish leaders dare to challenge President Obama about Iran's plan to develop a nuclear bomb.

But just as Prime Minister Begin minced no words, Israeli leaders continued this legacy when dealing with leaders attempting to punish Israel, if she refuses to comply to the demands of Western leaders. During the Holocaust, American Jews continued to feel nervous. Our fathers and mothers did not want to stir the pot. I recall speaking with Rabbi Arthur Hertzberg (1921--2006), who was a famous Conservative rabbi and prominent Jewish-American scholar and activist. He told me about his Hassidic father who dared to question Roosevelt from the pulpit and the Board of Directors fired the rabbi the following evening. Nobody wanted to upset the non-Jews—especially those who worshipped Roosevelt. For generations, the American Jew felt comfortable in his skin. Anti-Semitic incidents seldom occurred with ubiquity. As American Jews, we grew used to hearing how "America is *andrish*," the Yiddish word for "different."

The Church Needs to Fight Anti-Semitism

Despite decades of trying to promote better Christian-Jewish relations, it appears as though our time cultivating interfaith programs has fallen short of the mark. One gets the impression the Christian community does not concerned appear to be overly-concerned about the spread of anti-Semitism. Who could imagine Christian ministers blaming the Jew for COVID-19? I realize the fanatics and zealots do not reflect the overall philosophy of the American church. But I have bone to pick with the mainline churches such as the Presbyterian Church and other Protestant churches, who choose to remain silent and apathetic.

The San Francisco Theological Seminary is one of the main theological centers of the Presbyterian Church. On one occasion, Professor Walt Davis, the Dean of the Seminary, came up to me in 1996 and apologized for his Church's indifference toward the Jewish community of Europe during the

Holocaust. Not only didn't the Presbyterian Church refuse to assist the Jews in escaping, they utilized the Holocaust to convert those Jews who managed to flee the death-camps! Davis asked me as a representative of the Jewish faith what he could do to atone for his Church's sins. I told him that he should make sure the Church becomes a tireless critic of anti-Semitism and anti-Zionism.

Unfortunately, over the past several decades, the Presbyterian Church has been hijacked by some of its radicals. Nevertheless, I believe there are fine people who must take the reins of power away from the anti-Semitic wing of its church. I came across an old email someone from the Church had written a few years ago after the terrible Pittsburg synagogue shooting in Squirrel Hill:

> Although we ourselves may not have promoted anti-Jewish theologies, we nonetheless confess, before God and our Jewish sisters and brothers, the ways in which the Christian church has promoted hate through fear, false narratives, and poor interpretation. Although it may not be our fault, it is our responsibility to set the record straight in proclaiming that the God of Jesus Christ, who we worship, is also the God of Israel, and that our hope is in the reconciliation, not the division, of all peoples.[162]

Europe still retains the crown for enabling anti-Semitism in their societies. They have demonstrated they have learned nothing from the horrors of the Holocaust. Perhaps the most profound Christian interpretation of this question comes from the early 19th century Baptist preacher, C.H. Spurgeon (1834-1892), where he writes about Cain's question: "Am I my brother's keeper?"

> I put it to the consciences of many silent Christians, who have never yet made known to others what God has made known to them—How can you be clear from guilt in this matter? Do not say, "Am I my brother's keeper?" for I shall have to give you a horrible answer if you do. I shall have to say, "No, Cain, you are not your brother's keeper, but you are your brother's killer." If, by your effort you have not sought his good, by your neglect you have destroyed him."[163]

Lutheran theologian, Dietrich Bonhoeffer who used to cite the verse, "Where is Abel your brother?" whenever he engaged leaders of the Lutheran community to assist in rescuing the Jewish people from the Nazis. To his chagrin, he felt bitter over the bishops' lack of nerve. Bonhoeffer used to frequently quote the verse, "Who will speak up for those who are voiceless?" (Prov. 31:8). Consequently, Bonhoeffer felt compelled by God to be *the* voice defending the Jews in Nazi Germany—a price he ultimately paid for with his life. [164]

In the "Parable about the Last Judgment" mentioned in Matthew 25:31-46, Jesus left a message in a bottle for the future theologians of the 20-21st century to reflect whenever they think about the Jewish people— Jesus's own flesh and blood family:

> ". . . for when I was hungry and you gave me food, I was thirsty and you gave me something to drink, I was a stranger and you welcomed me, I was naked and you gave me clothing, I was sick and you took care of me, I was in prison and you visited me.' Then the righteous will answer him, 'Lord, when was it that we saw you hungry and gave you food, or thirsty and gave you something to drink? And when was it that we saw you a stranger and welcomed you, or naked and gave you clothing? And when was it that we saw you sick or in prison and visited you?' And the king will answer them, 'Truly I tell you, just as you did it to one of the least of these who are members of my family, you did so to me."

Next time Protestant theologians think about the Jewish people and everything we have gone through because of hateful theological supersessionism, they would be wise to remember this parable from their master and teacher. Jesus' humanity makes him an excellent model for people to emulate themselves after—wouldn't it be nice if his followers took his words more seriously? "Therefore, what God has joined together, no human being must separate." (Mark 10:9)

The Jew as the Scapegoat

Why do people scapegoat the Jews? Whenever we scapegoat, we project the darkest part of our own personalities rather than take ownership of these unpleasant features we possess. Carl Jung, as we noted earlier, describes the dark, shameful, hidden topography of our souls as the "shadow archetype." and denied about ourselves onto others. As Jung observed, the "shadow" side of our personality, "the thing a person has no wish to be," (*Collected Works,* Vol. 16) and spontaneously acts out when its owner refuses to acknowledge these anti-social traits exists within his one psyche. To cover up our shadow, we wear a psychological mask, which Jung identifies as the persona.

In ancient Greek plays, the actors wore the persona to depict the characters they played. In societies, we use the term "scapegoat" to individuals and groups who are accused of causing misfortune. Scapegoating serves the relieve oneself, or one's social clique of assuming any responsibility for victimizing the Other who is not a part of their community. This behavior could explain why the United Nations routinely singles out the State of Israel for human rights violations. And although numerous countries deny freedoms to their populace, they are almost never singled out for criticism. This is a topic we will return to at another time. The animus against Israel reflects an age-old animus toward the Jew, who has been regarded as a danger to civilization. Criticism toward Israel serves as a smoke-screen for the world's most enduring hatred of the Jews. It is arguably a fig-leaf for anti-Semitism.

As an autonomous nation, Israel does not permit other countries to impose their will on the Israeli Jew whenever they feel like it. The Israeli Jews believe that their destiny is literally in their hands; they know they can both act and impact history around them. Israelis do not have an inferiority complex. They can stand toe-to-toe, eye-to-eye with the most influential leaders of the world.

Anti-Semitism in the Age of the Coronavirus

We thought we would never hear new libels accusing the Jew of being a carrier of disease and pandemics. But now the plague is, here again, we're beginning to listen to that same old rhyme again. We thought these libels were behind us; it turns out we were wrong. This is very hard for Jews because we want to believe that human nature is fundamentally good. Today's political climate is undergoing dynamic changes. Anti-Semitism is rebounding in every part of Europe, the United States, and Canada. Anti-Semites still regard the Jew as a threat to the social wellbeing of society.

With the coronavirus claiming over 400,000 lives across the world, we are hearing the chords of hateful rhetoric mantras blaming the Jewish people for economic unrest and global disasters. At a political rally that was organized by Neo-Nazi groups in Ohio, one could see large signs depicting a rat wearing a Star of David and yarmulke that read "the real plague." Lest we think Ohio is the exception, think again. In Rockland County, there are more than 325,000 residents. It has become one of the epicenters of the coronavirus in the United States. Some of the residents blame the spread of the coronavirus to a failure of "certain religious groups" failure to adhere to the standards of social distancing laid out by the government. Some advocated that "these people" ought to be wearing badges with the letter "C" sewn on to their lapel, indicating those who are infected by the virus.

Sound familiar?

The FBI has warned the Jewish community that neo-Nazi and white supremacist groups have called on members to spread the virus among Jews and police officers. Relentless and determined anti-Semites often target Jewish institutions and synagogues. Not even Zoom is insulated from their attacks, where the haters will "Zoom-bombed" and interrupted by anti-Semitic hackers.

In other countries, Jews are accused of poisoning a country's water resources, which is an accusation that also dates back to the time of the Black Death in Europe. Such attitudes are nothing new in Jewish history. Anti-Semites often justified attacking and destroying Jewish communities because they were considered the primary cause of the Black Death. From Italy, through the Rhineland, France, as far west as Spain. The Jew was singled out as a scapegoat.[165]

Between the years 1348 and 1351, European Christians accused the Jews of poisoning food, wells and streams. They were, tortured into making confessions, then rounded up in city squares, along with other Jews gathered at their synagogues, where *they were exterminated en masse.* Historians note that in the city of Strasbourg alone, 2,000 Jews were burnt alive by orders of the local council. In France, someone made a caricature of Agnes Buzyn, France's previous health minister who happens to be Jewish. In this cartoon, Buzyn is pouring poison into a well poisoning the well—but this time it's in 2020. The posting has been shared tens of thousands of times.[166]

The recent collapse of the stock market is also blamed on the Jews. Some Christian ministers on YOUTUBE claim that the coronavirus outbreaks in the synagogues, in particular, is God's judgment upon the Jews for rejecting Christ. For people incapable of critical and self-reflective thought, there is always a simple reason for the problems of today's world: The Jews! Today's Anti-Semitism is no longer willing to operate from the shadows; it has skillfully learned to weaponize its hatred across the Internet. Today, its members act brazenly "in your face."

Postscript 1: After the wrongful death of George Floyd, the Black Lives Matters leaders led followers into the Jewish district of Fairfax, Los Angeles, one of the oldest Jewish areas of Los Angeles. Allyson Rowen Taylor, the former Associate Director of the American Jewish Congress in LA, and a co-founder of StandWithUs, passed on an account of hearing chants of, "F___ the police and kill the Jews." Israeli-born philanthropist and activist Adam Milstein, who lives in Los Angeles, concurred. He said, "The Jewish community is in denial. The fact that synagogues got tagged and Jewish businesses were looted with [signs saying] 'Free Palestine' and 'Kill the Jews,' is not a coincidence. The rioters are Antifa and Black Lives Matter and they are inherently antisemitic."[167]   As another witness to the riots observed, "And yet the vandalism of synagogues and businesses, the cries of, "F___ Jews", and the "F___ Israel" graffiti on a synagogue eloquently testify to the inescapable truth of anti-Semitism that it is about Jews. And if Jews don't stand up when their synagogues and stores are attacked, who will?"[168]

Mayor de Blasio & His "Jewish" Problem

Friction between New York Mayor Bill de Blasio and the Jewish community came to boil recently after he scapegoated the Orthodox community for attending the funeral of a prominent rabbi named Chaim Mertz, who died from the coronavirus. The Mayor had on a previous occasion threatened to close any synagogue or church that did not adhere to his social-distancing rules.

> "Members of the Jewish community were putting each other in danger, they were putting our police officers in danger," he said. "Now, if I see it in any other community,

I will call it out equally." "I have no regrets about calling out this danger and saying we're going to deal with it very, very aggressively," he added.

De Blasio directed a tween directly to "the Jewish community, and all communities, that police can proceed to summons or arrest those found in large groups."

The Jewish community of New York bristled at this response. Rarely does the entire Jewish community agree on much of anything. But this was different. Every Jewish leader concurred: They needed to stand up to the Mayor. More than 100 rabbis, Jewish community leaders, elected officials, temples and organizations signed a letter sent to de Blasio on Thursday, calling for a meeting to 'discuss constructive approaches' to fighting the pandemic. The letter was organized by the New York Jewish Agenda to 'express our anger and disappointment at your scapegoating the Jewish community in response' to Tuesday's funeral. [169]

Their letter pointed out that Mayor had no right to characterize the funeralgoers as "the Jewish community," saying it "flattens a diverse group of New Yorkers into a single bloc and fuels the anti-Semitic hatreds that bubble beneath the surface of our society." Moreover, "this singling out is especially potent because it aligns with longstanding antisemitic tropes that have, for millennia, blamed Jews for societal ills," the letter continues.

The Mayor made no reference of how the Jewish groups have offered a variety of social services to the general community, such as organizing blood plasma donations, testing facilities and food banks for those suffering from the coronavirus. The letter went on to say, ""As Jews, we come together, at times of prayer, celebration, and mourning, making social distancing particularly crushing for our community," the letter said. "Jews have overwhelmingly led and acted responsibly in this moment of social distancing. To suggest otherwise on the actions of a few is the deepest form of marginalization."

You Cannot Have It Both Ways

Postscript 2: States across the country would not allow more than ten people to attend the funeral of a loved one, forcing men mourners to remain home. Three people riding together on a boat in Michigan is considered a "dangerous" activity. Attempting to go back to work? You can be fined thousands of dollars. But worshiping at a church or a synagogue cannot be tolerated? Police officers across the country keep a watchful eye on those neighborhoods where people want to pray, often ticketing them for insubordination.

But after the dreadful death of George Floyd, cities soon forgot about the social-distancing rules as thousands marched screaming down the streets. Are we to assume the coronavirus does not mind if people gather for protesting social injustice? Picture thousands of Americans standing shoulder to shoulder in the streets of several large American cities can be seen coughing and spitting upon each other. The police refuse to disperse them. Has this not spread the disease?

Mayor Bill de Blasio claims the protests are much different from the matter of the "aggrieved store owner or the devout religious person." They don't have good reasons to break quarantine. But apparently, the protestors and the looters do have good reason to be on the streets.

The Mayor cannot have it both ways.

According to the NYT, "Many epidemiologists, including Dr. Bedford, have noted in recent days that America's entrenched racial inequalities themselves translate into disproportionate early deaths and illness among African-Americans. That has been especially evident in the coronavirus pandemic, in which black Americans are dying at about twice the rate of white Americans." [170]

The time has come to treat the COVID-19 pandemic seriously and not make any exceptions for social justice warriors, or for those who are addicted to virtue-signaling. [171] They need to express their view via YOUTUBE or some other form of media. The double-standard here reeks of hypocrisy and pretentiousness.

It is regrettable to how politics is hopelessly triangulated in the coronavirus pandemic.

America, we must do better!

CHAPTER 33

"You will do well to try to inoculate the Indians by means of blankets, as well as to try every other method that can serve to extirpate this execrable race"

British General Jeffrey Amherst on the Smallpox Blankets

Weaponizing the Coronavirus

Troubled times often lead to rash misinterpretations.

At a time when the world ought to be banding together for the common good, there is another segment of the human population that is contemplating new ways of weaponizing the coronavirus. In Gaza, Hamas came up with a new way harming Israeli citizens. By raining missiles on Israel from Gaza, they are well-aware that Israelis will crowd themselves into bomb-shelters, an environment that would make it very easy to spread the pandemic among Israelis.

It is a diabolically clever attempt to cause harm unto the Israelis. But if any country can find a vaccine for the coronavirus, Israel has a pretty good shot. Interestingly, today Egypt announced they are building a physical wall to keep Gaza out of their country. Clearly, more and more moderate Arab countries are starting to realize that Gaza is a failed state that is incapable of acting like a civilized nation. Attempts to make peace with Gaza are doomed for failure. The coronavirus pandemic may have something to do with this; they do not think the Palestinians are serious about containing the pandemic.

Many people in the West cannot comprehend the thinking of the terrorist mind and its relentless pursuit of weapons of mass destruction through any means possible. There is no doubt, Jihadi preachers of Gaza inspired the idea. On the official Palestinian Authority TV, a Muslim preacher speaking said that corona is "one of Almighty Allah's soldiers" and he is unleashing it on those who attack his believers." Hamas' use of coronavirus is theologically consistent with a world view that sees utility in spreading pandemics to strike at an enemy. One would hope that in the event Israel discovers the vaccine for the coronavirus, they would be wise not to share it with enemies who are hellbent determined to destroy her through any means. One Turkish news commentator points to a wider trend: Islamists are planning on weaponizing coronavirus against Jews—wherever they congregate—and that goes double for the State of Israel! In one ISIS newsletter, the virus is a 'torment sent by God on whomsoever He wills.' 'Illnesses,' it continues 'do not strike by themselves but by the command and decree of God.'

Erich Fromm in my opinion rates as one of the greatest psychologists of the 20th century. One of Fromm's greatest theories pertains to two opposite impulses that are struggling for supremacy in the world. He refers to this great psychological conflict as the forces of necrophilia vs. biophilia. Fromm stresses that not all violence is necessarily immoral; a war that is fought for the preservation of human life and dignity cannot be compared to a war that seeks to end human life and dignity, as we see with the Nazis and the Jihadis of the 20th-21st centuries. According to Fromm, "Necrophilia constitutes a fundamental orientation: it is the one answer to life which is in complete opposition to life."[172] Fromm further added,

> Characteristic for the necrophile is his attitude toward force. Force is, to quote Simone Weil's definition, the capacity to transform a man into a corpse. Just as sexuality can create life, force can destroy it. All force is, in the last analysis, based on the power to kill. I may not kill a person but only deprive him of his freedom; I may want only to humiliate him or to take away his possessions—but whatever I do, behind all these actions stands my capacity to kill and my willingness to kill. The lover of death necessarily loves force. *For him the greatest achievement of man is not to give life, but to destroy it; the use of force is not a transitory action forced upon him by circumstances—it is a way of life.*[173]

Necrophilia, or the "love of the dead" is an ideation that is attracted to everything that is dead, e.g., corpses, decay, filth, dirt. As an illustration, Fromm mentions how the Nazi concentration camps were dedicated to the industry of death and genocide. Aside from killing the Jew, the Nazi genocide machine aimed to create an atmosphere of filth surrounding the Jew, who seldom ever had the opportunity to bathe. My father once told me that while he was in Auschwitz, he often bathed in the snow to keep his body clean, while the Nazi officers laughed at his behavior.

According to Fromm, the goal of necrophilia as political and religious phenomena is to transform everything that is living into death. This culture dedicated to death defined Nazism for the evil scourge it was. And yet, in our postwar illusions, we never dared to imagine that we would ever see this kind of menace threatening civilization again. It seemed too inconceivable.

But we were wrong—dead wrong. The continuous attacks on Israeli citizens sitting in pizza parlors, or at local parks and beaches only proves that the spirit of Nazism is alive and well–even thriving–in the Jihadist world today. If Hitler could see what Hamas and its allies are doing, he would be green with envy. The Nazis were miserable human beings, but not even the Nazis ever imagined they could use their young children as a human bomb when it comes to murdering Jews.

Whereas Nazism always remained a secular political philosophy dedicated to eradicating the world of Jews and other undesirables, today's Jihadist movement poses a far greater threat to all of civilization because the engines that run its campaign of genocide derives from religion itself. Let us be clear: Jihadism is a death-force that aims to destroy life as we know it for the glorification of Allah, who behaves more like the bloodthirsty deity of the Bible known as Moloch.

In fact, it is impossible to differentiate between the two.

Jihadists love saying, "We love death more than you love life."[174]

The worse part of necrophilia is that the people this philosophy affects makes them totally indifferent to life and even attracted to death. This would explain why being a martyr for the admirers of Jihad is so important. In the West Bank and Gaza, Palestinians have museums celebrating the sacrifice of his human bombs; museums decorated with Israeli body parts across the wall.[175]

Sounds like a museum made for Freddie Kruger.

The culture of Israel in contrast, corresponds to what Fromm calls, biophilia–the love of life, the attraction to everything that lives and grows. Preserving life and preventing death is one form of biophilia. Biophilia aims to integrate and unite, to fuse with different and opposite. Biophilia celebrates the perpetuity of human life—it looks to promote life wherever and whenever possible. Fromm believed that for biophilia to emerge, there has to be certain circumstances to enhance its growth, e.g., the absence of injustice, the love of creativity, the presence of freedom, and the spirit to innovate. In the battle against the coronavirus, Israeli physicians and scientists are working around the clock to come up with the medical technology that will create vaccines for those afflicted with this virus.

Decent people consistently transcend their religious families of origin.

In spiritual terms, biophilia encourages people to search for self-awareness, aspirations, and moral growth. Israel continues to develop technologies that improve the fabric of life while the Palestinian culture of death, which worships a god who loves *shihads* (martyrs) has produced a moral decadence that threatens the peace of humanity.

The time has come for the Palestinians and Israelis to work together and embrace a new paradigm of life that brings prosperity to all of its people. The leaders of Hamas routinely go to Israel whenever they or a loved one needs an operation that could save their relative's life. Israelis try to promote its philosophy of biophilia by giving a Palestinian baby a life-saving bone marrow treatment worth $55,000—paid by an Israeli pediatrician. And sometimes Palestinian mothers have donated the heart of their child in organ transplants--even if it meant that heart would save the life of an Israeli child. In the West Bank, it is not at all uncommon to see Israeli and Palestinian children participating at a summer camp; Israeli and Palestinian comedians have proven to be a dynamic duel; there is a substantial number of Palestinian students studying at the finest universities. The path of biophilia is a fruitful one—provided people are willing to take it and see where it goes.

We are living in extraordinary times in many ways. More and more moderate Sunni Muslims are doing their best to promote a new paradigm for peaceful and respectful relations with Israel. The Palestinians need to start embracing a philosophy of life rather than promote a religion centered on valuing death. Every American Jew ought to be proud of Israel's commitment to further the culture of life.

Golda Meir said it best, "We can forgive the Arabs for killing our children. We cannot forgive them for forcing us to kill their children. We will only have peace with the Arabs when they love their children more than they hate us."

On June 26, 2020, the U.S. District Court Judge Gary Sharpe issued a preliminary decision saying that de Blasio and Cuomo (as well as Attorney General Letitia James) exceeded their authority by putting restrictions on people of faith while simultaneously condoning the protests. By doing so, the de Blasio and Cuomo essentially said: "What is freedom for me, but not for thee."[176]

CHAPTER 34

*"The Stasi's sole function was to keep the Communist
Party in power. They didn't care how. To think what the
Stasi went through to spy on us. Even they couldn't dream
of a world in which citizens voluntarily carried tracking
devices, conducted self-surveillance, and reported on
themselves, morning, noon and night."*

Adam Johnson
Fortune Smiles

COVID-1984?

It is hard to believe seventy-one years have passed since the publication
of George Orwell's seminal book on the unbridled power of the modern
totalitarian state—*1984*. Orwell possessed a prescience seldom seen in
modern political writers.

The story is about a man named Winston Smith, who lives in the
nation of Oceania, where is governed by constant surveillance; Winston is
a low-ranking member and bureaucrat. Although there is no police force or
laws, the "Thought Police" is always present. Everywhere one goes, the signs
read, "Big Brother is Watching You." The pervasive power of the
government is so ubiquitous, rebellious crimes are considered the worst
kind of political offense. In Orwell's novel, the "telescreen" is a piece of
technology that resembles today's television. It is constantly streaming a
single channel of news, reflecting the view of Big Brother. But unlike the
television, the telescreen can never be turned off. In addition, the telescreen
has a built-in surveillance camera. This kind of power makes the State for
all practical purposes like God in the lives of the people.

As a child of the sixties, most of my generation can recall a show called
"Candid Camera." The show played practical jokes on people or caught
them behaving in funny ways. The show was not mean-spirited; it
characterized a happier time in our country's history. Nobody was ever

recorded without the consent of the individual taped. Candid Camera was harmless fun.

Recalling American History

Throughout our 230-year-old history, we have always thought that a descent to fascism was impossible. Yet, there have been times where our government has flirted with authoritarianism. Who could forget the time Abraham Lincoln suspended Habeas corpus, the law that defends the accused of unlawful detention or imprisonment without first bringing the person to court to determine whether the detention is lawful or not?

Habeas corpus is a recourse in law through which a person can report an unlawful detention or imprisonment to a court and request that the court order the custodian of the person, usually a prison official, to bring the prisoner to court, to determine whether the detention is lawful. FDR did the same thing when he interned Japanese Americans in internment camps. The suspension of civil rights often occurs in times of a national crisis. This is a problem all countries face—especially now with the coronavirus crisis that we have.

Fast-forward to 2020; wherever you go, whether to the local corner market or to the mall, the all-seeing eye of surveillance monitors virtually every segment of modern life—whether you go to the hospital, or to a school—even the sidewalks. Nobody ever thinks to question its legitimacy; it is a fact of today's modern technological age.

But today's world, video-taping individuals is something that has taken on a new significance. Aside from Big Brother observing us, Little Brother—the ordinary citizen—has been deputized by New York's Mayor to spy and snitch on one's neighbor if there is any violation of the social-distancing rules. The government is threatening to arrest Americans who wish to reopen their businesses, or arrest people walking on the beach and fine them. This is the kind of behavior one would expect from North Korea, but not the United States. Just mail in a picture of the suspected culprit to the NYPD.

Will life return to normal once the pandemic is over?

Hopefully. But for authoritarians who have tasted the nectar of power, the temptation to keep that power might prove too seductive. Orwell's society existed in a perpetual state of crisis. Some politicians and health experts would like to see the country remain shut down for another couple of months. Contrary to what certain politicians would like to see, already the public is demanding to return back to work. Restaurant owners want to keep their businesses open, as do hairstylists and bars. Sweden provides a fine example for how to make a transition to normalcy.

In Mayor de Blasio's dystopian vision of New York City, seasoned felons and other criminals roam the streets, lest they be infected by the coronavirus in prison. Yet, if someone is attending a Jewish funeral for a revered rabbi, that person risks getting arrested. He announced after he dispersed the mourners:

> If your congregation continues to meet, you could be done for good. If you go to your synagogue, if you go to your church and attempt to hold services, after having been told so often not to, our enforcement agents will have no choice, but to shut down those services," "I don't say that with any joy. It's the last thing I would like to do, because I understand how important people's faiths are to them, and we need our faith in this time of crisis. But we do not need gatherings that will endanger people.[177]

One would have gotten the distinct impression that churches and synagogues did not abide by the need for social-distancing. Yet, this has not been the case. Pictures of the Hassidic Jews at the Williamsburg funeral show that the majority of them wore facemasks. Across the religious divide, synagogues and churches both committed to closing their services in the interest of halting the pandemic. De Blasio's use of threats has made everyone more nervous than before—and in do so has exacerbated tensions in an anxious community. In addition, the Mayor could have acknowledged how 3,000 Orthodox Jews in New York who donated blood plasma in the last week, helping victims of this pandemic who are desperately in need. He could have spoken about the 45,000 members of the Jewish community who are expected to follow suit and give aid.

But he didn't.

Becoming a Society of Snitchers

Beyond that, the Mayor wants people to snitch on their neighbors.

FOX news analyst Judge Andrew Napolitano on Thursday warned America is turning into a police state and civil disobedience is on the horizon if governors do not come to their senses with civil liberties.

"Yesterday, the Supreme Court of Wisconsin... said to the governor's people, you do not have the authority for the lockdown, only the legislature does and the legislature told us they don't want it and you can't write your own laws and enforce laws that you have just written. That violates the Wisconsin constitution and by the way, the American constitution and therefore the lockdown is ended," Napolitano said on FOX News' 'Tucker Carlson Tonight[178]

But the list of infractions seems to increase daily.

- A Michigan resident is facing up to 93 days in jail for planting a vegetable garden in her front yard.[179]
- A SWAT team is sent to a bar that reopened.
- A hair salon owner gets sent to jail.
- Attempted use of drones to take citizens' temperatures.
- Hotlines set up for citizens to snitch on each other.
- A woman is arrested by the police for not wearing a facemask.
- Jewish worshippers in the Hassidic community get arrested for attending a funeral or service.
- Synagogues threatened with being closed.
- People receiving tickets for playing baseball with their children on a beach.
- Jogging alone without wearing a mask.
- Worshiping on Easter while sitting isolated in one's car parked at a church parking lot.

I am astounded by the A.C.L.U. acts as though everything is normal—when our most fundamental rights are being trampled. Instead of the State being accountable to the people, now the people are always accountable to the State. Since when did sitting on a park bench become a seditious act? What Orwell conceived as fiction is threatening to become a reality—not just in Europe, but also in the United States—especially in New York. The A.C.L.U. ought to be blasted as hypocrites who do not believe in the principles they espouse. They are tacitly endorsing the police state we are witnessing in our country today

It is disturbing to see American politicians praise China's handling of the coronavirus—especially since it was through their neglect, the virus spread throughout the world. Parenthetically I would add, with the help of IBM, Google, and other major American computer companies together have enabled China's authoritarian government to conduct mass surveillance against its people. China has produced tracking devices, facial recognition cameras, online data gathering technologies—all of which serve at the pleasure of the Chinese totalitarian state. Even more disturbing is China's vision of a "social credit system," not only based on the individual's ability to pay bills in a timely fashion, but is also monitor's the citizen's "social trustworthiness." China is no role-model in how they handled COVID-19 pandemic. Rather than salivating at the technologies China uses to monitor the threat of a pandemic, Americans ought to be very concerned that no measures be enacted that compromise the citizen's right to privacy.

In this picture, Democrat Virginia Gov. Ralph Northam is coming under heavy criticism in the last few hours after a photo was published showing him on a crowded beach but without wearing a mask. Yet, just before the Memorial Day holiday, Northam decreed that he would issue a statewide policy on Tuesday requiring all Virginians to wear masks in inside and outside spaces. This kind of duplicity can be seen in many other states all around the country that routinely issue tickets for failing to wear a facemask.

Jewish Tradition on Privacy

Rabbi Norman Lamm, the Dean of Yeshiva University once offered a priceless interpretation on the importance of privacy in Jewish tradition. Commenting upon the Mishnah's teaching, "Know what is above you—a seeing eye, a hearing ear, and a book in which all your deeds are recorded," Lamm explains:

> For moderns, who have become easy victims of both sinister designs of professionals of intrusion and the self-indulgence of the amateurs, that sage advice should be paraphrased to counsel us on how to avoid the breakdown of our privacy. "Know what is above you and below you, and in front of you, and in back of you—a seeing eye, a hearing ear—not of God, but of man's electronic

gadgets—and magnetic tape on which all your words are recorded." That awareness and that sensitivity are the moral and psychological background for successful legislation and for interpretations of the right to privacy by the courts. They will have been largely anticipated by Jewish law. . .[180]

Rabbi Lamm's advice is no less relevant in an age where authoritarian leadership threatens the civil liberties that have defined the United States since 1776.

Flash-forward to 2020; wherever you go, whether to the local corner market, or to the mall, the all-seeing eye of surveillance is monitors virtually every segment of modern life—whether you go the hospital, or to a school—even the sidewalks. Nobody ever thinks to question its legitimacy; it is a fact of today's modern technological age.

CHAPTER 35

"The most difficult struggle of all is the one within ourselves. Let us not get accustomed and adjusted to these conditions. The one who adjusts ceases to discriminate between good and evil. He becomes a slave in body and soul. Whatever may happen to you, remember always: Don't adjust! Revolt against the reality!

The dream of my life has risen to become fact. Self-defense in the ghetto will have been a reality. Jewish armed resistance and revenge are facts. I have been a witness to the magnificent, heroic fighting of Jewish men in battle."

Mordechai Anielewicz
Leader of the Warsaw Ghetto Uprising

Lessons from the Warsaw Ghetto Uprising

This week we observed Yom HaShoah—Holocaust Memorial Day, which corresponds to the start of the famous Warsaw Ghetto uprising. On April 19th, 1943, the Jews fought back and attempted to prevent the Nazis from deporting them to the concentration camps. This holiday helped the Jews realize that they cannot passively accept their fate. Their heroism is all the more incredible when we consider how the Jews lived in the Warsaw Ghetto. These Jews lived within the mall confines of the Warsaw ghetto were wholly unthinkable. About 400,000 people were crammed inside an area of 3.4 km. But they decided they would not passively walk to their deaths.

Brave people must fight for their freedom.

From the pages of the Bible, we read much about the power of civil-disobedience. In the early chapters of Exodus, two Egyptian women named Shiphra and Puah dared defy Pharaoh's murderous decree and genocide of the Hebrew babies, ordering them to drown the infants in the Nile River (Exod. 1:8-22).

When David fled King Saul's attempt to execute him, he fled to the priestly city of Nob. There, David was well-received with a meal; he left with the sword he used to kill the giant Goliath. Saul felt outraged that the High Priest Ahimelech assisted his enemy. The King orders his soldiers, "Make the rounds and kill the priests of the LORD, for they assisted David. They knew he was a fugitive and yet failed to inform me." But the king's servants refused to lift a hand to strike the priests of the LORD.[181]

Is it not any wonder why Jews have been leaders in a variety of social causes where we have defied the immoral policies of the State? Our tradition teaches us that moral people must decide to make a difference.

Consider the following illustration:

Snoopy, the loveable beagle in the Peanuts cartoon, once broke his leg. He received hundreds of letters to Snoopy expressing their sympathy. But Snoopy philosophized about his plight while he was perched on top of his doghouse. Looking at his huge white cast on his leg, he mused, "My body blames my foot for not being able to go places. My foot says it was my head's fault, and my head blamed my eyes...My eyes say my feet are clumsy, and my right foot says not to blame him for what my left foot did..." Snoopy then looks out at his reading audience and confesses, "I don't say anything because I don't want to get involved."

This story ought to serve as a homily for the dangers of remaining indifferent or apathetic in the face of great danger. Totalitarian regimes cannot tolerate dissidents willing to challenge and defy their status quo. Beyond that, dictators do their best to spy and tattle on their neighbors or friends. In the perfect Orwellian world, the eye of Big Brother is everywhere. But not even George Orwell could have imagined the genesis of "Little Brothers," i.e., ordinary citizens who serve the State and enforce its ruthless policies.

Celebrating the Heroes and Heroines of the Holocaust

As we remember the Holocaust, let us celebrate the heroes and heroines—ordinary people—who decided to stand up and make a difference. The brave French and Dutch people wore the yellow Star of David and demonstrated their solidarity with the Jewish people. The Danish people, led by King Christian X refused to cooperate with the Nazis and did not deport a single Jew living in their country.

Michael Bar Zohar's excellent book, "Beyond Hitler's Grasp" narrates perhaps the most amazing story of all about the righteous gentiles of WWII. During World War II, hundreds of thousands of Jews were deported from the Balkan states to labor and extermination camps in Germany and Poland. Bulgaria, with a Jewish population of only 50,000, sided with Hitler's government early on, its king having become convinced that only with German aid could he successfully press his territorial claims to land lost to Greece and Romania. Yet, in the face of constant German demands, Bulgaria's government refused to deport the nation's Jewish citizens. Instead, as the Bulgarian-born Israeli politician Michael Bar-Zohar writes in this fine contribution to Holocaust studies, "the Bulgarian Jews became the only Jewish community in the Nazi sphere of influence whose number increased during World War II."

Standing up to totalitarian regimes is so vital today for the majority of people living on this planet are governed by dictators who have no respect for human rights. Amazingly, Communist China and Iran has both won seats on the Human Rights Council of the United Nations—where it will play a key role in picking the world body's human rights investigators — including global monitors on freedom of speech, health, enforced disappearances, and arbitrary detention—in a move that has sparked a protest by international human rights activists.

Chinese Heroes of Conscience

To the Chinese people, l must urge them to look at the Warsaw Ghetto uprising as an inspiration. Although their country has no civil liberties to speak of, there are many heroes who dared to defy the Chinese dictatorship and regime.

Their stories need to be told. A courageous Chinese physician named Dr. Li Wenliang tried to warn his fellow medical practitioners about the situation in Wuhan. One day before Dr Li's death, lawyer Chen Qiushi released videos describing chaotic scenes in Wuhan hospitals with coronavirus victims lying in corridors were shared with an audience of more than 400,000 YouTube and 250,000 Twitter followers. He too went missing. His family was told the following day he was being held in medical quarantine at an undisclosed location. And not surprisingly, he was soon dead of the very plague he tried to warn about. Other physicians have also mysteriously disappeared or died because they tried to warn their people about the danger of this pandemic.

Consider the story of Fang Bin, a forty-year-old businessman who felt compelled to speak out against the government's attempt to suppress what really happened. What did Fang Bin do? He had the audacity to expose the truth about the coronavirus outbreak, but refused to remain silent. To get his message out to the Chinese people, he posted a video of people dying of the virus, along with scenes of body bags piling up outside the hospital. Over 200,000 saw this video before it was taken down. In another video he had posted, he urged the people, "Citizens resist, Hand back power to the people."[182] And then Fang Bin received an unexpected visit from the state police, dressed in hazmat suits took him away to medical quarantine.

Voices of conscience exists in China, who fight valiantly against a rogue and totalitarian regime, determined to suppress the truth no matter what the cost. Normally, Fang Bin is a shy person, but he could not believe what was happening in his city. He felt compelled to do something and protest. It is believed he and other dissidents are being tortured and forced to sign a confession that they were guilty of making mischief.[183]

Our media and politicians must hold the Communist government of China responsible. We cannot look the other way.

As we recall the bravery of people in the past who stood up against rogue regimes from the time of the Exodus and through the Holocaust, let us give support to the modern-day heroes of Communist China who continue to challenge its government by telling the truth of what really happened in China.

CHAPTER 36

"Political correctness is America's newest form of intolerance, and it is especially pernicious because it comes disguised as tolerance. It presents itself as fairness, yet attempts to restrict and control people's language with strict codes and rigid rules. I'm not sure that's the way to fight discrimination. I'm not sure silencing people or forcing them to alter their speech is the best method for solving problems that go much deeper than speech. Political correctness is Fascism pretending to be manners."

George Carlin

"Those who are determined to be 'offended' will discover a provocation somewhere. We cannot possibly adjust enough to please the fanatics, and it is degrading to make the attempt.

I'm very depressed how in this country you can be told "That's offensive" as though those two words constitute an argument."

Christopher Hitchens

Pandemics in an Age of Political Correctness

It is purported the Chinese have a saying: May you live in interesting times." Although it sounds like something you would expect to hear from Confucius, there is no source in Chinese literature that confirms the origin of this statement. Yet it seems to describe a people who seem to move from one crisis after another.

Yes, regardless of its origin—we are living in interesting times. This is especially evident when we examine the political arena.

When President Trump referred to the coronavirus, he referred to it several times as "the Chinese Virus." This led to a barrage of criticisms claiming the President was stigmatizing Chinese Americans and other Asian ethnicities in this country.

Looking at the comment, I thought it reaffirmed Rahm Emanuel's cynical remark: "Never let a good crisis go to waste." Actually, it was not Emanuel who originated this remark, it was Winston Churchill who first said, "Never let a good crisis go to waste." When seen through the lens of realpolitik, Nancy Pelosi's and Joe Biden's accusation that Trump is a racist is clever—especially in an election year.

Asian Americans in particular have long felt uneasy about their Asian status as perpetual foreigners, endowed with an "outsider status." As Jews, it is easy for us to relate to many of the negative stereotypes Asian Americans have endured. In communities across the United States, there is a genuine fear that the Chinese living among them need to be quarantined. They are blamed for the pandemic that originated in Wuhan, China. They are singled out—regardless whether the Chinese students living among them have been to China or not. As one critic expressed why we should refer to it as "COVID-19."

In another new story, California Democratic Sen. Kamala Harris introduced a resolution to prevent lawmakers from using the terms "Chinese Virus" and "Wuhan Virus" to reference the novel coronavirus that originated in Wuhan, China. Such designation is, "anti-Asian and racist."

The argument goes that this type of conflation between a place and an ethnicity can lead to the racist harassment of people who are perceived to be linked to disease. It also creates the illusion that they are safe because the disease affects the Other.

I get it.

As one friend of mine put it, "How would we like it if someone spoke about the "Jewish Virus?"

But we are living in interesting times; people have to be super sensitive not to say anything that may sound racist or come across as intolerant. Actually, naming pandemics after places is actually quite common.

One of the deadliest flu viruses that killed over 50 million people worldwide between 1918-1919 is known as the Spanish Flu. Nobody knows to this day where it originated, but since the Spanish media were the first to bring it to the world's attention, and the fact the Spanish king contracted it—the name stuck. Other possibilities include: France, China and Britain as the potential birthplace of the virus. In the United States, the first known case was reported at a military base in Kansas on March 11, 1918. On the other hand, the Spanish used to call it the "The French Flu."

By today's standards of political correctness that would be the equivalent to blaming the French!

This is pure silliness.

Nobody in Europe thought of hating the Spanish because of the "Spanish Flu," despite Spain's neutrality during World War I. No, nobody spoke ill of the Spaniards. Nor is there any evidence that the names of any of the other diseases inspired "racism or xenophobia" toward races or ethnicities commonly identified with such regions. Here is how other diseases were named through recent history: Middle East respiratory syndrome (MERS): A coronavirus outbreak, first reported in Saudi Arabia, in 2012-13; Ebola: a rare and deadly disease named for a river in Zaire, now DRC, in the 1970s. Guinea Worm: Known for centuries under various names, but named for the Gulf of Guinea, West Africa in the 17th century. West Nile virus: A mosquito-borne virus, named for West Nile region of Uganda where it was first isolated in the 1930s. German Measles: Rubella, named not for its origin, but because German physicians were first to identify it in the 19th century. Note that nobody blamed the Germans for introducing this disease. Marburg virus: An Ebola-type hemorrhagic virus named for a town in Germany where an outbreak occurred in a lab in the 1960s. Lassa fever: A hemorrhagic fever named for a town in Nigeria where it was identified in the 1960s. Hantavirus: Linked to rodents, some strains can be lethal to humans. Named for the Hantan river in South Korea, where it was isolated in the 1970s.

The comic and social commentator Bill Maher is no friend of the President or the Republican Party. Yet, even he felt compelled to admit that as the world is facing a global pandemic, this was "no time for political correctness."

> "'What if people hear Chinese virus and blame China?' The answer is we should blame China. We can't afford the luxury anymore of non-judginess towards a country with habits that kill millions of people," Maher thundered Friday in a monologue at the end of his HBO show "Real Time."

The longtime liberal said there were bigger "tainted fish to fry," saying if the sun exploded many of the online lefties would whine about the first person who called it a dwarf star. "Jesus f–king Christ can't we even have a pandemic without getting offended. When they name Lyme Disease after a town in Connecticut the locals didn't get all ticked off," Maher laughed. "It scares me that there are people out there who would rather die of the virus than call it by the wrong name," he said. "This isn't about vilifying a culture. This is about facts.[184]

When you look at from this perspective, calling COVID-19 "Chinese Coronavirus" is factually accurate. It originated in China. I suspect the Chinese government is doing its best to change the name of the pandemic for an altogether different but political reason. Simply put, it is not the Chinese people who are at fault here; nor are the descendants of Asian Americans to blame for the virus. But China's Communist Party rulers are the ones who are really to blame. Since its outbreak, the Communist Party did its best to cover their tracks. They acted totally irresponsibly in allowing thousands of Chinese nationals to travel throughout the world while obscuring the potential consequences. The Communist Party of China alone are the ones to blame.

Just as beauty is in the eye of the beholder, so too political correctness exists only in the eye of the beholder. Some scholars are debating whether to rename the Spanish Flu to the "1918 Influenza Pandemic," a clear reaction to the Chinese Virus/Coronavirus argument.

Most normal and reasonable people are not singling out the Asian people—except for those politicians who wish to evoke memories of past behavior as a political weapon in their endless will-to-power. As far as racists are concerned, there is little one can do to prevent them from espousing their animus towards Jews, Asians, Women, and others. Racists will always find a reason to justify their hatred of minorities.

Ironically, the same Chinese citizens who have suffered massively from the outbreak, have a better name for it: "Xi's Disease," after the Prime Minister, Xi Jinping.

Now that is the best name I have seen yet!

We would be far wiser to stay focused on ending the pandemic.

CHAPTER 37

"Nothing teaches us about the preciousness of the Creator as much as when we learn the emptiness of everything else."

Charles Spurgeon
Morning and Evening, Daily Readings

Should Worship be Considered an Essential Service?

The question has come up: Should churches and other houses of worship be considered, "an essential service"? The President recently announced that he would override governors who do not open up the houses of worship for services. Moreover, it has been argued by many that places of worship are no less "essential" than liquor stores or supermarkets. Both these places should not be reopened before religious services.[185] The President's position here is logical; by insisting that houses of worship be reopened, he is appealing to his evangelical supporters. Presidents in office often use the "bully pulpit" to promote an agenda that the President personally endorses.

I have wonder.

Had the President opposed the reopening places of worship, I suspect the opposition party would probably have clamored that they be open. Sometimes it does not matter what position a President takes when it involves a controversial issue. There will always be a host of critics, who consider the President a mortal enemy.

Still, the question concerning the status houses of worship being an "essential services" is a relevant question intelligent people ought to be able to discuss dispassionately and intellectually—without rancor, and without accusations of acrimony.

Confining people to their homes can also prove dangerous for one's health—and one's mental health. The number of suicides has experienced a dramatic increase since the coronavirus lockdown began. The stories we read in the papers are legion and tragic.

- In Germany, the state finance minister commits suicide because he was worried about a looming economic disaster.
- A British teenager takes her life because she was distressed by the social distancing measures, keeping her away from her friends.
- An Italian nurse who feared spreading the virus to other people succumbed to her depression and committed suicide.
- One county in Washington State reported a surge in suicide, mostly among men in their 30's and 40s.

Some studies claim that COVID-19 threatens tens of thousands of lives stemming from rampant unemployment, isolation and an uncertain future. This could well lead to 75,000 deaths from drug or alcohol abuse and suicide, new research suggests.[186]

Aside from the rise in suicide, many couples are feuding more with one another since the lockdown began. The absence of personal space can also take its toll on relationships. In general, suicides are a social problem that can be measured in numerous studies. This year, may well be a recent all-time high.[187] We are living at a time that is reminiscent of Charles Dickens' introduction in his "Tale of Two Cities":

> It was the best of times, it was the worst of times, it was the age of wisdom, it was the age of foolishness, it was the epoch of belief, it was the epoch of incredulity, it was the season of Light, it was the season of Darkness, it was the spring of hope, it was the winter of despair, we had everything before us, we had nothing before us, we were all going direct to Heaven, we were all going direct the other way – in short, the period was so far like the present period, that some of its noisiest authorities insisted on its being received, for good or for evil, in the superlative degree of comparison only.

Despite the great success we have seen in our economy, we are now witnessing hard times that challenge our ability to come back. When we consider the millions of unemployed people who are in lockdown, we must remember that this dilemma threatens the mental health and spirit of our nation. This situation makes a persuasive case for why the houses of worship play an "essential service" in keeping the mental and spiritual health of our nation healthy.

Learning from the Spanish Influenza

In my research over the last few months, I have read about the numerous pandemics that have occurred in recorded history. In the beginning of this book we touched upon the great pandemics of Late Antiquity. Now we shall attempt to compare the Coronavirus Pandemic to the most severe pandemic of the last 150 years—the Influenza Pandemic of 1918-1919, also known as the "Spanish Flu."

Historically, the influenza pandemic was caused by the H1N1 influenza It began in Spain, in the spring of 1918, and lasted till the summer of 1919. Over 500,000 people were infected—which was a third of the world's population. The number of deaths attributed to this pandemic have been estimated anywhere from 17 million to a 100 million people. Although it was not as deadly as some of the earlier pandemics, most notably, the Black Death, the Spanish Influenza is one record as one of the most dangerous pandemics of history.

As I began reading about the Spanish Influenza pandemic, I came across the response of religious institutions of that time. I wondered: Were places of worship opened throughout the pandemic? The answer I came across was enlightening. During the Spanish Influenza pandemic, churches and synagogues remained closed, along with cinemas, theaters, music halls, and Sunday schools. As with today, the closure of churches generated considerable controversy. Even the closing of schools also proved controversial. However, Catholic Church took a different approach. Churches remained open throughout the epidemic, and many religious ceremonies and processions were celebrated for the time being, which only exacerbated the spread of the disease. One historian observed:

> In the first days of October, for example, the Bishop of Zamora [Castile], concerned 'because the reigning evil is due to our sins and ingratitude', organized a week-long series of religious acts in honor of the Virgin Mary. Although the sanitary officials protested and tried to prevent people crowding into churches, it was to no avail.

> At the end, the Bishop congratulated himself on the large
> attendance "as one of the most significant victories
> Catholicism has obtained." Zamora was the capital that
> registered the highest mortality during the epidemic. But
> although some religious authorities can be accused of
> unjustified ignorance during the epidemic, it must not be
> forgotten that among the thousands of anonymous heroes
> and heroines who put their lives in danger so that the sick
> could have care and assistance, there were many nuns and
> priests.[188]

In Philadelphia, all churches, schools, theaters were closed. Even public funerals were prohibited. Curiously, only one public gathering place was allowed to remain open: the saloon. It is odd that today, the liquor stores are considered an essential service for people.

And while there are obvious similarities to the coronavirus, let us make this point perfectly clear: the coronavirus was mild when compared to the dangers of the Spanish Influenza. Unlike the coronavirus, the Influenza pandemic geometrically exploded, as the historian John Barry noted, "In ten days—ten days! —the epidemic had exploded from a few hundred civilian cases and one or two deaths a day to hundreds of thousands ill and hundreds of deaths each day." Furthermore:

> Federal, municipal, and state courts closed. Giant placards
> everywhere warned the public to avoid crowds and use
> handkerchiefs when sneezing or coughing. Other placards
> read "Spitting equals death." People who spat on the street
> were arrested—sixty in a single day. The newspapers
> reported the arrests—even while continuing to minimize
> the epidemic. Physicians were themselves dying, three one
> day, two another, four the next. The newspapers reported
> those deaths—on inside pages with other obituaries—even
> while continuing to minimize the epidemic. Health and
> city workers wore masks constantly.[189]

Barry goes on to say that every city in the United States closed down its churches and places of worship. But beyond that:

It was as if the virus were a hunter. It was hunting mankind. It found man in the cities easily, but it was not satisfied. It followed him into towns, then villages, then individual homes. It searched for him in the most distant corners of the earth. It hunted him in the forests, tracked him into jungles, pursued him onto the ice. And in those most distant corners of the earth, in those places so inhospitable that they barely allowed man to live, in those places where man was almost wholly innocent of civilization, man was not safer from the virus. He was more vulnerable. . .

When we think about worship as an "essential service," we might be wise to remember the great pandemics of the past. When we look at it from that perspective, the overreaction to the coronavirus begins to make more sense.

However, one could counter by saying that the coronavirus is bad, but it cannot begin to compare to the great pandemics of the last 200 years.

And maybe they might be right.

In defense of the position that worship is an essential service, we could counter that congregations are communities that provide love and support to the young and old alike. Worship centers are often in the front lines when it comes to ministering to those who are sick and suffering.

If people can maintain proper social- distancing in Walmart or the local liquor store, they can't they act that way in a house of worship? Sometimes I think our leaders treat their people as if they were immature children—incapable of following the social-distancing guidelines. Threatening worshipers with fines and incarceration is lame—especially when considering the number of dangerous felons who have been released to roam the streets for their next target.

Perhaps the "essential services" argument has merit.

The State of Israel recently opened up synagogues on the condition that the worshipers observe the social-distancing. Those who object to the opening up of houses of worship claim the danger of contagion has not fully abated in all the states.

Re-Inventing Worship

Regardless where one stands on the issue, new challenges often force us to reinterpret our faith. Jewish tradition has always possessed the ability to reinvent itself since biblical times. The only thing etched in stone is the Ten Commandments—and everything else is negotiable! Community worship has always been one of the most important ways people show solidarity with one another. Yet, with the social-distancing rules, most places of worship that I am familiar with are reluctant to hold services for fear of contagion.

Enter the Internet and livestreaming. And admittedly, I have noticed that in some ways we have attracted larger crowds from all over the country who wish to participate in our services. But such a concept was unknown to many members of the clergy like myself. This is a whole new experience. To paraphrase Captain Kirk, "We have boldly gone to places no other synagogue has gone before." Livestreaming a service is fine and good, but there is one important question every faith community ought to address.

Is this how services will be conducted in the future once we return to normalcy? `

I am reminded of an old story. On the Eve of Yom Kippur, a man came to his rabbi and asked him the following question, "I have a quandary. Tonight, is the first night of the World Series, but it is also the night of Yom Kippur. What should I do?" Feeling annoyed, the Rabbi quipped, "Have you ever heard of a VCR?" The congregant replied, "Oh thank you Rabbi, I will videotape the Kol Nidre Services!" There is a real danger if our services become a video facsimile of a real service. Live participation grabs the worshiper in a way that livestreaming cannot.

As the coronavirus continues to abate, the pathway to resuming services in the faith communities will have to move incrementally. If history has taught us anything, rash behavior advocated by leaders of the faith community does not serve it well.

NOTES

[1] BT Sanhedrin 98a and 98b.

[2] Epictetus: *Discourses and Selected Writings* (New York: Penguin Books, 2000) *On Providence* I:6:33-34.

[3] III.24·20f, 5; IVS·27)·

[4] In Judaism, the model of the Exodus because the foundation of the social laws governing Israelite society. The memories of their collective travails at the hand of a powerful and ruthless Egyptian leadership taught them how authoritarian power regarded the Israelites as a mere commodity, to be used, swapped, and disposed at will. Every moral law that followed in the other books of the Tanakh serves to highlight the dignity and sacredness of human life—regardless of the social status of the individual.

[5] Michael B. A. Oldstone, *Viruses, Plagues, and History: Past, Present, and Future* (New York: Oxford University Press, 2010), p. 148. Comp. See Y. Furuse, A. Suzuki and H. Oshitani, "Origin of the Measles Virus: Divergence from Rinderpest Virus Between the 11th and 12th Centuries," Virology 7 (2010), pp. 52–55.

[6] Manolis J. Papagrigorakis, Christos Yapijakis, and Philippos N.Synodinos, 'Typhoid Fever Epidemic in Ancient Athens,' in Didier Raoult, Michel Drancourt, Paleomicrobiology: Past Human Infections, *Springer Science & Business Media,* 2008 pp. 161–173.

[7] Edwin G. Pulleyblank points out "One such source of information would have been the so- called embassy from the king of Da Qin, Andun t-uan twan, that reached the Han court by sea in 166 C.E. Since the name Andun can be plausibly identified either with the emperor Antoninus Pius (reg. 138-161) or his successor Marcus Aurelius Antoninus (reg. 161-180)." See Edwin G. Pulleyblank, (1999). "The Roman Empire as Known to Han China". *Journal of the American Oriental Society.* 119 (1), 1999, p. 78.

[8] Rafe de Crespigny, (2007). *A Biographical Dictionary of Later Han to the Three Kingdoms--23–220 AD* (Leiden: Koninklijke Brill, 2007), p. 600, Comp. Edwin G. Pulleyblank, (1999). "The Roman Empire as Known to Han China". *Journal of the American Oriental Society.* 119 (1), 1999, pp. 71–79. John E. Hill, *Through the Jade Gate to Rome: A Study of the Silk Routes during the Later Han Dynasty, First to Second Centuries* CE. BookSurge, 2009), p. 27

[9] William H. McNeill, *Plagues and Peoples* (Garden City, NY: Anchor Press, 1976), p. 121.

[10] Julius Capitolinus, Verus in G. P. Goold (Ed.), D. Magie (Trans.), *The Scriptores Historiae Augustae: Translation* (Cambridge, MA; London: Harvard University Press, 1921). Vol. 1, p. 223.

[11] See J. F. Gilliam, "The Plague under Marcus Aurelius," *American Journal of Philology* 82 (1961), p. 249.

[12] *Meditations* 4:49.

[13] *Meditations,* 9:2.

[14] *Meditations* Book 5:14.

[15] Donald Robertson, *How to Think Like A Roman Emperor* (New York: St. Martin Press, 2019), 18-19.

[16] The Roman historian Tacitus disapproved of Jewish customs of which he declares "to be sinister and abominable. Hate and enmity towards other people are the counterpart to the strong solidarity which the Jews display towards one another. Their proselytes follow the same course and are imbued with contempt for the gods and indifference to their country and families." See M. Stern, *Greek and Latin Authors on Jews and Judaism Volume Two: From Tacitus to Simplicius* (Jerusalem: Publications of the Israel Academy of Sciences, 1980), p. 2.

[17] The Roman statesman and historian Dio Cassius in his voluminous works on Roman history record that around 189 C.E., a pestilence occurred during Commodus' reign in which 2,000 persons often died in Rome in a single day (*Dio Cassius* 72.14.3-4).

[18] "Pontius of Carthage, *The Life and Passion of Cyprian*"Transl. Ernest Wallis, c. 1885 published in The Ante-Nicene Fathers: The Writings of the Fathers of the Third Century, Volume 5, p. 270.

[19] Gary Ferngren, "A New Era in Roman Healthcare: How the Early Church Transformed the Roman Empire's Treatment of Its Sick" *Christian History Magazine: Healthcare and Hospitals in the Mission of the Church*, (no. 101), 11–12.

[20] Mekhilta Beshalach Vayassa 6:5; BT Berachoth 33a.

[21] Preuss, Julius and Fred Rosner (trans.). *Biblical and Talmudic Medicine* (New York: Jason Aronson Inc. 1978, 1993), p. 163.

[22] JT Ta'anit 3:5, I.1.

[23] BT Ta'anit 21b.

[24] See Aaron Amit, "The Death of Rabbi Akiva's Disciples: A Literary History" *Journal of Jewish Studies,* vol. lvi, no. 2, autumn 2005, pp. 265-284.

[25] Eugene Borowitz, *Reform Judaism Today,* Book one. *Reform in the Process of Change* (New York: Behrman House, 1978), 65.

[26] Elie Wiesel, *The Town Beyond the Wall, op. cit.,* 190.

[27] https://theprint.in/opinion/mecca-to-vatican-covid-19-proves-when-human-beings-are-in-peril-gods-flee-first/382851/

[28] A. I. Kook, B. Z. Bokser, (Trans.) *Abraham Isaac Kook-: The Lights of Penitence, The Moral Principles, Lights of Holiness, Essays, Letters, and Poems.* (Mahwah, NJ: Paulist Press, 1978), pp. 264-265.

[29] Cited by Louis Jacobs, *Faith* (New York: Basic Books, 1968), p. 134.

[30] Martin Buber and Maurice Friedman (ed.), *Martin Buber and the Human Sciences* (Albany, NY: State University of New York Press, 1996), p. 8.

[31] Blaise Pascal *Pensées* ("Thoughts") No. 233.

[32] Richard Dawkins, *The God Delusion* (London: Bantam Press, 2006), p. 104.

[33] Voltaire had already articulated this point in his *Candide* (chapter 6) where pundits of his time thought the Lisbon earthquake was a divine punishment for human sins—the Portuguese Inquisition/

[34] *Jean-Jacques Rousseau* and Christopher Kelly Roger D. Masters, and Peter G. Stillman (Editors) *The Confessions and Correspondence, Including the Letters to Malesherbes (*Hanover: University Press of New England, 1995), p. 360.

[35] *Voltaire's Correspondence*, vol. 30 (Geneva: Institute et Musee Voltaire, 1958), quoted in *Discovering the Western Past: A Look at the Evidence: Since 1500* Merry E. Wiesner, Julius R. Ruff, and William Bruce Wheeler (Boston, Ma: Houghton Mifflin Company, 2003), pp. 102-115.

[36] Cited from Roger D. Masters, *The Political Philosophy of Rousseau* (Princeton: Princeton University Press,1968), p. 68

[37] Stephen Sobriner, *What really happened in San Francisco in the earthquake of 1906. 100th Anniversary 1906* San Francisco Earthquake Conference, 2006

[38] https://www.nytimes.com/2015/05/24/us/decade-after-katrina-pointing-finger-more-firmly-at-army-corps.html

[39] https://govinfo.library.unt.edu/katrina/levees.pdf

[40] *Summa* 2, Q. 85, A. 6.

[41] Translated by Jaroslav Jan Pelikan, *The Christian Tradition: A History of the Development of Doctrine, Vol. 1 The Emergence of the Catholic Tradition* (100-600) (Chicago: Chicago University Press, 1971), 315. *Cf. Anti-Pelagian Writings* 11:23 published in Vol. V of the *Early Church Fathers Nicene–Post/Nicene Part* I (New York: T. & T. Clark, 1887).

[42] Translated by Jaroslav Jan Pelikan, *The Christian Tradition: A History of the Development of Doctrine, Vol. 1 The Emergence of the Catholic Tradition* (100-600) (Chicago: Chicago University Press, 1971), 315. *Cf. Anti-Pelagian Writings* 11:23 published in Vol. V of the *Early Church Fathers Nicene–Post/Nicene Part* I (New York: T. & T. Clark, 1887).

[43] NT John, 9:1–12,

[44] Robert Funk and Roy Hoover, *The Jesus Seminar: The Search for the Authentic Words of Jesus* (San Francisco: Harper Collins, 1993), pp. 432-433.

[45] For a comprehensive list of examples, see Elizabeth Wayland Barber and Paul T. Barber's *When They Severed Earth from Sky: How the Human Mind Shapes Myth* (Princeton, N.J.: Princeton UP, 2004).

[46] Ibid., 6-7.

[47] *Guide* 2:48.

[48] See Joshua Lederberg, "Pandemic is a Natural Evolutionary Phenomenon" in *Social Research*, Vol. 55, No. 3, "In Time of Plague" (AUTUMN 1988), pp. 343-359, especially p. 348.

[49] Peter Kropotkin, *Mutual Aid: A Factor of Evolution* (New York: McClure Phillips & Co., 1902), p. 293

[50] Ibid., p. 12.

[51] For a comprehensive list of examples, see Elizabeth Wayland Barber and Paul T. Barber's *When They Severed Earth from Sky: How the Human Mind Shapes Myth* (Princeton, N.J.: Princeton UP, 2004).

[52] http://www.nbcnews.com/id/12358223/ns/health-infectious_diseases/t/skeptics-warn-bird-flu-fears-are-overblown/#.XqdDYGhKiUk

[53] https://www.cidrap.umn.edu/news-perspective/2020/01/officials-say-most-americans-not-risk-coronavirus

[54]https://www.politico.com/news/magazine/2020/04/11/america-two-decade-failure-prepare-coronavirus-179574

Comp. https://billingsgazette.com/news/state-and-regional/wyoming/leavitt-urges-people-institutions-to-take-precaution-against-flu/article_f9fc1a64-9f6e-5b86-9591-ce03f1bd4665.html

[55] https://www.aei.org/op-eds/we-were-caught-unprepared-by-a-pandemic-9-11-the-failures-began-long-before-trump/

[56.]Michael Shevack & Jack Bemporad, *Stupid Ways, Smart Ways to Think About God.* (Liguri, Miss., 1993) p 18.

[57.]Martin Buber, *Meetings* (Open Court, Laselle, Ill. 1973) pp. 52-53.

[58] Martin Buber, Meetings (Open Court, Laselle, Ill. 1973) pp. 52-53. [iii] In her psychological study, *The Birth of the Living God,* Ana-Maria Rizzuto argued a child's concept of God is determined by a variety of factors, e.g., parents, family, siblings, and other significant people) or circumstances (e.g., a lightning-storm or an earthquake etc.). Prevailing conditions will alter the person's God representation at any given time. Children project their internal parent images (both good and bad) onto their God-concept. If her father sexually abuses her, then the image of God as Father may have a negative meaning in her life. Rizzuto writes, "Reshaping, rethinking, and endless rumination, fantasies, and defensive maneuvers, will come to help the child in his difficult task. This second birth of God may decide the conscious religious future of the child. This is the critical moment for those interested in catechesis. If they want to understand the progress of an individual child, they must have some knowledge of the private God the child brings with him. No child arrives at the 'house of God' without his pet God under his arm" (Ibid, p.8). Similar to Rizzuto, Edward Stein writes, "God is projected father (psychologically), and... this basis of trust is the sustaining, binding meaning that makes religion crucial to men.... It is perfectly possible that the way in which the Ground of Being makes himself known, revealed himself, was by making man biologically dependent upon his human parents and prone to such projections." Edward Stein, *Guilt: Theory and Therapy (*Philadelphia: Westminster Press, 1968), 139.

[59] William James, *The Will to Believe: And Other Essays in Popular Philosophy* (New York, London: Longmans Green and Co. New York, 1907), p. 246.

[60] https://www.thetimesnews.com/zz/lifestyle/20200402/is-coronavirus-gods-will-jewish-christian-and-muslim-leaders-debate-tough-questions-amid-pandemic

[61] Billy Prewitt, *The Coronavirus in Biblical Prophecy (Self-published),* p. 5.

[62] https://www.nytimes.com/2020/03/14/opinion/coronavirus-church-close.html

[63] BT Ta'anit 21b, op. cit., p. 152.

[64] https://www.msn.com/en-us/news/world/pope-coronavirus-pandemic-could-be-natures-response-to-climate-crisis/ar-BB12jOw8?ocid=sf2

[65] 28 J. Hanska, *Strategies of Sanity and Survival*, Chapter Three. Compare with R. Horrox, The Black Death, 111–120.

[66] Justin Stearns, "New Directions in the Study of Religious Responses to the Black Death" *History Compass* 7 (2009): 1–13,

[67] Zohar, Genesis 88a

[68] Ravindra Varma, *Spiritual Perceptions of Mahatma Gandhi* (New Delhi: Rupa Publications, 2006), p. 122.

[69] The participial form of which is the common word for "enemy."

[70] According to the midrashic literature, Job actively took up the cause of the widows and orphans. He was accustomed to visiting the sick—regardless of whether they were wealthy or poor. Job used to bring a physician with him and offered consolation when a death occurred in their homes. He even went out of his way to provide financial support to those who were hungry. He encouraged the hopeless to place their trust in the LORD, and prayed for a suffering family when someone got ill. According to one legend, Job provided sustenance to a bereaved family continuously, thus earning the blessings of all who benefited from his countless acts of kindness. See *Leket Midrashim* , 6b–7a.

[71] In the Tanakh, the word *śaṭan,* means, "adversary" or "obstructer." Originally, *śaṭan* was originally a common noun (e.g., 2 Sam. 19:22). Over time, it came to refer to an angelic being who acts as God's instigator (1 Chron. 21:1), and prosecuting attorney (Job 1–2). During the Intertestamental period Satan becomes an adversarial to seeks to thwart God at every opportunity.

[72] "Devil" derives from Late Latin diabolus (also the source of Italian diavolo, French diable, Spanish diablo; German Teufel is Old High German tiufal, from Latin via Gothic *diabaulus*). In Jewish and Christian the term "the Devil, Satan," conveyed "accuser," and "slanderer."

[73] The term is associated with "complaint," "calumniation," "accusation," and "slander." The word "devil," derives from the verb δια-βάλλω "accuse") which is derived from *dia*, "through," and *bollen*, "thrown apart," or to "cast asunder," or "to divide." Thus, the name "Devil" aptly refers to the Chief Adversary, whose task is to create obstacles between humankind and its Creator. In many ways, διάβολος is the exact opposite of the Greek word for symbol—σύμβολον (*sýmbolon*= συν- [*sym*-] meaning "together" and βολή [*bolé*], "throw"; hence, "to throw together"). In a theological context, the symbolic functions to unite both spirit and matter. Jung and others have pointed out that the science of etymology deals with the unconscious side of language and often provides valuable psychological insights with respect to faith development.

[74] Mother Teresa and Brian Kolodiejchuk, *Mother Teresa: Come Be My Light* (New York: Image, 2009), 187.

[75] According to some rabbinic legends, Job served as one of three advisors to Pharaoh, who counseled the ruler on what to do with the Israelites. One midrash says that Job came from Aram, and he told Pharaoh that he was free to do whatever he felt like doing—it made no difference to him. Louis Ginzburg, *Legends of the Jews*, 468.

[76] Rashi explains that the Book of Job teaches us two important things: (1) that we may learn from it a response to those who condemn God's attribute of justice (2) Job also serves to instruct us that no person ought to be blamed for words that he utters because of personal pain (Rashi's commentary to BT *Bava Batra* 15a). Elsewhere, Rashi adds on the verse "For you did not comfort me with your 'verbal defense' as did my servant, Job" (Job 42:7). His only sin consisted of saying, "He destroys both the innocent with the wicked..." (Job 9:23). And whatever else Job said came from his suffering which weighed heavily upon him and forced him to speak thusly. But *you* [the friends], on the other hand, were wrongful to accuse him of being wicked. In the end, it was you who were silent and defeated before him. Instead of attacking him, you should have comforted him as Elihu did. *As if Job didn't have enough suffering, you added guilt to your sins by angering him.*

[77] BT *Ta'anit* 23a; BT *Bava Bathra* 16a.

[78] Cited from Richard C. Trench, "On the Study of Words," 1852, cited from http://www.etymonline.com/index.php?term=schadenfreude.

[79] Aristotle, *Nicomachean Ethics* 1107a8–27.

[80] See *Ramban's Commentary* on Leviticus 19:18. There he stresses the biblical imperative stresses that one must also rejoice with the success of one's neighbor and not begrudge the Other his shared of happiness and success.

[81] Renée Girard, *Job: The Victim of his People* (Palo Alto: Stanford University Press, 1987). In *Things Hidden Since the Foundation of the World,* René Girard discusses the implications of his theories in relationship to the Bible and the NT. According to Girard, the Gospel narratives describe a ritual murder when the mob demanded that the victim-god be lynched for all to see. This ritual murder later came to be commemorated by Christians who symbolically reenact the ritual sacrifice through a ceremony known as the Eucharist.

[34] James Frazer the *Golden Bough*, Chapter 58 Human Scapegoats in Classical Antiquity Section 1: The Human Scapegoat in Ancient Rome; Section II The Human Scapegoat in Ancient Greece (pp. 574-77).

[82] https://theintercept.com/2020/03/24/trump-cabinet-bible-studies-coronavirus/

[83] Sam Keen, *Faces of the Enemy: Reflections of the Hostile Imagination* (San Francisco, Harpercollins,1986), 12-13.

[84] Emmanuel Lévinas, *De l'existence à l'existant* (Paris: Vrin, 1986), 139.

[85] Maimonides, *Guide* 3:22

[86] *Guide* 3:22.

[87] Abraham Isaac Kook, op. cit., p. 171.

[88] Colette Strat, *Philosophy in the Middle Ages* (Cambridge: Cambridge University Press, 1993), 363-364

[89] M. H. Pope, *Job: Introduction, translation, and notes* (New Haven; London: Yale University Press, 2008), p. 350.

[90] See Ramban's commentary.

[91] Cf. Genesis 1:4, 10, 12, 18, 21, 25, 31.

[92] Gen. Rabbah 9:12; *Meshekh Hokhmah* notes in a homiletical vein, the word טוב (*ṭôb* = "good") is purposely missing from the creation of humankind, for humankind's goodness involves a moral choice that must be consciously and freely made (see notes on Gen. 1:26 regarding Pelagius's attack on Augustine regarding this particular point).

[93] M. Kalisch pointed out, "The biblical attitude toward the leper was by no means unique. Other Semitic and Oriental peoples excluded the leper from their society. Among the Persians, the Zoroastrians forbade the leper to enter a city; he was to have no social intercourse with his fellow citizens. If he happened to be a foreigner, the authorities expelled him from their country. Among the medieval Christians, a priest would hold up his crucifix and demand that the lepers dress up in a black garment and performed for him a service for the dead. When the leper was taken to the sequestered house, the priest would throw dirt on the leper's feet, and warned him he was never to appear without his black garment and be barefooted. Nor could he approach a well or field of wheat; if he owned property, he could not sell it to anyone; nor could he inherit. For all practical purposes, the leper was like a 'walking dead man.'"

[94] Steinsaltz Talmud on Tractate Bava Kama 61b.

[95] See Igrot Rabbi Akiva Eiger (Makhon Da'at Sofer, 5754), letters 71-73.

and Natan Gestetner, Pesakim ve-Takanot Rabbi Akiva Eiger (Jerusalem, 5731), letter 20, 70ff.

[96] https://nypost.com/2020/03/20/todays-coronavirus-update-trump-closes-borders-new-york-locks-down/

[97] (Source: https://www.thewanderingrv.com/car-accident-statistics/)

[98] https://www.creators.com/read/dennis-prager

[99] Ecclesiastes 3:1–8.

[100] Henri Nouwen, *Bread for the Journey: A Daybook of Wisdom and Faith* (New York: Harper, 1989), p. 43.

[101] Henri Nouwen, *Ibid.* p. 44.

[102] Viktor E. Frankl, *Man's Search for Meaning* (Boston: Beacon Press, 2006), p. 113.

[103] https://www.jpost.com/Israel-News/Chief-Rabbi-of-Israel-Due-to-Coronavirus-stop-kissing-the-mezuzah-619753

[104] When Rabbi Menachem Mendel Schneerson was alive leading the Lubavitcher Hassidic movement, he created controversy over a terrible terrorist attack in the northern border town own of Ma'alot on May 15st, 1974. Tens of Jewish children were cruelly murdered in their school. At the time, the Schneerson advised that the school check its *mezuzot*, and a number were found not to be Kosher. The number of *mezuzot* that were found to be *pasul* [invalidated] was the same as the number of children who were murdered. See *Beis Moshiach* Issue 788, "Moshiach and Ge'ula," pp. 41-42.

[105] https://www.beliefnet.com/faiths/2005/06/kabbalah-faqs.aspx

[106] MT *Hilkhot Avodat Kochavim* 11:12. Cf. Maimonides was opposed to the use of amulets. Cf. *Guide* 1:61.

[107] Scott, Susan, and C. J. Duncan, *Biology of Plagues: Evidence from Historical Populations.* (New York: Cambridge University Press, 2001).

[108] Sherwin Nuland, *The Doctors' Plague: Germs, Childbed Fever, and the Strange Story of Ignac Semmelweis* (New York: W. W. Norton & Company; Reprint edition, 2004).

[109] *Taharoth*, 1, 5.

[110] Kelim, 1.

[111] Yadaim 3:1,

[112] https://hub.jhu.edu/2020/03/20/sars-cov-2-survive-on-surfaces/

[113] BT Bava Kama 23b.

[114] Jean-Paul Sartre, *Existentialism is a Humanism* (New Haven: Yale University Press, 1946, repr. 2007), p. 29.

[115] https://newstalk1130.iheart.com/featured/common-sense-central/content/2020-03-29-how-china-infected-the-world/

[116] https://www.japantimes.co.jp/news/2020/03/27/asia-pacific/science-health-asia-pacific/china-corona-toll/#.XokimIhKiUk ; https://foreignpolicy.com/2020/04/01/china-coronavirus-official-figures-underreporting-pandemic-response-xi-jinping/

[117] https://www.nytimes.com/2020/04/04/us/coronavirus-china-travel-restrictions.html

[118] https://www.nytimes.com/interactive/2020/04/13/technology/coronavirus-doctor-whistleblower-weibo.html

[119] See https://www.nytimes.com/2020/02/14/business/wuhan-coronavirus-journalists.html ; https://www.dailymail.co.uk/news/article-8233203/Chinas-disappeared-happened-dared-speak-coronavirus.html?ito=facebook_share_article-top&fbclid=IwAR2Bl4wopeYz1uXD5pCCClCLt7wFYUjr5pŁFHXpGyNTSrcLlEbEKRpw4SqF,

[120] https://www.nytimes.com/2020/03/13/business/masks-china-coronavirus.html

[121] https://www.dailymail.co.uk/news/article-8160931/Spain-returns-faulty-coronavirus-testing-kits-bought-Chinese-company.html?fbclid=IwAR1RDix6ejgC2qM_XO_gGaLJxIxCbodsLh_F4XNohTUHJ97qkIdVMeV_CQ8

[122] https://fortune.com/2020/04/14/coronavirus-face-masks-n95-respirators-price-gouging-ppe-medical-supplies-covid-19/

[123] https://www.cnn.com/2020/04/12/asia/china-coronavirus-research-restrictions-intl-hnk/index.html?utm_term=link&utm_content=2020-04-12T18%3A06%3A56&utm_source=fbCNN&utm_medium=social&fbclid=IwAR2u0MqEcFce8nHq2smjVkQIBSrDhCXNbP_G38TdOwpPfWftdAIe36Abfv4

[124] https://www.foxnews.com/world/china-arrested-hundreds-speaking-out-coronavirus?fbclid=IwAR0rEYJ0lc7hszDNv4AUbKlDGIxX_852YCxWNw5_7HugNOXsj8XBWk_SXUQ

[125] — Sigmund Freud, The Future of an Illusion

[126] JT Sotah 3:4, f. 19a, line 13.

[127] http://www.rationalistjudaism.com/2020/04/daas-torah-on-how-to-avoid-getting.html?spref=fb&fbclid=IwAR25__gSLj-qS2F3sSHsa510jiu0W4q51IZCTwmWgMuk6cRfqoP1coxq_mE

[128] Rabbi Tzvi Fishman Tzvi, *The Corona Bible: Coronavirus and Faith in Troubled Times* (Seattle: Kindle, 2020), p. 1.

[129] B*T Sanhedrin* 97a.

[130] *Antiquities*, xx. 5, § 1.

[131] *Antiquities*, xx. 5, § 1.

[132] BT Sanhedrin 98a.

[133] Josephus, *Wars of the Jews*. ii. 17, § 9).

[134] JT Ta'anit 4:7; Lam. R. to Lam. 2:2), and JT Hagigah 2:21-22.

[135] JT. Ta'anit 4:8, 68d. According to Rav Hai Gaon (938-1038), R. Akiba's disciples died in the failed Bar Kochba revolution against Rome (132-135 C.E.).

[136] *Avoth d'Rabbi Nathan* 31

137 *Mishpetei Uziel, Orach Chaim,* 19; *Hilchot Rabata LeShabbat.a* Comp. Rabbi Tzvi Pesach Frank, *Kol Torah,* (5694);

[138] Mishnah: Bava Kama 8:1; cf. BT Bava Kama 83b-85b.

[139] BT Sanhedrin 71a); cf. 1 Sam. 15:1-11; comp. 2 Sam.1-9.

[140] https://www.nytimes.com/2020/03/30/world/middleeast/coronavirus-israel-cases-orthodox.html

[141] https://www.the-daily-record.com/news/20200320/amish-taking-coronavirus-seriously-health-officials-say

[142] Carl Gustav Jung and Aniela Jaffe (trans.) *Memories, Dreams and Reflections* (New York: Vintage Books, 1961, 1989), p. 252.

[143] Carl Gustav *Jung, Man and his Symbols* (New York: Doubleday, 1964), p. 90.

[144] https://www.kupat.org/Project/166?source=105

[145] http://www.rationalistjudaism.com/2016/12/the-manipulative-lies-of-kupat-hair.html

[146] OH Hilkhot Tefilah 55:15.

[147] יְרוּבַּעַל בְּדוֹרוֹ כְּמֹשֶׁה בְּדוֹרוֹ; בְּדָן בְּדוֹרוֹ כְּאַהֲרֹן בְּדוֹרוֹ; יִפְתָּח בְּדוֹרוֹ כִּשְׁמוּאֵל בְּדוֹרוֹ. לְלַמֶּדְךָ שֶׁאֲפִילּוּ קַל שֶׁבַּקַּלִּין וְנִתְמַנָּה פַּרְנָס עַל הַצִּבּוּר הֲרֵי הוּא כְאַבִּיר שֶׁבָּאַבִּירִים

[148] Rosh Hashanah 25b.

[149] Judges. 11:34-35.

[150] שפה פנימית - ר"ל דמקום סגירת הדלת הוי כלחוץ אף שעכשיו היה הפתח פתוח ועיין במ"א שכתב שיש שחולקין ע"ז ומכריע כמותם דמקום זה הוי כלפנים ועיין בספר אבן העוזר שפסק ג"כ בפשיטות דהיכא דהמעיוט עומדים תוך המקום הזה מצטרפים לעשרה דלא גרע מחצר קטנה שנפרצה לגדולה המבואר בסט"ז וכן משמע מביאור הגר"א

[151] דאף דיש הפסק מחיצה ביניהם כיון דמראה להם פניו דומה למה שמבואר לקמן בסימן קצ"ה לענין זימון דאם מקצתן רואין אלו את אלו דמצטרפין וא"כ לפ"ז פשוט העומדים בעזרת נשים ובמחיצה המפסקת יש חלון ומראה להם פניו משם מצטרף עמהם לעשרה וכ"ש דאם יש בלעדו עשרה נחשב תפלה בצבור עי"ז ואעפ"כ יותר טוב אם בנקל הוא לו לירד לבהכ"נ שירד דיש מהאחרונים שחולקין על עיקר הדין וסוברין דעניינו אינו דומה כלל לזימון

[152] *Journal of Halacha & Contemporary Society,* No. XXI - Spring 91 - Pesach 5751. For the online edition of this study, see: http://www.daat.ac.il/daat/english/journal/broyde_1.htm

[153] Berachoth 7:5; see BT Berachoth 50a.

[154] According to R. Yechiel Mikal Epstein's Aruch HaShulchan (OH 55:20), God is always present whenever ten Jews gather to pray. He touches upon a theme reminiscent of William Blake's woodcarvings of Job, where the face of Job and the face of God (so to speak) mirror one another.

[155] *The Commentary of Rabbi David Kimchi* on 2 Kings 23:10.

[156] The Greek historian Diodorus Siculus describes how common was the practice of child sacrifice in Phoenicia and her colonies (xx. 14). He notes that in one siege, the Carthaginians sacrificed 200 boys to Kronos. Other Greek and Roman authors wrote extensively about the practice of sacrificing children as burnt offerings in Phoenicia and the Punic colonies of N. Africa, and especially in the ruins of the Phoenician city of Carthage, located in North Africa. It is there archaeologists discovered the remains of hundreds of children sacrificed to the goddess Tanit and the god Baal-Hammon have been excavated (L. E. Stager and S. R. Wolff, *BAR* 10/1 [1984] 31–51). Other Phoenician sanctuaries or sacrificial precincts have been discovered on Sicily and Sardinia, one which contains a cremation pit full of burnt matter (cf. G. Moore, "The Image of Moloch," in *JBL,* 1897, xvi. 161; et seq.; M. J. Lagrange; Donald Harden, *The Phoenicians,* London: Thames & Hudson, 1962, pp. 94–104; A. R. W. Green, *The Role of Human Sacrifice in the Ancient Near East* [Missoula, MT: Scholars Press. 1975] esp. 173–87); W. F. Albright, *YHWH and the Gods of Canaan,* Garden City: Doubleday, 1968, pp. 234–244).

[157] https://www.timesofisrael.com/state-mandated-cremation-a-posthumous-mitzvah-says-leading-orthodox-rabbi/

[158] R, Ḳimchi's Com. *ad loc;* comp. השרשים ס"ע, (*s.v.* מסרף).

[159] See R. Solomon b. Adret, Responsum No. 369; Moses Isserles to Yoreh De'ah, 363, 2). Responsa She'vut Yaakov 2:97. See also Chatam Sofer, YD 2:334.

[160] Midrash Wayasha' cited in Jellinek, "Bet ha-Midrash," 1:37.

[161] Ibid. xliii, p. 394.

[162] https://www.gtownpres.org/news-archive/a-pastoral-note-around-the-pittsburgh-synagogue-shooting

[163] C.H. Spurgeon and T. Carter, *2,200 Quotations: From the writings of Charles H. Spurgeon: Arranged topically or textually and indexed by subject, Scripture, and people* (Grand Rapids, MI: Baker Books, 1995), 228. Vol. 33. 672.

[164] *Christian History Magazine-Issue 32:* Dietrich Bonhoeffer: Theologian in Nazi Germany" (Carol Stream, IL., Christianity Today 1991).

[165] S. K. Cohn, Jr., "The Black Death and the Burning of the Jews," *Past and Present,* 196 (2007): 3–36.

[166] https://www.jta.org/2020/04/02/global/an-unwanted-symptom-of-the-coronavirus-crisis-in-france-anti-semitic-conspiracy-theories

[167] https://www.jpost.com/diaspora/jewish-business-describe-vandalism-looting-of-businesses-in-la-630089

[168] https://www.frontpagemag.com/fpm/2020/06/farrakhan-supporter-led-la-black-lives-matter-daniel-greenfield/?fbclid=IwAR0iCbj6cC_A-kywaHfnOJVpP2bdGYURNIl2Q67cNRf5Vha4e0CqcjPEu7M#.XuzEDolZYdE.facebook

[169] https://thehill.com/blogs/blog-briefing-room/news/495530-jewish-leaders-elected-officials-condemn-de-blasio-for

[170] https://www.nytimes.com/2020/06/07/us/Protest-coronavirus-george-floyd.html

[171] Virtue signaling is the popular modern habit of indicating that one has virtue merely by expressing disgust or favor for certain political ideas or cultural happenings.

[172] Eric Fromm, *The Heart of Man: Its Genius for Good and Evil* (New York and London: Religious Perspectives Vol. 12, Harper & Row, 1964), p. 45.

[173] Eric Fromm, *The Heart of Man: Its Genius for Good and Evil* (New York and London: Religious Perspectives Vol. 12, Harper & Row, 1964), p. 39.

[174] See https://www.youtube.com/watch?v=PAOzy2zwyxo

[175] https://www.youtube.com/watch?v=THTksFG6Zlg

[176] https://gellerreport.com/2020/06/de-blasio-and-cuomo-get-creamed-in-court-federal-judge-rules-cuomo-de-blasio-wrong-to-limit-worship-services-condone-mass-protests.html/ See also: https://vosizneias.com/2020/06/26/federal-court-says-new-york-governor-cuomo-is-wrong-to-limit-worship-services/

[177] https://politicodailynews.com/de-blasio-threatens-to-permanently-shutter-churches-that-continue-to-hold-worship-services-2/

[178] https://www.realclearpolitics.com/video/2020/05/15/andrew_napolitano_the_country_has_gone_from_a_free_state_to_a_police_state_in_a_period_of_six_weeks.html?fbclid=IwAR0AxHEdXU8gn6TraaVWJmWDVd4qikX4UK4n9oNoVVrzSREG0KIZJuO51w0

[179] https://www.foxnews.com/us/michigan-resident-faces-93-days-in-jail-for-vegetable-garden?fbclid=IwAR3-qSYKWABEfEv7lMzBsjoZvVcixGYCAXVLNufes0Zy2izvyecaotyERZk

[180] Norman Lamm, *Faith & Doubt: Studies in Traditional Jewish Thought* (Jersey City: KTAV, 2006), p. 299.

[181] 1 Samuel 22:17–18.

[182] https://www.dailymail.co.uk/news/article-7961571/Whistleblower-arrested-China-secretly-filming-piles-body-bags-coronavirus-hospital.html

[183] https://www.dailymail.co.uk/news/article-8233203/Chinas-disappeared-happened-dared-speak-coronavirus.html?ito=facebook_share_article-top&fbclid=IwAR2Bl4wopeYz1uXD5pCCClCLt7wFYUjr5pEFHXpGyNTSrcLlEbEKRpw4SqE

[184] https://nypost.com/2020/04/11/bill-maher-defends-calling-coronavirus-chinese-virus/?utm_source=facebook_sitebuttons&utm_medium=site+buttons&utm_campaign=site+buttons&fbclid=IwAR2YGjuPHY2JTIjT92Cs0uoIVl__kY7wI46uvjLzvx1HpOToXtKFCOqhEfs

[185] https://www.businessinsider.com/trump-declares-houses-of-worship-essential-says-hell-override-governors-2020-5

[186] https://www.cbsnews.com/news/coronavirus-deaths-suicides-drugs-alcohol-pandemic-75000/

[187] In 2018, the most recent year for which data is available, more than 48,000 Americans died by suicide, according to the Centers for Disease Control, ranking it the country's 10th-leading cause of death. And while many countries have seen their suicide rates decline in recent years, in the U.S. the rate has increased 35% since 1999, from 10.5 deaths per 100,000 people to 14.2, an alarming rise that's also prompted a call to action among health professionals. See https://www.usnews.com/news/healthiest-communities/articles/2020-05-22/experts-warn-of-a-surge-of-suicides-tied-to-the-coronavirus-pandemic

[188] See Beatriz Echeverri, "Spanish influenza seen from Spain" in Howard Phillips and David Killingray, *The Spanish Influenza Pandemic of 1918-1919: New Perspectives* (New York: Routledge, 2001), p. 180.

[188] John M. Barry, *Influenza: The Epic Story of the Deadliest Plague in History* (New York: Penguin, 2004), p. 221.

Made in the USA
Monee, IL
23 September 2021